EDWARDS, T.J.

Standards, Guidons and colours of the commonwealth forces

8\12

Hertfordshire
COUNTY COUNCIL
Libraries, Arts
& Information

355.15

**Please return this book
on or before the last
date shown or ask for
It to be renewed.**

 100% recycled paper.

L32

D1614944

Please renew/return this item by the last date shown.

So that your telephone call is charged at local rate,
please call the numbers as set out below:

	From Area codes 01923 or 0208:	From the rest of Herts:
Renewals:	01923 471373	01438 737373
Enquiries:	01923 471333	01438 737333
Minicom:	01923 471599	01438 737599

L32b

STANDARDS, GUIDONS AND COLOURS
OF THE
COMMONWEALTH FORCES

By the same Author:

REGIMENTAL BADGES
MILITARY CUSTOMS
MASCOTS AND PETS OF THE SERVICES

Standard of Ligonier's Regiment of Horse
(afterwards 7th Dragoon Guards)
carried at the Battle of Dettingen, 27th June (or 16th
June, old style), 1743.

STANDARDS, GUIDONS
AND COLOURS

OF THE

COMMONWEALTH FORCES

By

MAJOR T. J. EDWARDS

M.B.E., F.R.Hist.S.

Member of the Society for Army Historical Research

WITH A FOREWORD BY

SIR GERALD WOLLASTON, K.C.B., K.C.V.O.

Inspector of Regimental Colours

ALDERSHOT

GALE & POLDEN LIMITED

1953

First Published, May, 1953

PRINTED AND MADE IN GREAT BRITAIN BY
GALE AND POLDEN LTD. AT THEIR WELLINGTON PRESS,
ALDERSHOT, HAMPSHIRE

CONTENTS

ILLUSTRATIONS

Gerald W. Wollaston
Garter.

FOREWORD

BY

SIR GERALD W. WOLLASTON, K.C.B., K.C.V.O.
Inspector of Regimental Colours

THE historical associations of Regimental Colours, and the fact that they embody the traditions of famous regiments, ensure for them the interest not only of Service men but of the public generally.

A Standard Book on the subject, giving, both to the initiated and the uninitiated, information concerning the origin and meaning of Colours and the Regulations which govern them, has long been needed. This want has now been supplied by Major Edwards in the following pages.

As Inspector of Regimental Colours, and responsible for them throughout the Empire, it is a pleasure to me to commend this book to all those who desire to learn something of the subject, as well as those who wish to extend their knowledge of its historical and practical details.

The book is well documented and its statements are based on quoted authority, as becomes a text-book on so important a subject. It covers a wide range of kindred historical matters associated with Colours and should be invaluable both to the student and to the general reader.

Gerald W. Wollaston
Garter.

Inspector of Regimental Colours.

COLLEGE OF ARMS,
QUEEN VICTORIA STREET,
LONDON, E.C.4.

INTRODUCTION

THE compilation of this book has necessitated many years of research. I started collecting material concerning Regimental Standards, Guidons and Colours soon after the close of the Great War of 1914-18, but did not seriously begin research with a view to writing a book on the subject until after retirement in 1926. The late war of 1939-45 interrupted work on the project, which was not renewed until two years ago.

Dealing with a subject that has been a feature of life from the dawn of history down the centuries to the present day, and to compress it into a few hundred pages, entailed much sifting, writing and rewriting, correspondence with every British Dominion, some foreign countries, numerous regiments and Military Academies and Colleges. But first and foremost I wish to express my gratitude to the War Office, where I served continuously from 1921 to 1951, for providing opportunities to investigate and verify material ; from all ranks, both military and civil, I enjoyed most sympathetic co-operation. In addition, information and illustrations have been obtained from the Board of Admiralty, Royal Marines Office, Air Ministry and College of Arms as well as from gentlemen either in possession of old Colours or descendants of those who performed gallant feats connected with them in "battles long ago." In every single instance the response to my requests has been most generous, and I am happy to acknowledge it in this manner.

Among those I wish to mention specially is A. S. White, Esq., F.R.Hist.S., Librarian of the War Office, who guided my researches in the early days; he has also read the proof of this book and made suggestions which I have adopted; the five Officers Commanding the Regiments of Foot Guards, who kindly loaned to me their Regimental Colour Books; the College of Arms, who readily accorded me every facility to examine the records of the Inspector of Regimental Colours (then the late Sir Henry Farnham Burke); and Sir Gerald W. Wollaston, the present Inspector, who has not only favoured me by writing the "Foreword" to this work, but also checked the manuscript. J. D. Heaton-Armstrong, Esq., M.V.O., Chester

Herald and Inspector of Royal Air Force Badges, was most helpful in connection with the Colours and the Standards of the R.A.F. I also wish to mention the considerable assistance received from Flight Lieutenant M. J. Creighton and Squadron Leader J. F. D. Elkington in this matter. I am much indebted to Major L. M. Arnold, the War Office, who very kindly checked the proof of this book and who made a number of suggestions, which have been adopted.

I have received considerable assistance from the makers of Regimental Standards, Guidons and Colours, and wish to mention particularly in this connection the late Lady Olive Smith-Dorrien, D.B.E., Principal of the Royal School of Needlework, South Kensington, Miss Clare Miller, of Messrs. Hobson and Sons, 1 Lexington Street, London, W.1, and Miss Rhoda M. Rasey, of the Royal School of Needlework.

Owing to the length of time that the work has been compiling it is possible that my acknowledgements have not included all those who have assisted me in some way. I hope that any such will acquit me of discourtesy in omitting to mention them.

It may be added that the material upon which this book is based had its adventures during the late war. A considerable number of my papers were stored in the cellar of my house. When a German bomb burst a sewer in the neighbourhood this cellar became flooded. Many papers were rescued, but a large number became pulped under a foot of water and I had the disappointing task of shovelling these latter into buckets for removal by the dustmen. On examining the rescued papers I was pleased to find that those dealing with the book had been placed on top and were therefore above the water line and among the first "saved."

T. J. E.

SOMLI,
THAMES DITTON, SURREY.
December, 1952.

CHAPTER I

THE SIGNIFICANCE OF REGIMENTAL COLOURS*

REGIMENTAL Colours are the memorials to the great deeds of a regiment and the symbol of its spirit as expressed in those deeds. When Colours were carried on active service, acts of heroic self-sacrifice were often performed in their defence, for they were the rallying point of a regiment and the scene of its last stand. From this association with deeds of epic gallantry has evolved that attitude of veneration which Colours have acquired. An expression of this attitude may be seen in the Service of Consecration which attends their commencing service, the salutes accorded to them during service, and the Laying-up Service when they are retired.

This great respect for Regimental Colours in the days of long ago may also be traced to the ancient customs associated with the purging of a soldier's sin. Writing of the "Sanctity of the Colour," the late Sir John Fortescue, author of the famous "History of the British Standing Army," stated concerning the German Free Companies, or Landsknechte, that when a company of German mercenary infantry was formed, the Commanding Officer read the terms of service to the men who, each raising three fingers, swore in the name of the Trinity to observe them. Then a ring was formed and the Commanding Officer, calling the Ensigns into the midst of it, delivered to each the Colour of his company and exhorted him to defend it to the death. If any crime were committed which brought disgrace on the regiment, the Provost-Marshal laid his complaint before the Ensigns, who thereupon thrust their Colours, point downwards, into the ground and vowed that they would never fly again until the reproach was wiped off. Thus we see that the Colours were already the symbol of the regimental honour. The men then inquired into the case without the intervention

* The term "Colours" embraces Cavalry Standards and Guidons and Infantry Colours, except where it obviously applies exclusively to Infantry Colours only.

B   1

of any officer, and if the culprit was found guilty the Ensigns flew their Colours again before the whole regiment on parade.

In the eighteenth century the Colours were sometimes passed over a soldier's head to remove from him any infamy that a crime may have brought upon him. In the army of the Prince of Orange it was customary to sentence a deserter to be chained to a wheel-barrow and work at the public works for a term of years, after which, if he had conducted himself well, he was returned to his regiment and, the man kneeling, the Colours were waved over his head, the Colonel pronounced him an honest man and he was received into the ranks and got his arms (*Journal of the Society for Army Historical Research*, IV, 59).

In Thomas Simes's "The Military Guide for Young Officers, &c.," published in 1772, he deals with the punishment for certain offences, and after explaining why an offence committed by a soldier should not have the same lasting effect upon his character as upon a civilian who committed the same offence, states, in the case of the soldier, because "it is a punishment which he receives at the hands of his comrades," but for civilians the offenders fall within the province of the hangman, "the consequence of which is, that one is obliged to pass the Colours over a soldier's head after he has received this punishment, in order, by such an act of ceremony, to take off that idea of ignominy which is attached to it" (*Journal of the Society for Army Historical Research*, II, 157).

That this custom continued into the nineteenth century is evident from the following extract from "The Letters of Private Wheeler, 1809-1828" (p. 41). Writing under the date 17th June, 1810, from Horsham Barracks, Wheeler states:

> "We formed square in the Barrack yard, when the Colonel began a lecture that lasted some time, he was in one of his best good humours—an act of grace was to be performed, the prison doors were to be opened and the prisoners set free, but there was one unfortunate man whose crime was so great, that it required something extraordinary to be done before he could be purged from his guilt. It was Sergeant Harrison, he had been on Command and had lost or spent the public money intrusted to him, about £2—and deserted. He had been brought back on the 2nd inst. The Colonel lectured poor H--- a long time, was afraid if he released him without

thorou'ly wiping away all his guilt, it would be of little or no benefit to him or to the service. After a little consideration, he shouted out, 'is there none can advise me in this important affair?' All was silent, no one tendered their advice. 'What,' he cried, 'will no one put their shoulders to the wheel. Then I must lift the waggon myself, spread the Colours.' The Colours were brought to the middle of the square, the tops put together, thus forming a kind of arch. 'Now H---,' said the Colonel, 'pass uncovered under those honourable Colours.' This done, he shouts out, 'He's half clean, he must pass under them again, let the Colours touch him this time; now his crime he's blotted out for ever, he is regenerated, the new born babe is not more innocent, and, woe to the first man who ever mentions the affair to him.' No one had been appointed in his place, he was therefore ordered to join his Company and retain his rank. He was not disliked, so everyone was pleased to see him restored in his former situation again.''

On reading the names of battles and campaigns emblazoned on Regimental Colours it is not difficult to realize what it cost in courage, endurance, patience, determination and other fine qualities to get those names on to those Colours. In their country's cause regiments have been almost wiped out either by the sword or disease, or both, yet the only memorial to this heroism may be a name on a Colour. The charge of the famous Light Brigade in the Crimea, and what it meant in devotion to duty in the face of great odds and the consequent loss of life, is summed up in the solitary word "Balaklava"; months of patient endurance in agonizing circumstances, perpetually under fire from the enemy, with food at starvation point, is crystallized in "Lucknow"; eighteen years of incessant warfare under most adverse conditions is epitomized in "Tangier 1662-80." The story of the world-wide nature of British military heroism is written in a few words on Colours.

Now that Colours are no longer carried in action it will not be possible for them to become battle-scarred as formerly, but, nevertheless, each successive set of new Colours, like the heir to a great family, inherits the traditions, glory, honour, and veneration acquired by its predecessors.

"The flag is a symbol, intrinsically valueless—extrinsically priceless," says Andrew Ross in "Old Scottish Colours"; and

STANDARDS, GUIDONS AND COLOURS

Sir Edward Hamley expressed much the same thought in the following lines, written on seeing some old Colours of the 32nd Foot* in Monmouth Church:

"A moth-eaten rag on a worm-eaten pole.
It does not look likely to stir a man's Soul,
'Tis the deeds that were done 'neath the moth-eaten rag,
When the pole was a staff, and the rag was a flag."

In a practical sense "to keep the flag flying" has been a prime duty of soldiers at all times owing to its inspiring effect†. The life of individuals, even of those in high authority, was not of such importance as the preservation of the symbol of the tribal or regimental spirit. The Vikings were successful against Alfred the Great until he captured their famous Raven banner; at the battle of Hastings all hope was not abandoned when Harold was killed, but it was when the Standard was lost.‡ In our seventeenth-century campaign against the Moors at Tangier, Lord Teviot captured an enemy standard which was promptly displayed upon one of our forts. The effect was instantaneous; the Moors considered it a bad omen and drew off, much disheartened. During the Peninsular War (1808-14) we captured so many French Eagle Standards that Marshal Soult ordered the remainder to be sent back to France for safety. The French soldiers, however, soon improvised some standards from all sorts of material, as they could not endure being without their emblems.

This feeling of despondency at the loss or absence of the ensign, colour, etc., has a long history, for we read in Isaiah x, 18, "They shall be as when a standard-bearer fainteth," and the context clearly shows that if the standard-bearer faints and the standard falls to the ground, the cause is lost.

* Since 1881 1st Battalion The Duke of Cornwall's Light Infantry.

† Extract from a letter "From His Majesty's Camp before the Castle oJ Namur ye 1st of September, 1695" written by "Wm. Blathwayt." (PRO/ SP/Class 87. Vol. 1, Folio 123).

"When the officers of the Bavarian Guards were allmost all kill'd or wounded, and the rest of the Troops very much shatter'd, My Lord Cutts (finding the Terra Nova too difficult) sustain'd them with some of his English; and among others, commanded a Lieut. to pass the Pallisadoes with 30 men and attack a Batterie of the Enemy's; and immediately the English and Bavarians, planting their Colours upon the Pallisadoes, the men took fresh courage, march'd briskly up to their Colours, and they soon made a lodgment."

‡ Sir Edward Creasy in "Fifteen Decisive Battles of the World—The Battle of Hastings."

**The Standards of The Life Guards, presented by H.M. King George V
on 24th June, 1927.**

CHAPTER II

THE ORIGIN OF COLOURS

REGIMENTAL Colours are a development of the banners of medieval nobility, which in turn trace their origin back through the ensigns and standards of the Romans, Greeks, Egyptians and Children of Israel to the totem poles of the prairie brave. Their invention was due to two practical requirements—viz., the need of some mark of distinction between families, tribes and races,* and a conspicuous rallying point in battle.

At the dawn of history every man was very much like his neighbour in appearance and his scanty clothing was not sufficient to achieve that distinction between families, tribes and races necessary for many reasons, particularly rapid identification in battle.† To overcome this, primitive man painted on his body the image of some animal or bird with which he was familiar and whose qualities he considered he possessed or wished to acquire. For instance, the fleet of foot painted on themselves the figure of a galloping horse or a bird in flight, the strong adopted a lion or bear, the wise an owl or serpent. This family sign was also painted on the tent, tepi, or other form of dwelling-place.

When a tribe went to war the badge of the tribal chief was hoisted upon a pole so that it could be seen at a distance and in close country, and it is in the use of these badges for war

---

* In the fulfilment of the first requirement may be seen the origin of heraldry, *vide* "Heraldry as Art" (Chapter 1), by G. W. Eve—

"Heraldry, in its essence, began when man first used natural forms to symbolize, and ascribe to himself, those qualities—strength, courage, cunning—which he had full cause to recognize in the beasts with whom he struggled for existence; when he reproduced, as well as he could, their ferocious aspect, to strike terror into his human enemies while satisfying his own warlike vanity, and so adopted them as badges or even as totems."

† The adoption of a universal dress for active service by modern armies presents much the same kind of problem. In the British service this is overcome by placing distinctive features (*e.g.*, Formation Badges, etc.) on battledress. (See "Heraldry in War," by Lieut.-Colonel H. N. Cole, O.B.E., T.D., F.R.Hist.S.)

purposes that the origin of Regimental Colours lies. It is not difficult to appreciate that the badge or totem of a persistently successful family or tribe would acquire an atmosphere of veneration and give rise to a superstitious belief in its power to lead to victory. Such an attitude the Roman soldier adopted towards his Eagle Ensigns.

The symbolic aspect of the subject is concisely summed up by Hulme ("Flags of the World"):

> "So soon as man passes from the lowest stage of barbarism the necessity for some special sign, distinguishing man from man (*i.e.*, individual desire), tribe from tribe, nation from nation, makes itself felt; and this prime necessity once met, around the chosen symbol spirit-stirring memories quickly gather that endear it, and make it the emblem of the power and dignity of those by whom it is borne. The painted semblance of grizzly bear, or beaver, or rattlesnake on the canvas walls of the tepi of the prairie brave, the special chequering of colours that compose the tartan of the Highland clansman, are examples of this; and as we pass from individual or local tribe to mighty nations, the same influence is still at work, and the distinctive Union Flag of Britain, the tricolor of France, the gold and scarlet bars of the flag of Spain, all alike appeal with irresistible force to the patriotism of those born beneath its folds, and speak to them of the glories and greatness of the historic past, the duties of the present, and the hopes of the future—inspiring those who gaze upon their proud blazonry with the determination to be no unworthy sons of their fathers, but to live, and if need be to die, for the dear home-land of which these are the symbol."

Following on this statement it will not be difficult to appreciate that regimental *esprit de corps* grew up naturally round the Regimental Colours of our modern armies.

**The Standards of Royal Horse Guards (The Blues), presented by
H.M. King George V on 24th June, 1927.**

CHAPTER III

THE TERM "COLOURS"

THE precise origin of the term "Colours," as applied to military flags, does not appear to have been established. In "Certain Discourses, written by Sir John Smythe, Knight" in 1585, but not published until 1590, he refers to some modernists who had introduced new terms into military vocabulary, and remarks: "Their Ensigns also they will not call by that name but by the name of Colours, which terme is by them so fondly and ignorantly given." There is also an early reference to them in Barret's "Theorike and Practike of Modern Warres," published in 1598, wherein he writes: "We Englishmen do call them of late Colours, by reason of the variety of colours they be made of, whereby they be better noted and known." There is a slightly earlier reference in Peele's "Battle of Alcazar," a play performed in 1591 and published three years later:

> "And now, behold, how Abdelmetic comes,
> Uncle to this unhappy traitor King,
> Arm'd with great aid that Amarath had sent,
> Great Amarath, Emperor of the East,
> For service done to Sultan Soliman,
> Under whose Colours he had served in the field."

Sir John Fortescue, in "A History of the British Army," states, with a note of confirmation, that "Before the end of the (sixteenth) century the flags of infantry, from their diversity of hues, had gained the name of Colours."

A number of references to Colours will be found in Shakespeare's plays. In "King Richard II," IV, i, a reference to the Duke of Norfolk has

> "And his pure soul unto his Captain Christ
> Under whose Colours he fought so long."

In "King Henry VI," I, iv, Joan la Pucelle: "Advance our waving Colours on the walls"; and in Act 3, Scene iii, she says again—

> "There goes the Talbot with his Colours spread,
> And all the troops of English after him."

Coming to the seventeenth century, Markham (1622), in his

"Five Decades of Epistles of Warre," deals with the term thus: "Men began to forbeare the carrying of Arms, and only fixed a Device or Empresa, and some but the only variation of two severall Colours (and so are called Colours)."

The term seems to have become well established in the early years of the seventeenth century, and there is evidence of this in a book entitled "Munro": his expedition with the "Worthy Scots Regiment (called Mac.Keyes Regiment) levied in 1626." In the year 1627 "The Regiment mustered, received Colours"; and later, "to send Captain Robert Ennis into England (the regiment was then on the Continent), to know His Majestie of Great Britaines will, whether or no, they might carrie, without reproach, the Dannes Cross, in Scottish Colours."*

Gerat Barry, who published his book "A Discourse on Military Discipline" in 1634, refers to the Ensign carrying his "culores" in his left hand, and that he should display his "culores" in his window.

As to the present Standing Army, the Royal Warrant of 1661 by Charles II refers to "Colours and Ensigns," and subsequent Warrants and Regulations use the term "Colours" when referring to Infantry flags.

In the eighteenth century an Ensign's Commission was referred to popularly as "A pair of Colours."

STANDARD AND GUIDON

A Standard was the largest of the numerous flags flown in armies in the Middle Ages. As its name implies, it was a flag made to stand, as opposed to being carried. A Tudor manuscript definitely states, with reference to the Royal Standard: "The Standard to be sett before the King's pavilion or tente, and not to be borne in battayle." This Standard was eleven yards long and swallow-tailed.

Regiments of Household Cavalry had always carried Standards, which are practically square in shape.

The earliest Royal Warrant dealing with these matters of the present Standing Army is that of 1751, wherein it is laid down that Standards are to be carried by Dragoon Guards. Under a Royal Warrant of 9th January, 1746, the three senior Regiments of Horse commanded, respectively, by General Sir Phillip

---

* The Dannes Cross, or Dannebrog, is now carried in the Regimental Colour of The Green Howards.

The Standard of The Queen's Bays, presented by the Colonel-in-Chief of the Regiment (now Queen Elizabeth The Queen Mother) at Tidworth, 29th July, 1939.

The Reverse side of the Standard of The Queen's Bays, showing the ten selected battle honours for the Great War, 1914-1918

Honeywood, Lieut.-General John Duke of Montague and Field-Marshal George Wade, were "formed into Regiments of Dragoons" under the new title of "Dragoon Guards." They had previously carried Standards as Horse Regiments and on becoming Dragoon Guards were permitted to continue carrying Standards. These three regiments are perhaps better known as the 1st King's Dragoon Guards, The Queen's Bays and the 3rd Dragoon Guards. The remaining Horse Regiments were similarly formed into Dragoons in 1788 with the title of Dragoon Guards, and they also continued to carry Standards, as at present.

The term "Guidon" is derived from the old French *guyd-homme*, the flag carried by the leader of Horse. It has always been swallow-tailed and regarded as being junior to a Standard.

In medieval times superior knights bore a square standard in the field, whereas those of a lesser degree bore a swallow-tailed guidon. In the event of one of the latter performing some heroic service which was brought to the Sovereign's notice, he was sometimes elevated to the superior class by having the tails cut off his Guidon, thereby converting it into a square Standard. Hence today, Household Cavalry and Dragoon Guards carry Standards, while the junior arm, Dragoons, carry Guidons.

CHAPTER IV

THE EVOLUTION OF COLOURS

WHEN the dawn of civilization was breaking upon Western Europe, Rome and Greece were at their height, whilst Nineveh had had her day. Therefore when the early Briton was using a crude imitation of some bird or animal as his ensign, the Roman legions carried beautifully carved eagles, whilst the golden standards of Nineveh were things of the past.

As in later times, the ensigns of early man had to be clearly seen in the din and dust of battle and in forest or wooded country, so they were made of bright, flashing material to which coloured ribbons or feathers were attached to catch the eye. The prairie braves also fledged their poles with the wings of eagles. In the case of the Aztecs and Mexicans the ensigns

Aztec Ensign.

10

were attached to the backs of the standard-bearers, thus leaving both hands free for the use of weapons.

The Children of Israel had their tribal ensigns, for we read in Numbers, chapter 2, verse 2: "Every man of the Children of Israel shall pitch by his own standard, with the ensign of their father's house." These ensigns are supposed to be referred to by Jacob in Genesis, chapter 49: "Judah is a lion's whelp. . . . Issachar is a strong ass. . . . Dan shall be a serpent. . . . Naphtali is a bird let loose. . . . Joseph is a fruitful bough. . . . Benjamin shall ravin as the wolf."

In the army of ancient Rome a maniple consisted of 200 men (two centuries), and its original ensign was a simple bundle of hay tied to the top of a spear, from which circumstance the member of a maniple was referred to as *miles manipularis*, a common soldier. Later a spear with a cross-piece of wood at the top was used and sometimes the figure of a hand, probably in allusion to the word *manipulus* or to the fact that the soldiers on occasion fought with hands joined. The next development was to place a shield, either round or oval, below the cross-

Ancient Roman Ensign.

piece on which were representations of warlike deities, such as Mars or Minerva, and Emperors. From about 104 B.C. the Roman armies favoured the beautiful Eagle Standards, richly decorated, carrying the well-known initials "S.P.Q.R." (Senatus Populusque Romanus—the Roman Senate and People).

The progress made in body-armour in Western Europe was such that by the middle of the eleventh century much of the warrior's body and of his horse were covered. This made rapid identification in the heat of battle very difficult, a circumstance that was overcome by the use of pennons or banners bearing various devices. A record of such flags used at the battle of Hastings in 1066 is in the famous Bayeux tapestry, where at least thirty are recorded. Individuality is the keynote of their make-up, difference being found in their shape, number of tails and devices borne upon them. Here may perhaps be found the first beginnings of heraldry, though heraldry as we know it in this country cannot be proved back farther than the middle of the twelfth century. During the thirteenth century the nobility went into battle with their entire body and most of their horse hidden by defensive armour, thus increasing the difficulty of quick identification. This was overcome by the use of armorial bearings. Thus writes Charles Boutell in "English Heraldry":

"From the circumstance that it first found its special use in direct connection with military equipments, knightly exercises, and the mêlée of actual battle, mediaeval Heraldry has also been entitled armory. Men wore the ensigns of Heraldry about their persons, embroidered upon the garments that partially covered their armour— and so they called them Coats-of-Arms; they bore these same ensigns on their shields—and they called them Shields-of-Arms; and in their Armorial Banners and Pennons they again displayed the very same insignia, floating in the wind high above their heads, from the shafts of their lances."

It is from these banners carrying ensigns of heraldry that Regimental Colours are directly derived.

The banners borne at the Battle of the Standard on 22nd August, 1138, at Northallerton, Yorkshire, provide an example of consecrated ecclesiastical banners being borne in action. They were the standards of the three Yorkshire Saints: St. Peter

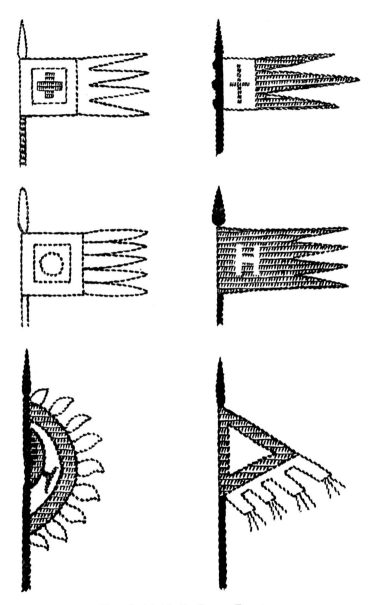

Flags depicted in the Bayeux Tapestry.

of York, St. Wilfrid of Ripon and St. John of Beverley. The yeomen of Yorkshire fought under Thurstan, Archbishop of York, and successfully withstood the wild charges of the Scottish clansmen.

By the end of the sixteenth century continental armies were throwing off their loose character as regards formations and adopting a systematized arrangement. One of the pioneers of this movement was Gustavus Adolphus, King of Sweden, who regimented his troops for the Thirty Years' War in Germany (1618-1648). His regiments of Horse and Foot were divided into a regular number of units, each composed of a definite number of men. Each unit had its Standard (Cavalry) or Colour (Infantry), and all in each regiment were of the same general pattern. This ushered in a period of standardization.

In his "Five Decades of Epistles of Warre," published in 1622, Markham lays down that "Captains (colours) ought to bee mixt equally of two several colours, that is to say (according to the Laws of Heraldry) of Colour and Metall."

He goes on to state his rules for Colours, which, in modern language, are:

Captain's Colour.—Should consist of the two principal colours in his coat-of-arms, with a small red Cross of St. George in the dexter chief canton (*i.e.*, next to the head of the lance or pole) not larger than one-sixth of the entire Colour.

Colonel's Colour.—To be the same as the Captain's, but of only one colour throughout.

Colonel-General's and Lord Marshall's Colours.—To be the same as the Colonel's, but with a smaller St. George's Cross, only one-eighth of the whole Colour.

General's Colour.—Of one colour throughout and without any St. George's Cross.

Ward, in his "Animadversions of Warre," published in 1639, when writing of the "Office and Duty of a Colonel over a Regiment," states:

> "Hee ought to have all the Colours of his Regiment to be alike both in colour and in fashion to avoide confusion so that the souldiers may discerne their owne Regiment from the other Troopes; likewise, every particular Captaine of his Regiment may have some small distinctions in their Colours; as their Armes, or some Emblem, or the

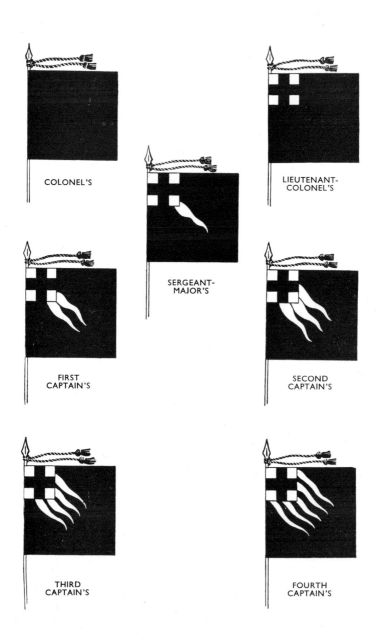

Colours of the Red Regiment of the Parliament Forces, 1643.

like, so that the one Company may be discerned from the other."

A particular feature to note is the St. George's Cross in the dexter chief canton. In the "Statutes and Ordinances of War" of Richard II (1385),* Article XVII states:

"Everyman of what estate, condition or nation he may be, so that he be of our party, shall bear a large sign of the Arms of St. George before and another behind, upon peril that if he be hurt or slain in default thereof, he that shall hurt or slay him shall no penalty pay for it; and that no enemy shall bear the said sign of St. George whether he be a prisoner, or otherwise, upon pain of death."

The red St. George's Cross was the mark of the English during the Crusades and is still borne in Regimental Colours, embodied in the Union Flag.

There is evidence that Markham's and Ward's rules were observed in the London Train Bands in the early part of the seventeenth century, the record being in the British Museum (Bibl. Harl. 986), entitled "Ensignes of the Regiments in London in 1643. Taken as they marched into Finsbury Fields, being the last General Muster—September, 26-1643," by "R. Symonds." The "Ensignes" are depicted in pen and ink quite roughly sketched, and one can imagine Symonds, from some point of vantage, jotting down hurriedly the outlines of the Colours as each company passed him by. The record shows the following:

Colonel's.—Of the same colour throughout without any kind of emblem thereon (except in the case of the Orange Regiment, where all the Colours have in the centre "IEHOVA PROVIEE BIT" within an ornamented circle).

Lieutenant-Colonel's.—Same as the Colonel's, but with the small St. George's Cross in the dexter canton.

Sergeant-Major's.—Same as the Lieutenant-Colonel's, but with a small "pile wavy," or a lozenge, a star, a ball, etc., near the lower inner corner containing the St. George's Cross.

1st Captain's.—Same as Lieutenant-Colonel's, but with two devices—lozenges, etc.

2nd Captain's.—Same as Lieutenant-Colonel's, but with three devices—lozenges, etc.

_____

* Grose, "Military Antiquities," 1788, II, 60.

3rd Captain's.—Same as Lieutenant-Colonel's, but with four devices—lozenges, etc.

4th Captain's.—Same as Lieutenant-Colonel's, but with five devices—lozenges, etc.

The book also contains a set of five sketches, headed "The Dragoons," showing swallow-tailed Guidons with rounded ends: the first has one ball, the second two balls, and so on.

A noteworthy incident of this period relates to Sir Edmund Verney, Charles I's standard-bearer. At the battle of Edgehill, 23rd October, 1642, Sir Edmund was surrounded by Parliamentarians and was offered his life upon the condition that he would surrender the Standard. To this he defiantly replied that his life was his own, but the Standard was his and their sovereign's, and he would never surrender it while he lived and he hoped that it would be rescued when he were dead. He fought on and killed sixteen of the enemy before he fell, his right arm being cut off. According to tradition, so tightly was the arm grasping the lance of the Standard that it could not easily be released.

The captured Standard was then placed in the care of the Secretary to Lord Essex, Commander of the Parliamentary army, but Captain Smith of King Charles' Life Guards, disguising himself with an orange scarf (the Parliamentary distinguishing badge on that occasion) which he had picked up on the battlefield, slipped through the enemy's ranks, snatched the Standard from Essex's Secretary, and made his way back safely to Charles and laid the Standard at his feet.

The Parliamentary "New Model Army" was formed in 1645 and the Colours were regulated on Markham's and Ward's plan, the hue of the Colour corresponding to the title of the regiments—*i.e.*, the Red Regiment had red Colours. Two Cavalry Standards of this period hang over the monument of Colonel Rice (or Rhys) Yate, in the Parish Church of Bromesberrow, Gloucestershire. Colonel Yate was a Royalist Commander of a troop of Horse. One Standard is that of his own troop and the other a Parliamentarian which he captured, and which has been identified by Sir Charles Firth, the great authority on the military forces of this period, as that of Captain Bragg. J. Peart Robinson, Esq., a descendant of Colonel Yate, kindly presented the author with a painting of each Standard, which are depicted on the opposite page.

Cavalry Standard of Parliamentary Forces.

Cavalry Standard of Royalist Forces.

C

In the British Museum is a MS. book entitled "Banners of the Parliamentary Army" (Bibl. Sloane 5247); on the back of page 119 are shown the Colours of a regiment—"The .Lord Inchequin's for Ireland, 1646." Their arrangement follows generally Markham's and Ward's rules: the field is red in every case and they have no fringe, cord or tassels. The list commences with the Lieutenant-Colonel's and is numbered "1," the detail being thus:

1. St. George's Cross in dexter chief canton with a golden harp in the middle.

2. No cross, but issuing from the dexter chief canton towards the middle a golden flame, with a golden harp in the middle.

3. All plain, but a golden harp in the middle.

4. Same as 3, but with two harps, one above the other.

5. Had three harps.

6. Had four harps.

7. Had five harps.

8. Had six harps.

9. Had seven harps.

This brings the evolution of Regimental Colours down to the eve of the Establishment of the present Standing Army.

CHAPTER V

THE PRESENT STANDING ARMY

EARLY PERIOD

CHARLES II was restored to the throne in 1660 and soon after the Army of the Commonwealth began to be disbanded. It would have entirely disappeared had not a rising in London of the Fifth Monarchy Men in January, 1661, given the King an excuse for retaining the remnant and raising new regiments. The remnant consisted of the Duke of Albemarle's Troop of Horse Guards and his Regiment of Foot (now the Coldstream Guards). The first establishment of the present army took effect from 26th January, 1661, and provided for*

Three Troops of Guards ...	Now The Life Guards
A Regiment of Horse of eight Troops	Now Royal Horse Guards
Two Regiments of Foot Guards	Now Grenadier Guards
Albemarle's Regiment ...	Now Coldstream Guards

As regards Standards and Colours, the numbers provided followed the previous practice of one Standard per troop of Cavalry and one Colour for each company. Perhaps the earliest Royal Warrant of this period on this subject is that reproduced below, which refers to the Regiment of Foot Guards commanded by Colonel Russell.† It reads:

CHARLES R.

Our will and pleasure is, and we do hereby require you forthwith to cause to be made and provided, twelve Colours or Ensigns for Our Regiment of Foot Guards of white and red taffeta, of the usual largeness, with stands,

---

* This is a brief summary : some of the regiments had existed a number of years before 1661, but there is not space here to detail these features.

† *Vide* the booklet, "The Colours of the Grenadier Guards."

19

heads and tassells, each of which to have distinctions of some of Our Royal Badges, painted in oil, as our trusty and well-beloved servant Sir Edward Walker, Knight, Garter Principal King-of-Arms, shall direct, and for so doing this shall be your warrant.

Given under our Sign Manual at Our Court at White-hall, this 13th day of February, 1661.

To our right trusty and right well-beloved cousin and Councillor Edward Earl of Sandwich, Master of our Great Wardrobe, or his Deputy.

By His Majesty's Command,

EDWARD NICHOLAS.

There was another Regiment of Foot Guards at Dunkirk commanded by Lord Wentworth, for which an identical Royal Warrant was signed a month later. Lord Wentworth died in 1665, and his and Colonel Russell's regiments were amalgamated to form the 1st Guards, which in 1815 was granted the honour title of "1st or Grenadier Regiment of Foot Guards" in commemoration of their having defeated the grenadiers of the French Imperial Guards at the battle of Waterloo on 18th June, 1815 (*London Gazette*, 29th July, 1815).

There are a few interesting points in connection with these warrants. In the Regimental Headquarters of the Grenadier Guards is a sketch purporting to be the original designs drawn in 1661 by Sir Edward Walker. This shows that the "First, or King's Company Colour" was pure white, with the King's cypher "C.R." in gold ensigned with a crown, while the remainder are all white with a red St. George's Cross covering the whole field, with a badge in the centre. The Royal badges referred to are still borne on the Colours in rotation. Originally these badges were "painted in oil," as were certain other features on Colours during this period, but gradually this was displaced by embroidery. The reference to the "Garter Principal King-of-Arms" is interesting from the fact that since 1806, when the office of Inspector of Regimental Colours was inaugurated, the appointment has always been held by an officer of the Heralds College who has become Garter during his tenure of it (see page 91). Until 1836 the Colours of Household Troops were provided by the Sovereign and not by the Colonel of the Regiment, hence the reference to the "Master of the Great Wardrobe."

An early reference to the Colours of the Coldstream Guards is to be found in "Travels by Cosmo, Third Duke of Tuscany, through England, 1669" (*vide* "History of the Coldstream Guards," p. 126, by Mackinnon), in which they are described as being green, with white balls and a red cross. This regiment was formed in 1650 under the colonelcy of George Monk, later Duke of Albemarle, as a regiment of the New Model, and the new Colours were no doubt similar in pattern to those previously borne during the Commonwealth. According to Francis Sandford's "History of the Coronation of James II," these Colours were soon afterwards changed to blue, with St. George's Cross throughout edged (fimbriated) white. Instead of Royal badges, numerals indicated the precedence of the companies. Royal badges were first granted to the regiment by William III in 1696.

Nathan Brooks wrote an account of a review held on Putney Heath on 1st October, 1684, from which it is noted that Royal regiments and those connected with Royalty bore Royal badges in their Colours. The Holland Regiment, later 3rd Foot, now The Buffs, is mentioned among those not connected with Royalty, and its Colours were green with St. George's Cross throughout, fimbriated white.

James II did not reign very long (1685-1689), but he abolished the Royal badges of the 1st Guards and replaced them with his cypher "J.R." multiplied according to the seniority of the Captain (*vide* Francis Sandford, *ante*). On the other hand, in the case of regiments not connected with the Sovereign the Colonels placed their own badges on the Colours of their regiments. On this point Samuel Milne Milne in "Standards and Colours of the Army," a standard work, referring to the pictorial record of the Colours of this period in the Royal Library at Windsor Castle, writes:

> "In the long list it will be found that the greater part of the infantry, and some of the cavalry regiments, bore on their Colours the armorial devices of the Colonels in some shape or other. The custom so prevalent in Civil War times seems to have been resuscitated even to a larger extent than before."

At this period Colonels practically owned their regiments,

and they appear to have used portions of their personal arms in the same way that Charles II had used his. Here are a few examples:

> The Earl of Shrewsbury's Horse (later 5th Dragoon Guards)—The Colonel's Standard bore a lion rampant from the arms of the Talbot family.
>
> The Royal Fusiliers, then commanded by the Earl of Dartmouth—The Colonel's Colour bore a stag's head from his arms.
>
> The Earl of Bath's Regiment (now The Royal Lincolnshire Regiment)—The Eldest Captain's Colour bore an organ rest (clarion), one of the Earl's badges. (The Royal Lincolnshire Regiment now have two clarions on their Regimental Colour.)
>
> The Duke of Norfolk's Regiment (now The Suffolk Regiment)—The Colonel's Colour has a Howard crest—viz., a lion statant on a cap of maintenance. The eldest Captain's Colour has a cross crosslet, from the Howard arms.
>
> Sir William Clifton's Regiment (now The East Yorkshire Regiment)—The Colonel's Colour bore a Clifton crest—viz., a demi-peacock issuing from a ducal coronet. The Lieutenant-Colonel's, Major's and senior Captain's Colours all bore another from the Clifton arms—viz., cinquefoils.

These badges, crests, etc., from the arms of the Colonels changed when the Colonel changed, a system which was in vogue through the Sedgemoor Campaign (1685), Marlborough's Campaign during the War of the Spanish Succession (1702-1711), and at Dettingen (1743), the latter being the last occasion that an English King (George II) commanded in the field in person.

One famous Cavalry Standard of the Dettingen period is still in existence, hanging in the museum of the Royal United Service Institution, in Whitehall, London (see Frontispiece). The regiment at that time was the 8th Horse; in 1788, however, it became the 7th Princess Royal's Dragoon Guards, which in 1922 was amalgamated with the 4th Royal Irish Dragoon Guards to form the present 4th/7th Royal Dragoon Guards. General Sir John Ligonier (later Earl Ligonier) was Colonel of the Regiment from 1740 to 1749 and his arms are borne upon the Standard,* together with a very small Union only three inches square. At the battle of Dettingen on 27th June, 1743, this Standard was borne by Cornet Richardson and his exploit is recorded in the regimental history thus:

> "It was in this charge that Cornet Richardson earned undying fame, not only by his gallantry, but also by his mother-wit. Surrounded by the French horse, he stoutly defended the Standard he carried, receiving no less than seven and thirty cuts and bullet holes upon his body and through his clothes, besides many another in his standard pole. Asked afterwards how he managed to save his charge, the gallant Irishman replied in right Irish fashion: 'If the wood of the Standard had not been of iron, it would have been cut off.' "

There is another exceptionally gallant deed connected with a Guidon during this battle: it belonged to the 3rd Dragoons (now 3rd The King's Own Hussars). The regiment charged on three occasions a vastly superior number of the French, who nearly annihilated them. Two of the three Guidons had been cut to ribbons, both the silk and the poles, and in the last charge the third Guidon had dropped from the wounded Cornet's hand and lay on the ground. A trooper of the regiment, Thomas Brown of Kirkleatham, Yorkshire, was in the act of dismounting to recover it when a French sabre cut off two of the fingers of his bridle hand. His horse promptly bolted and carried him to the rear of the French lines. Here he saw the regiment's Guidon being borne away in triumph by a French gendarme. This he could not bear, and, disabled though he was, he rode straight at the gendarme, cut him down, recaptured the Guidon and, gripping it between his leg and the saddle, fought his way back to the British lines, with three bullet holes through his hat and seven wounds on his face and body, but with the Guidon safe. For this most gallant exploit Brown was publicly rewarded.

As a result of the political Union of England and Scotland in 1707, the red Cross of St. George, which had hitherto been borne alone, either in the dexter chief canton or covering the whole field, was now joined by the white saltire of St. Andrew

---

* Ligonier's crest, a demi-lion issuing from a ducal coronet, with the motto "Quo fata vocant," was the clothing badge of the 7th Dragoon Guards for many years.

of Scotland in a blue field (see p. 8). The red Cross of St. Patrick was incorporated in 1801.

Just as the red Cross of St. George had been the banner of English troops, so the white saltire of St. Andrew on a blue field had been the battle flag of Scottish soldiery for centuries. In the British Museum there is a pictorial list of Scottish "Colours and Standards taken at Preston and Dunbar"* by the Commonwealth forces in which the St. Andrew's Cross figures fairly frequently. In 1662 the Colours issued to the Scots Guards were red, with St. Andrew's Cross in a blue field in the dexter canton, in the centre a thistle, crowned, with the motto "Nemo me impune lacessit." The Colours of The Royal Scots at the Putney Review in 1684 were, according to Nathan Brooks (*vide* p. 21), a St. Andrew's Cross with the badge and motto as for the Scots Guards.† At his Coronation the following year, James II changed the Scots Guards Colours to the white St. Andrew's Cross in a blue field, and they remained so until the Union in 1707.

It was about 1707 that the infantry arm was reorganized for tactical purposes, each battalion fighting in three divisions—*i.e.*, one of pikes in the centre with another of musketeers and grenadiers on each flank. The number of Colours carried by a battalion was correspondingly reduced, and probably only those of the three senior officers were carried—viz., the Colonel's, Lieutenant-Colonel's and the Major's. This assumption is based on the Colours now carried by the Foot Guards, where the Queen's Colours of the 1st Battalions are the previous Colonel's Colours, the Queen's Colours of the 2nd Battalions are the previous Lieutenant-Colonel's Colours, and the Queen's Colours of the 3rd Battalions (where they exist) the previous Major's Colours.

From this it will be seen that Markham's and Ward's rules still held good for the reduced number of Colours, but their abolition was in sight, except for Household Troops.

---

* Harl. MS. 1/460. The battle of Preston was fought in August, 1648, and that of Dunbar on 3rd September, 1650.

† The history of the Regimental Colours of The Royal Scots is excellently recorded in "The Regimental Records of The Royal Scots," by Leask and McCance: see Appendix II therein.

Colours of the 70th Foot, later 2nd Bn. The East Surrey Regiment, presented at Aldershot in 1867, by Lady Scarlett, wife of General the Hon. Sir J. Yorke Scarlett, Commanding at Aldershot.
Example of a black Regimental Colour.

CHAPTER VI

THE INTRODUCTION OF QUEEN'S AND REGIMENTAL COLOURS

WHAT are probably the first Regulations issued to control Regimental Colours of Infantry of the Line* is a manuscript document in the Royal Library, Windsor Castle,† entitled "Colours, Cloathing of Drummers, Grenadier Caps, Drums, Bells of Arms and Camp-Colours of the Marching Regiments of Foot, 1747. R. Napier, Adjutant-General."

The Regulations are reproduced at Appendix "A".

Whatever remnant of the personal aspect remained in Colours, as far as Colonels of Regiments were concerned, was swept away by the opening paragraphs of these Regulations, which read:

"No Colonel to put his Arms, Crest, Device or Livery on any part of the Appointments of the Regiment under his command.‡

"No part of the Cloathing or Ornaments of the Regiments to be altered, after the following Regulations are put into execution but by His Majesty's permission."

These Regulations also brought to an end the operation of

---

* Samuel Milne Milne (*vide ante*) states that "A Royal Warrant was issued 14th September, 1743," but adds in a footnote that he "only met a copy of this Warrant in a little work entitled 'Rudiments of War,' 2nd Edition, 1782, published by Egerton." The opening paragraphs of this Warrant resemble those of the 1747 Regulations. The authenticity of this Warrant is, however, not clear.

† I wish to acknowledge my indebtedness to Sir Owen Morshead, K.C.V.O., D.S.O., M.C., Librarian, and the late F. W. Barry, Esq., M.V.O., Assistant Librarian, Windsor Castle, for kindly placing at my disposal and assisting me in checking the information regarding Colours in the Royal Library, Windsor Castle.

‡ A few crests of Colonels of Regiments have, during the present century, been authorized to be borne as badges on Colours, *e.g.*:

Coldstream Guards (p. 72), Crest of Duke of Albemarle; Crest of Duke of Cambridge.

Irish Guards (p. 81), Crest of Earl Roberts; Crest of Earl Cavan.

Duke of Wellington's Regiment (p. 207), Crest of Duke of Wellington.

Gordon Highlanders (p. 211), Crest of Duke of Gordon.

the rules laid down by Markham and Ward, for they state:

> "The King's or First Colour of every Regiment or Battalion is to be the Great Union. The Second Colour to be the Colour of the Faceing of the Regiment with the Union in the upper canton, except those Regiments which are faced with White or Red, whose Second Colour is to be the Red Cross of St. George on a White ground and the Union in the upper canton."

This reduction of the number of Colours to two per battalion has remained to the present day, except that Rifle Regiments do not carry any Colours. The original employment of Rifles was as scouts or skirmishers, covering the whole force, where inconspicuity in movement was essential, a feature that would have been nullified had they displayed Colours.* For the same reason Hussars and Lancers, originally light troops of the Cavalry Arm, do not carry Standards or Guidons.

The "Second Colour" was popularly known as the "Regimental Colour," but it was not until 1844 that the name was officially recognized. As regards regiments "faced with White or Red," the objection to a regiment having a white Colour would be that it would resemble a flag of truce, and a red Colour would be confused with the Queen's Colours of the Foot Guards. In those days the facings were the lapels, cuffs, collars and turn-back of the coat.

The Regulations go on to state that:

> "In the centre of each Colour is to be painted or embroidered in gold Roman characters the number of the Rank of the Regiment within a Wreath of Roses and Thistles on the same stalk ; except the Regiments which have Royal Badges or particular ancient Badges allowed them; in these the number of the Rank of the Regiment is to be towards the upper corner."

"The number of the Rank of the Regiment" means in practice the order in which the Regiment stood in the precedence table, and it introduced the regimental aspect into the Colour. The wreath of "Roses and Thistles" agreed with the "Union," being the emblems of England and Scotland, and so these remained until 1800, when Ireland joined the Union and the red saltire of St. Patrick was incorporated into the flag by Royal

---

* The King's African Rifles, however, carry Colours.

Proclamation of 1st January, 1801, and the shamrocks joined the roses and thistles to form the Union Wreath.

The "Royal Badges" and "ancient Badges" are given in Appendix "A." At this time only a few regiments were permitted to have badges in the centre of their Regimental, or second, Colour ; in 1930, however (Army Order 170), the King approved of all Infantry regiments that had not already a centre badge having one. The same privilege was extended to the Standards and Guidons of Cavalry under Army Order 199/1931. A complete list of these centre badges is at Appendix "C".

THE ROYAL WARRANT OF 1ST JULY, 1751

The similarity of the wording of the 1747 Regulations and the 1751 Warrant justifies the assumption that the former was the basis of the latter. As there was only four years' difference in point of date of their issue, it may have been thought by the authorities that the Regulations should be elevated to the status of a Royal Warrant to give them more force. The Warrant is reproduced at Appendix "B". Some of the points of difference between the Regulations and the Royal Warrant are noted here:

(a) Whereas under the Regulations only the Sovereign could grant permission for alterations to be made, under the Warrant this power was also vested in "Our Captain-General." At that date, 1751, the Duke of Cumberland held that appointment.

(b) In the description of the "Devices and Badges" for the "1st Regiment, or The Royal Regiment," an important addition is made in the Warrant in that "the Distinction of the Colours of the Second Battalion is a flaming ray of gold descending from the upper corner of each Colour towards the center." This is the "pile wavy" already noticed as the distinction of the Major's (formerly Sergeant-Major's) Colour.

(c) Regulations for Cavalry Standards, Guidons and Drum Banners are introduced into the Warrant and provide for
    (i) Standards and Guidons for Dragoon Guards.
    (ii) Standards for Horse.
    (iii) Guidons for Dragoons and Light Dragoons.

In the first paragraph of the Cavalry Section "Horse Grenadier Guards" are mentioned. These were first raised in 1678, and later underwent reorganization; in 1788 there were two Troops which were merged with 1st and 2nd Troops of Horse Guards to form the 1st and 2nd Regiments of Life Guards.

(d) The badge of the White Horse of Hanover is ordered, under the Warrant, to be worn in the Grenadiers' caps, and all Standards and Guidons.

(e) The regimental element in the Cavalry was to be shown by the "Rank of the Regiment" on the King's or First Standard or Guidon and the "Badge of the Regiment" on the Second and Third Standards and Guidons.

(f) The distinction of the Third Standard or Guidon to be a figure on a circular ground of red under the motto "Dieu et mon Droit."

(g) In the "General View" is a list of badges, etc., authorized to be borne by Cavalry.

THE ROYAL WARRANT OF 19TH DECEMBER, 1768

Another Royal Warrant was signed on 19th December, 1768 (reproduced in Appendix "D"), but it made no radical changes in the appearance of Colours. It varied from the previous Warrant in the following points:

(a) Infantry Regiments with black facings are mentioned, and their second Colour "is to be St. George's Cross throughout; Union in the Upper Canton; the three other Cantons, Black." The following regiments wore black facings in 1768:

50th—later 1st Bn. The Queen's Own Royal West Kent Regiment.

58th—later 2nd Bn. The Northamptonshire Regiment.

64th—later The North Staffordshire Regiment.

70th—later 2nd Bn. The East Surrey Regiment.

(b) Exact measurements are now given for Colours. In 1751 the size of the Colours and length of the pike were "to be the same as those of the Royal Regiments of Foot Guards."

(c) The 60th or Royal American Regiment is mentioned. It was raised in America in 1755, and is now The King's

Colours of the 2nd Bn. The East Surrey Regiment, presented on behalf of H.M. King George VI by the Colonel of the Regiment, General Sir Richard Foster, K.C.B., C.M.G., D.S.O., at West Chiltington Camp, Sussex, on 30th November, 1945.

Example of a white Regimental Colour.

(The first Stand of Colours to be presented after the conclusion of the Second World War.)

Royal Rifle Corps. As in the case of The Royal Scots in 1751, in each of the 2nd Battalion Colours was a "flaming ray of gold." It became a Rifle Corps in 1824, and ceased to carry Colours from that year.

(d) In the Cavalry "General View" it will be noticed that in the last column, referring to the 15th King's Light Dragoons (later 15th Hussars), the word "Emsdorff" appears. The battle of Emsdorff was fought on 16th July, 1760, and this is the earliest instance of the grant of a battle honour in the form of the name of the action. The earliest campaign to be similarly commemorated is "Tangier, 1662-80," but this was not granted until 1909 (Army Order 180).

With the publication of this Royal Warrant the general form and design of Standards, Guidons and Colours became stabilized, and subsequent Warrants, Regulations, etc., have only introduced modifications in points of detail into the main structure.

CHAPTER VII

MODIFICATIONS IN DESIGN, Etc.

No important instructions regarding Standards, Guidons and Colours appear to have been issued between 1768 and 1844. (See extract at Appendix "E".) In the latter year the "Regulations and Orders for the Army" gave much detail and may be regarded as a "milestone" in description. The main features are: (*a*) For the first time it is laid down that the corners of Standards are "to be square." As a matter of fact they always were square, but the term "Standard" had previously been loosely used to include "Guidons." Further, these Regulations stated that the upper and lower corners of the Guidon were "to be rounded." (*b*) Queen Victoria came to the Throne in 1837, and these Regulations were the first since that date. The first Colour had been designated "The King's" in 1751, but a change was now required and it was called "The Royal," a term which lasted until 1892 when it was altered to "The Queen's." In the Clothing Regulations of 1936, page 182, it is described as "The Royal, or first, Colour, hereinafter called the King's Colour," thus embracing all descriptive elements.

In these 1844 Regulations the second Standard, Guidon or Colour is officially called the "Regimental" for the first time, since when it has been described as "The Regimental or Second" Standard, etc. (*c*) The Great Union is fully described. (*d*) Under a Commander-in-Chief's letter of 21st August, 1782, most Regiments of Infantry of the Line were allotted County titles—*e.g.*, 29th (or Worcestershire) Regiment. Long before this date a number of regiments had been granted Royal titles or titles connected with members of the Royal Family, or such titles as "Inniskilling" or "Cameronian." Under these Regulations it was laid down in regard to the Regimental Colour that "Those Regiments which bear a Royal, County or other Title are to have such designation on a red ground round a circle within the Union wreath of Roses, Thistles and Shamrocks. The Number of the Regiment in Gold Roman characters in the centre." This arrangement emphasized the regimental character of the second Colour. (*e*) Hitherto devices, distinctions and battle honours in general had been placed upon all Standards, Guidons and Colours, but under these Regulations they were to be placed on the Regimental, or second, third or fourth Standard or Guidon in the Cavalry and on the Regimental Colour in the case of the Infantry only.

As regards battle honours granted for service in the Great War of 1914-18,* Cavalry and Yeomanry regiments were permitted to emblazon on their Standards or Guidons a maximum of ten such honours selected from the total granted to each regiment, in addition to those already borne for previous service. In the case of Colour-bearing regiments of Infantry, they were permitted to emblazon on the King's Colour a maximum of ten such honours selected from the total granted to each regiment. These ten selected battle honours are shown in the Army List in thicker type than other honours granted for the Great War. (Army Order 470 of 1922.)

In the Foot Guards the old practice of placing all devices, battle honours, etc., on both Queen's and Regimental Colour is still maintained. In the Honourable Artillery Company battle honours are emblazoned on the Queen's Colour only, none being on the Regimental Colour.

In these Regulations of 1844 is a schedule giving the Titles, Badges, Devices, Distinctions and Mottoes authorized to be borne on Standards, Guidons and Colours. In the Queen's Regulations for 1892 these distinctions were to be "as given in the Army List," which is the present rule.

As Light Dragoons and Rifles did not carry Guidons or Colours, it was ordered under Horse Guards Memorandum of 28th August, 1854, that their honorary distinctions should be borne on their caps or helmet-plates.

In the King's Regulations of 1837 it was laid down that in making up new Standards, etc., application is first to be made to the "Inspector of Regimental Colours." This is the first mention of this official in Regulations, although he had been appointed in 1806 (see later), and no doubt the meticulous

---

* The battle honour "Afghanistan, 1919," granted to regiments under Army Order 92 of 1924, is not a Great War 1914-18 honour, and therefore does not come within the terms of this paragraph. It is borne among the honours for other campaigns.

Queen's Colour of the 11th Foot, now The Devonshire Regiment, issued at Cork on 23rd May, 1825, and laid up in Exeter Cathedral on 1st September, 1924.

details laid down in the 1844 Regulations were the result of his efforts to put Colours on a sound footing.

REGIMENTS AUTHORIZED TO CARRY STANDARDS, GUIDONS AND COLOURS

From the beginning of the Standing Army the rule was for

Horse and Dragoon Guards to carry square Standards;
Dragoons to carry swallow-tailed Guidons;
All Infantry to carry Colours.

The Parachute Regiment was authorized to carry Colours by Army Order 66 of 1948: the King's Colour to be the Union and the Regimental Colour maroon.

Regimental Colour of the 11th Foot, now The Devonshire Regiment, issued at Cork on 23rd May, 1825, and laid up in Exeter Cathedral on 1st September, 1924.
It will be noticed that the Small Union has been incorrectly repaired in the top right-hand corner.

On 24th May, 1834, a Horse Guards letter stated "that the use of Standards by Light Dragoon Regiments shall be discontinued." (Here "Guidons" should have been used instead of "Standards.") The reason for this is, apparently, that Light Dragoons were gradually being converted to Hussars, who do not carry any kind of flag. As a matter of fact, the 7th, 10th and 15th Light Dragoons had already been converted to Hussars in 1807, and the 8th in 1822.

As regards Lancers and Rifle Corps: in the Clothing Warrant of 1830, Standards or Colours, with belts, are laid down for them, but in the warrant of 12th March, 1834, no such provision is made.

D

In addition to Hussars, Lancers and Rifle Regiments, corps like the Royal Tank Regiment, Royal Artillery,* Royal Engineers, Royal Signals, Royal Army Service Corps, etc., have never carried Standards, Guidons or Colours.

The fact that Cavalry of the Line have now been converted to a mechanized formation, all belonging to the Royal Armoured Corps, has not affected their privilege of carrying Standards or Guidons. On dismounted parades they are carried in the same manner as formerly, and on mounted parades—*i.e.*, in vehicles—they are carried in a light tank (or whatever type of armament the regiment is equipped with) with an escort of two light tanks, echeloned in rear, one on each flank.

SIZE OF COLOURS

The early warrants are not very helpful in regard to the exact size of the Standards, etc. The Warrant of 1661, referring to the Foot Guards, states that they are to be "of the usual largeness." At the Coronation of James II in 1685 the Colours of the Foot Guards were 8 ft. 3 in. flying and 7 ft. 6 in. on the staff, and must have required considerable strength to bear them erect in even a modest breeze.

The 1751 Warrant states that the Infantry Colours were to be of the same size as those of the Foot Guards, but as those of the Guards are not mentioned nothing can be deduced from the statement. There is the same vagueness in the case of Cavalry Standards: "to be the same as those of the Horse and Horse Grenadier Guards."

---

* In the Royal Artillery the guns are regarded as their Colours. Writing of pre-eighteenth-century times, when the old Board of Ordnance organized the Trains of Artillery for expeditions, Lieut.-Colonel M. E. S. Laws, O.B.E., M.C., R.A., states in his pamphlet, "Outline History of the Development and Organization of the Royal Artillery, 1760-1950," that "The Train of Artillery took the Field, headed by a large Ordnance flag carried on the largest (or Flag) gun and embellished by a State chariot bearing the Ordnance kettledrums and the kettledrummer gorgeously arrayed."

Further information concerning the Flag Gun will be found in Vols. I and II of the *Journal of the Society for Army Historical Research*.

An illustration of the Standard of the Royal Artillery now used is on page 42. The flag is in R.A. Colours, red and blue (red below in the portion bearing the gun, and red above in the portion bearing the badge and motto) with the fringe in red, white and blue. The adoption of this Standard and its present use is explained on page 41.

The 1768 Warrant, however, gives definite measurements, and this practice was followed in all subsequent Warrants, Regulations, etc. The following table shows the sizes of Standards, Guidons and Colours at various periods. From this it will be seen that Infantry Colours were very large up to 1858.

Period and Authority	Size	
	Width	Depth on Lance or Pike
STANDARDS		
1768. Clothing Warrant	2 ft. 5 in. (without fringe)	2 ft. 3 in.
1873. Q.R.	2 ft. 6 in. (without fringe)	2 ft. 3 in.
1898. Q.R.	2 ft. 5½ in. (without fringe)	2 ft. 2 in.
1936. Clothing Regulations	2 ft. 5½ in. (without fringe)	2 ft. 2 in.
GUIDONS		
1768. Clothing Warrant	3 ft. 5 in. to the end of the slit of the swallow-tail	2 ft. 3 in. (Those of Light Dragoons to be of smaller size.)
1936. Clothing Regulations	3 ft. 5 in. (exclusive of the silk on the pole and of the fringe.)	2 ft. 3 in.
COLOURS		
1747. Regulations at Windsor	6 ft. 6 in.	6 ft. 2 in.
1768. Clothing Warrant	6 ft. 6 in.	6 ft.
1855. Submission dated 5th November	6 ft.	5 ft. 6 in.
1858. Submission dated 11th May	4 ft.	3 ft. 6 in. (exclusive of the fringe)
1868. Q.R.	3 ft. 9 in.	3 ft. (exclusive of the fringe)
1936. Clothing Regulations	3 ft. 9 in.	3 ft. (exclusive of the fringe)

As the Colour-bearers were very young officers, mere boys between fourteen and seventeen years of age, they had considerable difficulty in controlling the Colours when they were unfurled. Even a slight breeze would sometimes cause the Colours to carry them off their feet as they gripped the staves with all the power of which their small hands were capable. Occasionally they suffered the indignity of being thrown to the ground when a sudden gust of wind struck the Colours. In this connection Captain Cooke of the 43rd Light Infantry has recorded in his Memoirs (p. 24) that he joined the regiment in January, 1805, a month before his fourteenth birthday, and that a year later "The venerable Earl Fitzwilliam, who was Colonel of the Regiment, was there (at a party), and when I was introduced to him he asked me whether I did not find the Colours very heavy in my hands? My face instantly coloured up; the fact was, I had been blown down, Colours and all, while at a field day at Ashfield in Kent."

On 4th September, 1803, Major-General Sir John Moore wrote to Colonel Harry Calvert, the Adjutant-General, commenting upon "The Rules and Regulations" of General Sir David Dundas, in which he refers to the size of Colours in the following words: "I tried the mode pointed out by H.R.H. for directing the march in line. The objection to trust so important a charge as the direction of the march in line to the Ensigns, is that in our service they are the youngest, least experienced, and most giddy of the officers of a Regiment; and our Colours are so large and unwieldy that it is next to impossible to carry them upright and steady." (*Vide Journal of the Society for Army Historical Research*, IX, 162.)

Although these gallant lads may have lacked somewhat in physical strength, they were never wanting in courage on the battlefield and defended their Colours against the greatest odds. (*Vide* p. 173, "Brave Deeds around the Colours.")

Standards and Guidons always had fringes, but it will be seen from the table on the previous page that this adornment to Colours was not introduced until 1858. The reason for its introduction is mentioned in the following Horse Guards letter of 5th July, 1859:

"SIR,

"The new pattern Colours for the Infantry having, from their reduced size, a poor effect on Parade, I am directed by the General Commanding in Chief to intimate to you that Her Majesty has been pleased to sanction the addition of a silk and gold fringe of the pattern sent herewith.

"The Border for the Queen's Colour is to be of Crimson silk and gold, and that for the Regimental Colour of the Facings of the Corps and gold.

"I have the honour to be, Sir,

"Your obedient servant,

(*Sgd.*) "T. TROUBRIDGE, *D.A.G.*"

ALBERT WM. WOODS, ESQ.,
INSPECTOR OF REGIMENTAL COLOURS,
HERALDS COLLEGE,
DOCTORS' COMMONS.

The 1873 Q.R. stated that the depth of the fringe was to be about two inches, and that rule still holds good.

THE LANCE OR PIKE

The early poles to which flags were affixed appear to have been used as defensive weapons, and accordingly their length, balance and "war-head" were influenced by such considerations. In the Middle Ages a more ornamental lance was evolved, until the fluted pattern, usually associated with tournaments, arrives. This was the pattern adopted for Cavalry Standards and Guidons in the seventeenth century, excellent paintings of which may be seen in the Colour Books in the Royal Library, Windsor Castle. These lances had heart-shaped heads, with an ornamental design thereon.

The Infantry Colour pikes appear to have always been of a plain character, surmounted with a business-like sharp spear head, though somewhat ornamental also.

The head of the lances and pikes underwent a change in 1858, when the handsome Royal Crest displaced the spearpoint. (See Submission dated 11th May, 1858.)

The following table shows the patterns at various periods:

Period and Authority	Cavalry Lance	Infantry Pike
1768. Clothing Warrant	9 ft. (including spear and ferril)	9 ft. 10 in. (including spear and ferril)
1868. Q.R.	9 ft. (including Royal Crest)	9 ft. 10 in. (including Royal Crest)
1873. Q.R.	8 ft. 6 in. (including Royal Crest)	8 ft. 7 in. (including Royal Crest)
1898. Clothing Regulations	8 ft. 6 in. (including Royal Crest)	8 ft. 7½ in. (including Royal Crest)
1904. Clothing Regulations. Part I	8 ft. 6 in. (including Royal Crest)	8 ft. 7½ in. (including Royal Crest)
1936. Clothing Regulations. Part I	8 ft. 6 in. (including Royal Crest)	8 ft. 7½ in. (including Royal Crest)

NUMBER OF STANDARDS, GUIDONS AND COLOURS CARRIED

It has already been mentioned that in the seventeenth century each troop and company had a Standard, Guidon or Colour. In the Infantry the number of Colours per battalion was reduced to three in 1707 and to two in 1747 under the

Regulations of that year, and that number has continued to the present day.

As regards the Cavalry, Samuel Milne Milne (see *ante*) states, "The number of Standards carried by cavalry regiments during the latter part of the (eighteenth) century varied very considerably," and then, quoting from Inspection Returns, he shows that regiments had either three or two Standards or Guidons only, irrespective of the number of Troops per regiment.

Light Dragoons ceased carrying Guidons in 1834, as previously mentioned, and in August, 1858, the number of Standards or Guidons per Cavalry regiment authorized to carry them was reduced to one. As this involved the display of honorary distinctions, the order was in the following terms:

> "Her Majesty has been pleased to approve that regiments of Dragoon Guards and Dragoons henceforth carry but one Standard or Guidon; that the second, third and fourth Standards or Guidons, at present in use, be discontinued, and that the authorized badges, devices, distinctions and mottoes be, in future, borne on what is now called the Royal or First Standard or Guidon, in the Dragoon Guards and Dragoons."

Whether this was the result of experience in the Crimean War (1854-55) and Indian Mutiny (1857-58) is not known, but a reduction in the number of Standard and Guidon bearers, together with their escorts, no doubt increased the fighting strength to the same extent.

SUPPLY, DURATION AND REPAIR OF COLOURS

Before 1857 it was the practice for the Colonel of the Regiment to provide Standards, Guidons or Colours for his regiment if it were authorized to carry them, and in the Clothing Warrants before that date he was expressly directed to provide them.*

The Proprietary System came to a definite end in 1855,† and in 1857 the Regulations assume a different wording regarding

---

* See Clothing Regulations, 1819 (Sec. IV, para. XXIV), and Clothing Warrant for Cavalry, 14th July, 1827, Articles XXIV and XXVII, and corresponding references in the Regulations of 26th May, 1827, 30th July, 1830, 12th March, 1834, and 24th February, 1844.

† It had been gradually "dying" since the Peninsular War.

the supply of Colours, the relevant matter being found, not in the Clothing Regulations as heretofore, but in "The Queen's Regulations." The paragraph reads:

> "Previously to sending to the War Office requisitions for new Standards or Colours, application is to be made, through the Adjutant General, to the Inspector of Regimental Colours, for a drawing of the pattern as approved by Royal Authority."

The Army Clothing Regulations of 1857 give much more detail on this point, as will be seen from para. 46 reproduced here:

> "Colours will be supplied in infantry regiments and Standards or Guidons to Heavy Cavalry upon requisition addressed to the Secretary of State for War.

> "The period of duration assigned for Colours and Standards on home service and under ordinary circumstances is twenty years. On foreign stations the duration of these articles will vary according to the climate and nature of the service, and the above period must be kept in view as far as practicable.

> "Previous to a requisition being sent in for new Colours, the old ones must be examined by a Board of Survey, and the proceedings forwarded to the Secretary of State for War. Should the Colours not have lasted the prescribed period, a report must be made of the circumstances under which they have become unserviceable.

> "Repairs to Colours must be executed in the Regiment, and the expense thereof charged in the contingent accounts, supported by vouchers and a certificate of the Officer Commanding."

In course of time the instructions became more precise and detailed, and in the Clothing Regulations the instructions are distributed over three separate parts of the book: (a) general instructions, (b) a table setting out the numbers to be issued to each regiment and the duration of their "life," and (c) an Appendix giving the detail as to dimensions, design, etc.

As regards (b), the first table is published in the 1894 Clothing Regulations and is here reproduced, as it is the basis of those published in subsequent editions.

TABLE XX

COLOURS, STANDARDS, GUIDONS, ETC.

Household Cavalry	Four Standards and cases and belts for each regiment every 4 years.
Dragoon Guards	One Standard and belt for each regiment every 20 years.
Dragoons	One Guidon and belt for each regiment every 20 years.
Foot Guards	Two Colours and cases and belts for each battalion every 5 years.
Infantry (except Rifle Regiments) and West India Regiment	Two Colours and belts for each battalion every 20 years.
Cases for Standards and Guidons, Dragoon Guards and Dragoons, and for Colours for Infantry	Every 15 years.
For Guards of Honour at Ballater and Dublin	Queen's Colour and case and belt for each station, renewed when unserviceable.
Royal Military College	Two Colours and cases and belts, renewed when unserviceable.

This table is unchanged in the 1904 edition, except that the following schools are added to column one of the last item: "Duke of York's Royal Military School" and "Royal Hibernian Military School." In 1914 the "West African Regiments" were added to "Infantry" in column one.

Colours, etc., are made of a material which is adversely affected by atmospheric conditions, in view of which a definite "life" is assigned to them. Owing to the guards at Royal Palaces and numerous ceremonial parades in and about London, the Colours of the Household Troops are brought into use more than those of Line Regiments, and in consequence their Colours are replaced more often.

The "life" of Standards, Guidons and Colours has varied at different periods, the present scale being as in the table on the opposite page.

The repair of Colours is also mentioned in the Clothing Regulations of 1862, paragraph 85, which reads thus:

"Repairs to Colours are to be executed in the Regiment, and the expense thereof charged in the pay list, supported by vouchers and the usual certificate."

Regiment, etc.	Articles	Period
The Life Guards	Four Standards (one Queen's and three Squadrons'), cases and belts	10 years
Royal Horse Guards	Four Standards, cases and belts ...	10 years
Dragoon Guards	Each regiment one Standard and belt	20 years
	One case	15 years
Dragoons	Each regiment one Guidon and belt	20 years
	One case	15 years
Foot Guards	Each battalion two Colours, cases and belts	15 years
Infantry of the Line (except Rifle Regiments)	Each battalion two Colours and belts	20 years
	Two cases	15 years
Guards of Honour at Ballater	Queen's Colour, case and belt ...	Renewed when unserviceable
Royal Military Academy	Two Colours and cases ; three belts*	Renewed when unserviceable
Duke of York's Royal Military School	Two Colours, cases and belts ...	Renewed when unserviceable
Queen Victoria School	Two Colours, cases and belts ...	Renewed when unserviceable

This was repeated in 1865 in identical terms. In 1881 the instruction was slightly varied thus:

"Repairs to Colours, Standards or Guidons will be executed in the regiment after authority shall have been obtained from the Director of Clothing."

In 1894 the instruction was again varied to this: "Repairs will be executed regimentally and charged to the public." This was repeated in identical terms in 1898, but in 1904 the following was added: "but when the cost exceeds £5, authority should be obtained from the Royal Army Clothing Department before expenditure is incurred." The present Regulations are somewhat similar, but where the cost is estimated to exceed £10 for a Guidon or Colour, units serving at home will obtain authority, through the Assistant Director of Ordnance Services concerned, from the Commandant, Central Ordnance Depot, Branston, before expenditure is incurred.

ROYAL ARTILLERY STANDARD

The idea of having a Standard (not to be confused with the Cavalry Standards mentioned earlier) for the Royal Artillery was first proposed in an article in the *R.A. Journal* for July, 1945, written by "C.R.A." (Brigadier Siggers), and eventually the

---

* The third belt is for the King George V's Banner: see p. 153.

The Formation Sign (and Regimental Number) incorporated into the Royal Artillery Standard.
The Standard illustrated incorporates the badge of 100 A.G.R.A. (A.A.) (T.A.) as flown by 667 Heavy Anti-Aircraft Regiment, Royal Artillery (T.A.).   (A Hampshire Territorial Army Unit raised in 1947 with its headquarters in Aldershot).

Master Gunner's Committee approved it. A design submitted by Sir Gerald W. Wollaston, Inspector of Regimental Colours at the College of Arms, was approved by the King and the flag was adopted in August, 1947.

The Standard is flown at the Headquarters of R.A. Regiments and batteries and by independent R.A. units—*e.g.*, Schools, Independent Troops, etc., It is flown in peace and war, subject to security regulations.

It is made in the following sizes:

For use at Headquarters.

(*a*) 3 ft. by 1 ft. 1½ in., when a flag-pole 10 ft. high would be suitable.

(*b*) 4 ft. by 1 ft. 6 in., when a flag-pole 16 ft. high would be suitable.

For use in large camps, barracks, etc.

8 ft. by 3 ft., when a pole 35 ft. high would normally be used.

Variations from the standard pattern are authorized, in that traditional crests, badges, formation signs, etc., may be placed on the Standards.

The R.A. Standard is flown on the car of the Master Gunner, St. James's Park, on official R.A. occasions (*vide* Queen's Regulations, 1940, para. 988 (*xiv*), as amended by Amendment No. 87 in March, 1951).

The Standard illustrated incorporates the badge of 100 A.G.R.A. (A.A.) (T.A.) as flown by 667 Heavy Anti-Aircraft Regiment, Royal Artillery (T.A.).

CHAPTER VIII

HONORARY STANDARDS AND COLOURS

IT was a custom of the old Honourable East India Company to recognize particularly distinguished service of regiments that served under them, whether Imperial or their own, by granting them Honorary Standards or Colours—that is, Standards or Colours in addition to the regulation number. For instance, of their own regiments Honorary Standards were granted to the 35th Scinde Horse and 36th Jacob's Horse* for service in Sindh in 1843. The 35th Scinde Horse also carried a Standard surmounted by an open hand which had been captured at the battle of Meeanee on 17th February, 1843, and the 34th Prince Albert Victor's Own Poona Horse† carried a Standard

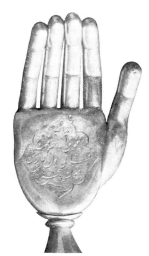

Detail of the silver hand on The Poona Horse Standard, showing the Persian inscription.

---

* These two regiments were amalgamated in 1921 to form The Scinde Horse (14th Prince of Wales's Own Cavalry).

† Amalgamated with the 33rd Queen Victoria's Own Light Cavalry in 1921 to form The Poona Horse (17th Queen Victoria's Own Cavalry).

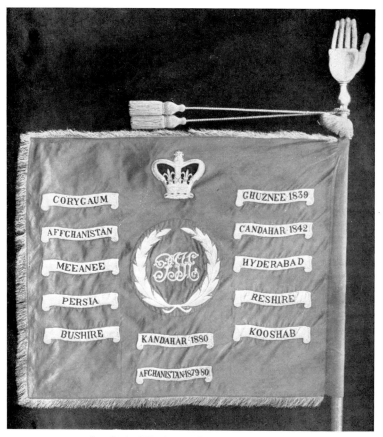

Standard of The Poona Horse, Indian Army.

surmounted by a silver hand bearing an inscription in Persian.

At the battle of Kooshab on 8th February, 1857, The Poona Horse captured the Standard of the 1st Khushgai Regiment of Fars of the Persian Army. This Standard bore at the top of the lance a silver hand, in the palm of which is inscribed, in Persian characters, "Yad Ullal Fauk Idebim," meaning "The Hand of God is above All Things." It bears a date corresponding to A.D. 1066.

Under India Government General Orders of 18th May, 1859, The Poona Horse were authorized to place this hand at the head of their Standard lance.

The 1st Battalion (Queen Victoria's Own Light Infantry) of the 7th Rajput Regiment was granted a third or Honorary Colour in 1803, bearing the words "Lake and Victory," for distinguished service. This was awarded in recognition of its distinguished service as the 15th Bengal Native Infantry Regiment at the battle of Delhi on 11th September, 1803, when serving under General Lord Lake. This is probably the only instance of the name of a Commander being borne on Colours as an award.

The Honourable East India Company granted Honorary Colours to three Imperial Regiments. Under a General Order dated Fort William, 30th October, 1803, the Governor-General

The Colours, including the Assaye Colour, Drums, Pipe Banner, etc., of the 2nd Bn. The Highland Light Infantry.

in Council granted an Honorary Colour to each of the 74th and 78th Regiments* in recognition of their distinguished service at the battle of Assaye on 23rd September, 1803, whilst serving under Major-General the Hon. Arthur Wellesley, later the great Duke of Wellington. Each Colour was to bear "a device properly suited to commemorate that signal and splendid victory."

The Colour granted to the 74th was burned at Fermoy, Ireland, on 6th April, 1918, and the charred remains are still preserved in the lid of a gold sarcophagus snuff-box, which is guarded by the officers of The Highland Light Infantry as a most sacred relic. To replace this Colour another was presented by Brigadier-General Sir Alfred Balfour, K.B.E., C.B., when a Major. This was laid up in 1931, and another was presented by the City of Glasgow.†

As regards the Colour presented to the 78th, according to Davidson's "History of The Seaforth Highlanders" (Vol. II, p. 49) there is some doubt about its fate, as shown by the following extract:

> "What became of the third or 'Assaye' colour has never been satisfactorily ascertained. It did not accompany the regiment to Europe in 1817, nor is any mention made of a third colour being carried by the 78th in any subsequent inspection report, though that of the 74th Regiment is frequently alluded to.

> "In the Spring of 1863 an application was made to the Horse Guards by the Colonel of the regiment, Sir Patrick Grant, G.C.B., for permission to again carry a third colour on ceremonial occasions, but this was refused in a letter of the 25th of September, stating it had never been intended that these honorary colours should be replaced. A similar application in the Jubilee year 1887 met with the same fate, but it was stated that there was no objection to a third colour being placed in the officers' mess, provided it was not carried on parade.

---

* Since 1881 these regiments have been, respectively, 2nd Bn. The Highland Light Infantry (City of Glasgow Regiment) and 2nd Bn. The Seaforth Highlanders (Ross-shire Buffs, The Duke of Albany's).

† *Vide The Highland Light Infantry Chronicle*, April, 1931.

"On the purchase of the Belmaduthy colours in 1889,* the officers accordingly determined to complete the stand by the addition of a third colour, which was duly carried out. The standard is of buff silk, bearing the 'Elephant' and 'LXXVIII' within two laurel branches; above on a blue scroll 'Assaye.' "

According to the inscription on the head of the Colour pikes of the pair of Honorary Colours granted by the Honourable East India Company to the 76th Regiment (since 1881, 2nd Bn. The Duke of Wellington's Regiment (West Riding)), they were granted "In Testimony of its meritorious services and distinguished bravery in the different actions recorded upon them."† The battle honours appropriate to the period referred to and now borne by The Duke of Wellington's Regiment are "Mysore," "Seringapatam," "Ally Ghur," "Delhi, 1803," and "Dieg."

The original Honorary Colours were carried through the Peninsular War (1808-1814), having been presented in 1807. In 1830 the centre portions of these Colours were transferred to new groundwork, and in 1888 the India Office supplied a pair of entirely new Colours. The Queen's Colour of this pair was lost by fire in Burma in 1900, and the Regimental Colour was laid up. In 1905 another new set was provided by the India Office.

As all of the above-mentioned Honorary Colours were presented to the regiments by the Honourable East India Company, simply as a means of recognizing distinguished service for a limited period in India, they have not the same status as those presented by the Sovereign, neither are they mentioned in the British Army List. In 1835‡ King William IV "was pleased to decide that no Regiment in His Majesty's service should be permitted to display a third Colour under any circumstances whatever," and this prohibition was confirmed by George V in January, 1933.

William IV's decision arose because the 5th Foot (now The

---

* "The first stand of Colours was for a long time at Belmaduthy, in Ross-shire, but were sold on the dismantling of the house in 1889, when they were purchased by the officers of the regiment" (*vide* Davidson, Vol. II, p. 49).

† "History of The Duke of Wellington's Regiment," p. 33, by Brigadier-General C. D. Bruce, C.B.E.

‡ Horse Guards letter dated 14th August, 1835.

The Royal Northumberland Fusiliers celebrating St. George's Day, with Queen's, Regimental and Drummers' Colour (in rear) all decked with wreaths of red and white roses.

E

Royal Northumberland Fusiliers) had preferred a claim to the distinction of bearing a third Colour on parade. The Colour referred to is a small green silk banner, a memento of a French Colour captured by the regiment at the battle of Wilhelmstahl on 24th June, 1762, during the Seven Years' War. It is now trooped on St. George's Day only, being carried with the drums when beating the Assembly, after which it remains at the saluting base. For this reason it is sometimes referred to as the "Drummers' Colour." The original banner was destroyed by fire at Gibraltar in 1833.

The Queen's Royal Regiment (West Surrey) also have a third Colour. It is sea green in colour, which was a favourite colour of Queen Catherine, Consort of Charles II. Tradition has it that the original of this Colour was presented to the regiment by Queen Catherine, from whom their title of "The Queen's" is derived. The Queen's had made a similar claim to the 5th regarding their right to carry a third Colour, and the letter of 14th August, 1835, after stating the above-mentioned prohibition, adds: "The King, however, expressed to Lord Hill His Majesty's earnest hopes that The Queen's Royals would regard this decision not as a mark of His Majesty's forgetfulness of the uniformly high character of the regiment, but solely as a proof of His Majesty's determination to establish uniformity in this, as in every other respect, throughout the army.

"The King was further pleased to observe that if it were wished, upon the part of The Queen's Royals, that the third Colour should be retained and preserved, His Majesty would not insist upon its being actually withdrawn, but in making that observation, His Majesty expressly ordered that on no account should the third Colour ever be displayed in the ranks of the Regiment."

In 1825 George IV had authorized The Queen's to bear their third Colour. This was represented to William IV, who none the less laid down as stated.

Colours of the 1st Bn. The Queen's Royal Regiment, with the third, or Queen Catherine's, Colour in the centre.

Colours of the 1st Bn. The Royal Northumberland Fusiliers, with the "Drummer's Colour" in the centre.

CHAPTER IX

REORGANIZATION OF INFANTRY
OF THE LINE

In 1881 a great reorganization of Infantry of the Line occurred. General Order 41 of that year inaugurated a system under which all single battalion regiments (except The Cameron Highlanders) were amalgamated in pairs, each pair forming one regiment. All Infantry regiments, amalgamated or otherwise, ceased being designated by their "Number of the Regiment" which they had borne since introduced in 1747 and were allotted a territorial or other descriptive title, their old numbers being abolished.

Since 1782 the majority of regiments had as their secondary title a county title, and the new amalgamated regiments adopted one of these titles. For instance, the 31st (Huntingdonshire) Regiment was linked with the 70th (Surrey) Regiment, the new title being "The East Surrey Regiment"; the 48th (Northamptonshire) Regiment was linked with the 58th (Rutlandshire) Regiment, the new title being "The Northamptonshire Regiment."

As might be expected, such an upheaval caused many heartaches among those regiments with fine records associated with the old number, but whose identity on amalgamation was now totally obliterated from the army. However this may have been, a study of the reasons for the introduction of the "Cardwell System" show that they were sound.

The main effect of the reorganization upon Infantry Colours was as follows :

(*a*) *The Royal or First Colour.*

To bear in the centre the territorial designation on a crimson circle with the Royal, or other, title within, the whole surmounted by the Imperial Crown.

(*b*) *The Regimental or Second Colour.*

(i) Previously this Colour had borne a Union in the upper

Colours and Escort of the 2nd Bn. The Northamptonshire Regiment.
These Colours were presented on the 10th May, 1860.

canton, but under the Queen's Regulations of 1881 this disappeared from Regimental Colours. Colours were not immediately changed to conform with these instructions, hence a number of the former pattern, with the Union in the upper canton, were in active use in the 1930's and, in fact, a few of the pre-1881 pattern are still in use (1952) by the express desire of the units concerned—*e.g.*, those of The Royal Lincolnshire Regiment are approaching their centenary, having been presented in Phœnix Park, Dublin, in 1863; and The Gloucestershire Regiment received new Colours on 26th April, 1952, the old ones having been in service since they were presented at Gibraltar in 1868.

(ii) The Colours of the 1st and 2nd Battalions to bear the ancient badges, devices, distinctions and mottoes which have been conferred by Royal authority.

Referring to battle honours in the form of names of actions, the 1909 K.R. stated: "In those regiments where the number of actions exceed nine, laurel branches are to be introduced, and scrolls bearing the names of the actions entwined thereon."

(iii) The Colours of the 3rd and 4th Battalions (*i.e.*, Militia Battalions) to be the same as those of the 1st and 2nd (or Regular) Battalions, but "without such devices and distinctions as specially refer to actions or campaigns granted in commemoration of the Services of the other two Battalions."

The effect of this instruction was to keep separate the distinctions granted to Regular battalions from those granted to Militia battalions. As they all belonged to the same regiment the reason for this is not clear, particularly as now all battalions, whether Regular or Territorial, bear precisely the same distinctions, thus making for regimental unity.

(iv) The number of each battalion (I, II, III or IV) to be placed in the dexter canton, formerly occupied by the Union. (Under the 1873 Q.R. "II BATT" was to be placed on a scroll below the Union Wreath in the case of 2nd Battalions.) A modification of the 1881 instruction was made in Q.R. of 1885 thus:

> "When regiments of Infantry are not entitled to a Royal or ancient badge, and have not a combination of territorial and Royal or other special designations, the number of the Battalion will be placed on the Colours within the

circle bearing the name of the regiment instead of in the dexter canton."

A further modification was made in 1894 in that "in the case of regiments which are entitled to carry honorary distinctions in all four corners of the Colours, the number of the battalion is to be placed below the honorary distinction" in the dexter canton.

(v) The territorial designation, if practicable, to be inscribed on a circle, within the Union Wreath of roses, thistles and shamrocks, and the Royal or other title in an escroll underneath, the whole ensigned with the Imperial Crown.

"If practicable" refers to regiments which had very long titles and could not be embroidered comfortably on the circle, except in ridiculously small letters, out of proportion with the remainder of the design.

1948 : Reorganization of Infantry of the Line

In 1948 another reorganization of Infantry of the Line took place under which many Regular battalions were disbanded and others amalgamated to form one battalion.

The Colours of disbanded battalions were laid up in accordance with current regulations.

In the case of amalgamated battalions the Colours of each separate battalion before amalgamation are permitted to be retained by the resultant battalion, but only those of one pre-amalgamated battalion are to be carried on a parade at any one time.

When the Colours of the former 1st Battalion become due for replacement, new Colours will be provided appropriate to the new 1st Battalion; but those of the former 2nd Battalion will continue in use until condemned as unserviceable and will then be laid up.

CHAPTER X

COLOURS OF THE FOOT GUARDS*

THE Foot Guards, by virtue of their close association with the Sovereign, have a history peculiar to themselves, which is reflected in the nature and emblazonment of features appropriate to royalty in their Colours. Briefly, these features are:

(a) The Grenadier, Coldstream and Scots Guards carry a Royal Standard of the Regiment or State Colour.

(b) All regiments carry Royal and other badges in rotation on their Regimental or Second Colour.

(c) The Queen's or First Colour is crimson and the Regimental Colour is the Great Union, whereas in the Infantry of the Line the Queen's Colour is the Great Union and the Regimental Colour generally of the same hue as the facings of the regiment.

(d) All battle honours authorized to be borne on Colours are borne on both Queen's and Regimental Colours, and not only on the Regimental (with ten selected for the Great War of 1914-18 on the Queen's) as in the case of Infantry of the Line.

Some of these special features are identical in each regiment of Foot Guards, and to obviate repetition they are dealt with in this section.

(a) *Royal Standard and State Colours.*

This Colour is closely associated with the Sovereign. In the

---

* I wish to acknowledge my indebtedness to the Officers Commanding the five Regiments of Foot Guards, who kindly loaned to me their Regimental Colour Books and other documents to assist in the preparation of this chapter, and also for granting permission to use any illustrations therefrom.

I wish further specially to acknowledge the great assistance obtained from the excellent memorandum prepared by the late Captain C. B. Balfour, Scots Guards (much of which also refers to the Coldstream Guards), kindly loaned to me by the Officers Commanding those regiments.—T. J. E.

Grenadier Guards it has always been the Colour of the Queen's Company and is usually referred to by its historic title, "The Queen's Company Colour, the Royal Standard of the Regiment." In the Coldstream and Scots Guards it is designated the "State Colour."

Nathan Brooks, the compiler of the list of regiments in 1684, refers to the Grenadier Guards Colour as "the Standard of The King's Own Company," and Sandford, the Herald who wrote the history of the Coronation of James II in 1685, uses identical language. The 1743 warrant mentioned by Milne states: "The Union Colour is the first stand of Colours in all regiments, royal or not, except the Foot Guards. With them the King's Standard is the first as a peculiar distinction."

In the "Standing Orders for the Army, 1755," para. 11 reads: "The King's Standard or Colours in the Guards can never be carried to any guard but that on His Majesty."

(b) *Royal Badges, etc.*

Royal and other badges are borne on the Regimental or Second Colours of all regiments of Foot Guards. When each company carried a Colour the badge was emblazoned in the centre. When Company Colours were abolished for the Infantry of the Line they continued to be issued to the Guards until 1838, when only one Regimental Colour was provided for each battalion. A different Company badge was selected to be borne upon each fresh issue of Regimental Colours.

In 1859 there was an attempt to compel the Guards to select one Company badge that should be borne permanently on all succeeding issues of Regimental Colours; but on the matter being referred to Queen Victoria, Her Majesty ruled that a different badge should be selected for each fresh issue of Colours, and this practice has continued ever since. The method of selecting the badge is dealt with in the sections dealing with each regiment.

(c) *The Queen's Colour being crimson and the Regimental Colour being the Great Union.*

The Colonel's, Lieutenant-Colonel's and Major's Colours were all crimson about 1750-1760. (The actual date varied in each regiment.) Until 1838 the Colours of the Foot Guards had been supplied by the Master of the Great Wardrobe, and later by the Lord Chamberlain, at public expense. In that year, however, the Colonels were informed that they were to provide the Colours in future in the same manner as in other regiments. In 1855 the Proprietary System was abolished and the State undertook to provide all Colours of the army, and accordingly published Regulations in 1857 and 1859 which were intended to apply equally to the Guards as to other regiments. Under these Regulations the Great Union was to be the First Colour and the Second Colour of the facing of the regiment, as in the case of Infantry of the Line. The Guards appealed against this, and the matter was referred to the Queen, who directed that the Queen's or First Colour should be crimson and the Regimental or Second Colour the Great Union.

In 1855 the Guards had already settled which of the crimson Colours should be the Queen's Colour of each battalion, the arrangement being:

Colonel's Colour	...	Queen's Colour of 1st Battalion.
Lieutenant-Colonel's Colour	... ...	Queen's Colour of 2nd Battalion.
Major's Colour	...	Queen's Colour of 3rd Battalion.

This arrangement was confirmed by Horse Guards letter of 24th November, 1859, and is still in force.

(d) Battle Honours on both Queen's and Regimental Colours.

When the honour "Gibraltar" was granted in 1784, it was directed to be placed upon the Second Colour, but the Vellum Colour Books in the office of the Inspector of Regimental Colours (see later) show that such honours were placed upon both Colours in the early years of the nineteenth century, and this practice remained until 1844, when it was directed that such distinctions should be placed upon the Second Colour only. However, in 1859 the Guards obtained authority to bear their distinctions on both Colours, which they do at present.

(e) Decking of Colours with a laurel wreath.

The occasions on which Colours are decked are shown in Appendix "E".

GRENADIER GUARDS

Note on the origin of the Regiment.

This regiment originated from two regiments of Guards raised by Charles II, which were amalgamated to form one later on.

Whilst the King was an exile on the Continent he raised a regiment of Guards of twelve companies from among his royalist followers in 1656, giving the command to Lord Wentworth. At the Restoration in 1660 this regiment went into Dunkirk, where it remained until the sale of that place two years later, when it came to England.

In 1660 Charles commissioned Colonel John Russell, a son of the Earl of Bedford, to raise another regiment of Guards in England, also of twelve companies, appointing him to the command. Therefore, from 1662 there were two Regiments of Guards in England. These two were continually disputing as to which was the senior: Wentworth's claimed it on the ground of age, and Russell's on the ground that it had been longest on the English Establishment. The King was at a loss as to how to settle this matter until Wentworth died in 1665, when he amalgamated both regiments to form one, the First Guards, a title it bore until 1815, when "His Royal Highness has been pleased to approve of the First Regiment of Foot Guards being made a Regiment of Grenadiers and styled the 1st or Grenadier Regiment of Foot Guards, in commemoration of their having defeated the Grenadiers of the French Imperial Guards upon this memorable occasion"—*i.e.*, at the battle of Waterloo on 18th June, 1815.

The new regiment therefore had twenty-four companies.

The Royal Standard of the Regiment.

The full title of this flag is "The Queen's Company Colour, the Royal Standard of the Regiment," its heraldic description being: Gules (crimson), in the centre the Royal Cypher reversed and interlaced or, ensigned with the Imperial Crown proper, in chief on the dexter the badge of England, viz., a rose stalked and leaved or, in chief on the sinister the badge of the Kingdom of Scotland, viz., a thistle stalked and leaved or, in base on the dexter the badge of Ireland, viz., a shamrock or, in base on the sinister the aforesaid badge of England, each ensigned with the Imperial Crown proper.*

By a decision dated 27th October, 1902, "the Colour is only carried when the Regiment is employed on ceremonial duties when the Sovereign is present, and on no other. If on such occasion the 1st Battalion is detailed to furnish a Guard of Honour, the King's Company will provide it and will carry the Colour. If either of the other Battalions is detailed to furnish the Guard of Honour the Colour will be carried by the Guard. If the Regiment is not detailed to furnish a Guard of Honour the Colour will be carried by the King's Company. If the Regiment is not detailed to furnish a Guard of Honour, and the King's Company is not present, the Colour will not be carried."*

By a decision of 11th May, 1914, "the Colour will only be lowered to His Majesty the King, Her Majesty the Queen and Her Majesty the Queen Mother. When the Guard of Honour is mounted on a Royal personage entailing the lowering of the Colour, the King's Company Colour will not be carried. This does not apply to a case where His Majesty the King is actually seated in a carriage or riding with the Foreign Royalty, but only applies when His Majesty arrives earlier or later than the Foreign Royalty at such function."* By a decision of 26th October, 1937, "the Colour is to be lowered on every occasion when the Sovereign is present, even if the Guard is mounted in honour of some other personage."

By a decision of 5th February, 1917, "when a Guard of Honour is furnished by the King's Guard the King's Company Colour will not be carried."*

In the sketch, in the Headquarters of the Regiment, purporting to be the original design drawn in 1661 by Sir Edward Walker, the Royal Standard is shown as white throughout with the King's Cypher "C.R." in gold, ensigned with a crown, in the centre. According to the accounts of the Great Wardrobe for 1661, the White Royal Standard belonged to Lord Wentworth's Regiment, while Colonel Russell's regiment had a crimson Standard. On the amalgamation of the two regiments in 1665 the white Standard ceased to be carried, there being only one King's Company from that time.

---

* *Vide* the booklet, "The Colours of the Grenadier Guards."

The original Standard had no fringe, and this feature has been maintained.

The Standard issued in 1704 was embroidered with Queen Anne's cypher ensigned with a crown, but another issued two years later was "embroidered with Her Majesty's cypher and crown in the middle, and the quarterly arms of the four kingdoms," *i.e.*, England, Scotland, Ireland and France. This latter arrangement, however, was short-lived owing to the union of England and Scotland in 1707, when the Royal Arms were arranged as follows: England and Scotland impaled in the first and fourth quarter, France in the second and Ireland in the third, and so the Standard remained until the accession of George I in 1714, when the arms of Hanover displaced those of England and Scotland in the fourth quarter. In 1801 the fleur-de-lis was removed from the Royal Arms, and on the accession of Queen Victoria in 1837 the arms of Hanover were removed, because Her Majesty did not succeed to that kingdom, and the design of the Standard became as it is now described above.

The Royal Standard is the personal gift of the Sovereign, and a new one is normally presented at the commencement of each reign. The Royal Standards carried during the reigns of Queen Victoria, King Edward VII and King George V are preserved in Windsor Castle.

The Company Colour of the Queen's Company.

The Grenadier Guards have thirty Company badges (see pages 63—65) which are made into Company Colours of crimson silk, about 20 in. × 18 in. in size. Upon them are embroidered, in the centre, the Company badges ensigned with the Imperial Crown: in the dexter chief canton is embroidered in gold the designation of the Company, and in the sinister chief canton is embroidered in gold the name of the Sovereign, etc., to which the badge in the centre refers.

The Company Colour of the Queen's Company has, in the centre, the Royal Crest ensigned with the Imperial Crown, in the dexter chief canton "QUEEN'S COMPANY," and in the sinister chief canton "QUEEN'S CREST."

It is this small Company Colour of the Queen's Company that is buried with the Sovereign, a custom which originated in 1910 at the funeral of King Edward VII, and later observed at

Grenadier Guards: The King's Company Colour. The Royal Standard of the Regiment, presented by H.M. King George VI.

Colours of 1st Bn. Grenadier Guards. The Regimental Colour (Union) on right carries the badge of the 28th Company.

Face p. 60

the funeral of King George V in 1936 and of King George VI on 15th February, 1952.

The Battalion Colours.

The 1661 drawings of these Colours show that they were all white with the red St. George's Cross covering the whole field, the only distinction being the badge borne in the centre of each. In his Army List of 1684 Nathan Brooks gives a little more detail, for he states:

"The Royal Regiment of Foot Guards (consisting of 24 companies, each of which has an Ensign).

"This Regiment flyes St. George's Cross in a White Field, viz.:

The Colonel's white, with a red cross, the Crown or,

The Lieut.-Colonel's, the same with C.R. crowned or,

The Major's with C.R. and Crown or, with a Blaze crimson."

In 1685 Sandford, in his "History of the Coronation of James II," described the Colours thus:

Colonel's	Crimson, not charged with any device.
Lieutenant-Colonel's	White, with St. George's Cross covering the whole field.
Major's	Same as Lieutenant-Colonel's, but with a pile wavy.
Captain's	Same as Lieutenant-Colonel's, but eldest Captain had a King's cypher ensigned with Imperial Crown in the centre; the Second Captain had two cyphers and crowns, and so on.

In the Colour Books at Windsor Castle the Colours are depicted as they were in 1745 and show the following:

Colonel's	Crimson throughout with crown in centre.
Lieutenant-Colonel's	The Union; in the centre the King's cypher "G.R.," crowned.
Major's	Same as Lieutenant-Colonel's, but with the pile wavy.
First Captain	Union; in the centre the crest of England ensigned with the Imperial Crown: figure 1 in dexter canton.

Milne states that "A little later (*i.e.*, after 1745) the Lieutenant-Colonel's and the Major's were changed from the 'Union' to 'plain crimson,' the former having a small Union in the upper corner, the latter the same, with the addition of a small blaze or flame of gold issuing underneath the corner of the union." This agrees with the 1768 Colour Book at Windsor.

As previously mentioned, the crimson Colours of the Colonel, Lieutenant-Colonel and Major were adopted as the Queen's Colours respectively of the 1st, 2nd and 3rd Battalions in 1855, and so they have remained.

The Royal Badges.

In the first Royal Warrant of 1661 twelve Royal badges were authorized for the "Regiment of Foot Guards," and another twelve were authorized in the second Warrant in the same year. Although twenty-four in all were authorized and issued, only twenty are shown in the drawing in the Regimental Head-quarters of the Regiment. One possible explanation is that the badges in the Royal Standard, the Colonel's, Lieutenant-Colonel's and Major's Colours in each regiment may have been identical, which would account for the other four badges.

In the above-mentioned drawing the Royal Standard is shown white, so also is one other Colour, which bears the red Rose of Lancaster; all the others are red St. George's Crosses.

On the amalgamation of Russell's and Wentworth's Regiments in 1665 the twelve badges of Russell's were retained, but twelve new ones were issued for Wentworth's late twelve companies. On his accession in 1685, James II abolished the Royal badges and substituted his cypher ensigned with the Imperial Crown, multiplied on the Company Colours according to the seniority of the Captain. The Junior Captain's Colour must have been fairly well covered with cyphers and crowns and of considerable weight. In the Coldstream and Scots Guards there were no cyphers in the Captains' Colours, their seniority being indicated by Roman numerals painted in the centre and ensigned with the Imperial Crown.

The repetition of cyphers and crowns did not last long, for William III abolished them and substituted a Royal Cypher and Crown in the centre only of each Colour.

The entries in the Great Wardrobe accounts for 1693 seem to imply that the Royal badges were restored that year because without them confusion arose between the Colours of the First Guards and Coldstream.

Although under the 1747 Regulations only two Colours were permitted, it is thought that for the First Guards the whole twenty-four Colours were provided up to 1838, but only two were actually carried.

In 1855, at the time of the Crimean War, Queen Victoria granted six more badges to the Regiment on augmentation.

The present description of the badges as laid down in the Colour Book of the Grenadier Guards is as shown below.

Note.—Each badge is ensigned with an Imperial Crown.

Com-pany	Description of the Badge	By whom and when granted
Queen's	The Royal Crest ... ... (The Queen's Crest)	Charles II ... 1661
2nd	A Rose gules, surmounted by another argent, barbed and seeded proper (A badge of Henry VIII)	Charles II ... 1661
3rd	A Fleur-de-lis or ... ... (A badge of Henry V)	Charles II ... 1661
4th	A Portcullis with chains pendant or ... (A badge of Henry VII)	Charles II ... 1661
5th	The Sun in its splendour or, thereon a Rose argent, barbed and seeded proper (A badge of Edward IV)	Charles II ... 1661
6th	A Thistle stalked and leaved proper ... (Badge of Scotland)	Charles II ... 1661
7th	A Harp or, stringed argent ... ... (Badge of Ireland)	Charles II ... 1661
8th	On a mount vert a Dragon passant with wings elevated gules (Badge of Wales borne by Henry VII)	Charles II ... 1661
9th	On a mount vert a Greyhound passant argent, gorged with a collar gules studded and ringed or (A badge of Henry VII)	Charles II ... 1661
10th	The Sun in its splendour or ... ... (A badge of Richard II)	Charles II ... 1661
11th	A Unicorn passant argent, armed, maned and tufted and unguled or, gorged with a Prince's coronet and the chain reflexed over the back of the last (A badge of James I)	Charles II ... 1661
12th	On a mount vert an Antelope statant argent, attired, tufted, ducally gorged and chain reflexed over the back or (A badge of Henry IV)	Charles II ... 1661

Com-pany	Description of the Badge	By whom and when granted		
13th	On a mount vert a Hart couchant argent, attired, unguled, ducally gorged and chain reflexed over the back or (A badge of Richard II)	Charles II	...	1661
14th	A Falcon with wings expanded argent, beaked, legged and belled or, within a fetter lock closed of the last (A badge of Edward IV)	Charles II	...	1661
15th	A Rose gules barbed and seeded proper ... (A badge of Henry IV)	Charles II	...	1661
16th	On a mount vert a Swan with wings expanded argent, beaked and legged gules, ducally gorged and chain reflexed over the back or (A badge of Henry IV)	Charles II	...	1661
17th	A Falcon, wings elevated argent, crowned and holding in the dexter talon a sceptre or, standing on the trunk of a tree eradicated, from the dexter side thereof sprouting a branch of white and red roses barbed and seeded proper (A badge of Queen Anne Boleyn, second wife of Henry VIII)	Charles II	...	1661
18th	The Trunk of a Tree couped and erased or, from the dexter and sinister side three leaves sprouting vert (A badge of Henry III)	Charles II	...	1661
19th	A Sceptre in bend dexter or, surmounted by a sword in bend sinister proper, pommel and hilt of the first (A badge of James I)	Charles II	...	1661
20th	On a mount vert an Oak Tree, therein a man's face Imperially Crowned, all proper (A badge of Charles II, who assumed it in commemoration of his escape after the battle of Worcester on 3rd September, 1651, when he eluded Cromwell's soldiers by hiding in an oak tree)	Charles II	...	1661
21st	The Sun rising or, behind clouds proper ... (A badge of Edward III)	Queen Anne		1713
22nd	A Beacon or, fired proper ... ... (A badge of Henry V)	Queen Anne		1713
23rd	Two Ostrich Feathers in saltire argent, quilled or, the dexter surmounted by the sinister (A badge of Henry VI)	Queen Anne		1713
24th	On a wreath or and azure a Tower triple towered of the first, from the portal a Hart springing argent, attired and unguled or (Crest of Ireland)	Queen Anne		1713
25th	Argent a Cross gules ... ... (Arms of St. George)	Queen Victoria		1855
26th	Azure billetee and a Lion rampant or ... (Arms of Nassau borne by William III)	Queen Victoria		1855

Colours of the 1st Bn. Coldstream Guards. The Regimental Colour (Union) on right carries the badge of the 22nd Company.

Colours of 1st Bn. Scots Guards. The Regimental Colour (Union) on right carries the badge of the 23rd Company.

Com-pany	Description of the Badge	By whom and when granted
27th	A representation of the Badge of the Most Honourable Order of the Bath, as established in 1727, or	Queen Victoria 1855
28th	Out of a ducal coronet a pillar proper, the top adorned with a coronet and plume of three peacock's feathers proper, charged with a star argent ; on either side of the pillar out of the coronet a sickle argent, handles gules, the backs adorned with small tufts of peacock's feathers and between the sickles before the pillar a Horse current argent (Crest of the House of Hanover)	Queen Victoria 1855
29th	A Trefoil vert ... ... (Badge of the Union of Ireland)	Queen Victoria 1855
30th	Out of a ducal coronet a pillar of the arms of Saxony crowned with a like coronet and thereon a plume of three peacock's feathers proper (Crest of the Prince Consort)	Queen Victoria 1855

COLDSTREAM GUARDS

Historical Note on the Origin of the Regiment.

When Oliver Cromwell was preparing for his campaign in Scotland in 1650 he wished to make George Monck Colonel of a Regiment of Foot, so he took five companies from Sir Arthur Hazelrigg's Regiment at Newcastle and another five from George Fenwick's at Berwick and organized them as a regiment, giving the Colonelcy to Monck. The first active service of this new regiment was at Dunbar on 3rd September, 1650, where it ably acquitted itself.

During the latter part of 1659 Monck was in command of the Commonwealth troops in Scotland, and for the last three weeks of that year he and his regiment were quartered at Coldstream on the River Tweed. On 1st January, 1660, he began his historic march on London, his regiment being referred to as "The Regiment from Coldstream" or "The Coldstream Regiment." In February, 1661, it became a regiment of Guards, hence Coldstream Guards, the regiment with the longest service on the English Establishment.

F

The State Colours.

The Coldstream Guards have two State Colours: they were presented by William IV. Their description is:

First State Colour.—Gules (crimson); in the centre the Star of the Order of the Garter proper, within the Union Wreath or, ensigned with the Imperial Crown; in each of the four corners a Sphinx argent between two branches of laurel fructed and tied with a riband or; in the centre, below the Star of the Order of the Garter, on a scroll azure, the word "Egypt" or.

The following battle honours are borne on this Colour: "Lincelles," "Talavera," "Barrosa," "Peninsula" and "Waterloo."

The Colour is fringed with gold and has gold and crimson cord and tassels.

Second State Colour.—Gules (crimson); in the centre the Star of the Order of the Garter proper, within the Union Wreath or, ensigned with the Imperial Crown; in each of the four corners a Sphinx argent between two branches of laurel fructed and tied with a riband or, superscribed "Egypt" also or.

The following battle honours are borne on this Colour: "Lincelles," "Talavera," "Barrosa," "Peninsula," "Waterloo," "Inkerman," "Alma" and "Sevastopol."

The fringe and tassels the same as the First State Colour.

There are two points of difference between these two Colours:

(i) The badge authorized under Horse Guards letter of 6th July, 1802, in commemoration of the Egyptian Campaign of 1801, under Sir Ralph Abercromby, was a Sphinx within two branches of laurel, superscribed "Egypt." In the Second Colour the badge is correctly placed thereon, but in the First Colour the Sphinx and "Egypt" are divorced from each other.

(ii) The Second State Colour bears the battle honours granted for the Crimean War, which do not appear upon the First Colour. It is thought that when the Crimean honours were granted in 1855 the First Colour was so old that any attempt to add more distinctions would probably tear the material, so it was decided to emblazon them on the Second State Colour only.

The Battalion Colours.

The earliest mention of the Colours of the Coldstream Guards is in MacKinnon's History of the Regiment (p. 126) and refers to a review by the Grand Duke of Tuscany in May, 1669. The Duke's record is quoted thus: "The Second Regiment, that of General George Monck, Duke of Albemarle, whose standard was *green* with six white balls and a red cross." The "six white balls" indicate a Captain's Colour: green was the colour of the facings at that time, being changed to blue in 1685. The hue of the Colours, however, had been changed to blue in 1670. In his Army List for 1684, Nathan Brooks notes: "The Cole-Stream, al, Cauldstream Regiment of Guards (consisting of 12 Companies, each of which has an Ensign) . . . Flyes St. George's Cross bordered with white in a blew field." Francis Sandford of the Herald's College devised the Colours of the Regiment for the Coronation of James II in 1685, and described them thus:

Colonel's	*Blue*, without any distinguishing feature.
Lieutenant-Colonel's	Blue with a white plain cross throughout, surmounted by a crimson cross.
Major's	Same as Lieutenant-Colonel's, but with a pile wavy issuing out of a canton of the first quarter.
Captain's	Same as Lieutenant-Colonel's, but with their seniority indicated by a Roman numeral painted in the dexter canton: the eldest Captain had a "I" and the youngest a "IX."

But, says Sandford, James II immediately altered that arrangement and "directed that the alterations following should be made in the Ensigns of His Second Regiment of Guards, that they might be more agreeable to the Colours of the First Regiment" (of Guards). The result was:

Colonel's	White throughout.
Lieutenant-Colonel's	White with crimson cross throughout.
Major's	Same as Lieutenant-Colonel's, but with the usual pile wavy.
Captain's	Same as Lieutenant-Colonel's, but with a Roman numeral in the centre ensigned with the Imperial Crown, indicating their seniority.

A booklet entitled "The Colours and Customs of the Coldstream Guards" states that

"In 1696 William III granted a further issue of 12 Colours, associating with the Regiment for the first time the Star of the Garter, and eleven of the present Company Badges (*i.e.*, down to the 9th Captain). The Colonel's Colour was *crimson*; the Lieutenant-Colonel's white with St. George's Cross, a Garter Star and Crown; the Major's the same, with a blaze; Captain's white with St. George's Cross; the 5th, 6th and 9th with Garter badges, the rest with Royal Badges."

The Wardrobe accounts for 1700-01 have evidence that the Colonel's Colour was crimson. The aforementioned booklet also records that the Lieutenant-Colonel's was probably crimson in 1707 and certainly by 1716, as also the Major's. By 1751, on the evidence of the Windsor Colour Book of that year, the Colours had become stabilized and show

Colonel's	Crimson, in the centre the star of the Garter ensigned with the Imperial Crown.
Lieutenant-Colonel's	Crimson, in the centre an eight-pointed star, ensigned with the Imperial Crown, in the dexter canton a Union.
Major's	Same as Colonel's, but with a Union in dexter canton, from the lower corner of which issues a pile wavy.
Captain's	Unions, in the centre a Company badge ensigned with the Imperial Crown, numeral of Company in dexter canton.

As in the case of the Grenadier Guards, the Colonel's, Lieutenant-Colonel's and Major's Colours have become the Queen's Colours of the 1st, 2nd and 3rd Battalions respectively, and their present description, as given in the Army List, is

1st Battalion	Gules (crimson): In the centre the star of the Order of the Garter proper, ensigned with the Imperial Crown; in base the Sphinx superscribed "Egypt."
2nd Battalion	Gules (crimson): In the centre a star of eight points argent within the Garter, ensigned with the Imperial Crown; in base the Sphinx super-

Regimental Colour of the 4th Battalion Coldstream Guards being marched past General Sir Charles Loyd, Colonel of the Regiment, at Pirbright Camp, on the 20th July, 1946, on the occasion of that Battalion's farewell parade prior to disbandment.

This Colour had originally been presented to the 4th (Pioneer) Battalion of the Regiment, which was raised for service in the Guards Division in the First World War. When that Battalion was disbanded in 1919 its one and only Colour was lodged in the Chapel of the Guards Depot.

In the Second World War the 4th Battalion was again formed, and on the conclusion of hostilities in the summer of 1945 they applied for permission to use this old Colour and it was accordingly sent to them in Germany. On the Battalion's disbandment in 1946 the Colour was once more returned to the Chapel of the Guards Depot, where it now is.

The 4th Battalion Grenadier Guards, raised for service in the First World War and subsequently disbanded, also had only one Colour.

	scribed "Egypt"; in the dexter canton the Union.
3rd Battalion	As for the 1st Battalion, with, for difference, in the dexter canton the Union and issuing therefrom in bend a pile wavy or.
Regimental Colours	The Union: In the centre a Company badge ensigned with the Imperial Crown; in base the Sphinx superscribed "Egypt."

The twenty-four Company badges are borne in rotation, three at a time, one on the Regimental Colour of each of the three Battalions.

A comparison will show that there is little difference between the Colours of 1751 and those of the present day.

Before leaving the Battalion Colour it may be noted that the Colonel's Colour changed its hue on four occasions, viz.:

1661.   Green to accord with the facings.
1685.   Blue and later to white.
1696.   Crimson as at present.

The Company Badges.

Company badges were first granted to the Coldstream in 1696 by William III. Previous to this the Company Colours were distinguished by the Roman numeral in the centre of each. The Regimental Booklet on Regimental Colours also records that only eleven badges were issued in 1696, four more in 1716 for the four companies raised in 1715—*i.e.*, 10th, 11th, 12th and 13th—and Unions were issued in 1729-30 for the 14th and 15th Companies bearing their present badges. There has been some doubt regarding the date of issue of the 16th Company badge, but correspondence clearly shows it to be 1814. The last eight (17th-24th) were granted by Queen Victoria in 1900 on raising the 3rd Battalion.

The list of badges as recorded in the Regimental Colour Book is as shown in the following table:

Bn. or Company	Description of the Badge	By whom and when granted
Queen's Colour of 1st Bn.	Star of the Order of the Garter proper ...	William III ... 1696

Bn. or Company	Description of the Badge	By whom and when granted	
Queen's Colour of 2nd Bn.	Star of eight points argent within the Garter proper	William III ...	1696
Queen's Colour of 3rd Bn.	Star of the Order of the Garter proper ...	William III ...	1696
1st	On a mount vert, a Lion sejeant guardant, his tail passed between his legs and reflexed over his back, argent	William III ...	1696
2nd	The Badge of the Prince of Wales, three ostrich feathers argent, quilled or, enfiled with a prince's coronet, with the motto "Ich Dien" in gold letters on a scroll azure	William III ...	1696
3rd	On a mount vert, a Panther guardant argent, spotted sable, azure and gules, and sending forth flames of fire proper from his mouth and ears	William III ...	1696
4th	Two Swords in saltire, with points upwards argent, hilts and pommels or	William III ...	1696
5th	St. George slaying the Dragon, all proper	William III ...	1696
6th	A Rose gules, barbed and seeded proper, within the Garter	William III ...	1696
7th	On a mount vert a Centaur with a bow and arrow proper	William III ...	1696
8th	Two Sceptres in saltire or	William III ...	1696
9th	The Knot of the Collar of the Order or, within the Garter	William III ...	1696
10th	An Escarbuncle or	George I ...	1716
11th	On a mount vert a Boar passant argent, armed, tusked, and bristled or	George I ...	1716
12th	On a mount vert a Bull passant argent, armed or	George I ...	1716
13th	A Rose gules, surmounted by another argent, barbed and seeded proper, impaled with a Pomegranate or, stalked also proper	George I ...	1716
14th	On a mount vert a Horse courant argent	George II ...	1729
15th	The Crown of Charlemagne all proper ...	George II ...	1729
16th	Out of a ducal coronet a pillar proper, the tops adorned with a coronet and plume of three peacock's feathers proper, charged with a star argent; on either side of the pillar, and out of the coronet, a sickle argent, handles gules, the backs adorned with small tufts of peacock's feathers, and between the sickles before the pillar a Horse courant argent	George IV ...	1814

Bn. or Company	Description of the Badge	By whom and when granted
17th	The Royal and Imperial Monogram of Her late Majesty Queen Victoria, Empress of India, in gold letters	Queen Victoria 1900
18th	On a mount vert an Heraldic Tiger argent, armed, unguled, tufted, ducally gorged and chain reflexed over back or	Queen Victoria 1900
19th	A Rose gules, seeded or barbed vert (a badge of Henry IV), within the collar of the Most Noble Order of the Garter with the George appendant, all proper	Queen Victoria 1900
20th	A representation of the Lesser George pertaining to the Order of the Garter or, encircled with the Garter and motto of the Order in their proper colours	Queen Victoria 1900
21st	An Eagle, wings expanded sable, beaked and legged or, with a Glory around the head or	Queen Victoria 1900
22nd	Two Laurel Branches in saltire vert, enfiled with the circle of the Imperial Crown proper	Queen Victoria 1900
23rd	The Crest of General George Monck, Duke of Albemarle, sometime Colonel of the Regiment—viz., on a chapeau gules, turned-up ermine, a Cat-a-Mountain statant guardant per pale sable and argent, between two branches of broom vert fructed proper	Queen Victoria 1900
24th	The Crest of the late Royal Highness, Adolphus Frederick, Duke of Cambridge, sometime Colonel of the Regiment—viz., a Lion statant guardant upon the circle of the coronet of His Royal Highness, with a like Coronet on its head, all or, the Lion charged on the breast with a label of three points argent, the centre point charged with St. George's Cross, and each of the others with two hearts in pale gules	Queen Victoria 1900

SCOTS GUARDS

Historical Note on the Origin of the Regiment.

Whilst on the links at Leith in October, 1641, news reached Charles I of a rebellion in Ireland. It was decided to send troops from Scotland to quell the outbreak, and one of the regiments raised for that purpose was that under the command of Archibald, Marquis of Argyll. It went to Ireland the following year, and finally returned to Scotland in 1649 to be disbanded. In 1650 Prince Charles (later Charles II) com-

Colours of 1st Bn. Irish Guards. The Regimental Colour (Union) on right carries
the badge of the 3rd Company.

Colours of 1st Bn. Welsh Guards. The Regimental Colour (Union) on right carries
the badge of the 2nd Company.

face p. 72

missioned Argyll to raise a regiment from amongst the recently disbanded soldiers, which he promptly did, his son, Lord Lorne, being appointed to the command. This regiment was designated a "Life Guard of Foot." Part of the regiment fought at Dunbar on 3rd September, 1650, and exactly a year later it was practically destroyed by Cromwell at the battle of Worcester.

When Charles II returned to England at his Restoration in 1660 a commencement was made to raise another regiment of Guards in Scotland, and gradually companies came into existence. On 1st May, 1661, the King signed a Warrant for the "Establishment of a New Regiment of Foot Guards to His Majestie consisting of six hundred soldiers," being the regimentation of six companies already raised. Another company was raised in 1665 and six more in 1666, thus rounding off the establishment of the Scots Guards with thirteen companies under the Colonelcy of George, Earl of Linlithgow.

In 1713 the title of the regiment became "The Third Regiment of Foot Guards"; in 1831 it was changed to "Scots Fusilier Guards," and in 1877 to "Scots Guards."*

State Colour.

On 15th July, 1899, Her Majesty Queen Victoria presented a State Colour to the Regiment, the description being: Crimson silk. The star of the Most Ancient and Most Noble Order of the Thistle within the collar and badge appendant of the said Order proper, encircled by the Union Wreath or and ensigned with the Imperial Crown, also proper; the whole surrounded by two branches of laurel or, having on each branch six scrolls argent bearing in black letters the honorary distinctions borne by the Regiment and, in base, the Sphinx superscribed "Egypt."

The six battle honours on the scrolls on the dexter side are: "Dettingen," "Talavera," "Peninsula," "Alma," "Sevastopol" and "Tel-el-Kebir"; those on the sinister side are: "Lincelles," "Barrosa," "Waterloo," "Inkerman," "Egypt 1882" and "Suakin 1885."

The Staff is surmounted by the Royal Crest in gold. The fringe is gold, and the cords and tassels are gold and crimson mixed.

---

* See *London Gazette*, 29th April, 1831, and *London Gazette*, 3rd April, 1877 for changes in those years.

The Battalion Colours.

Unlike the Colours of other regiments of Foot Guards, those of the Scots Guards are divided historically into two sections— *i.e.,* the Scottish Colours from 1650 to 1707, and the Union Colours from 1707 onward.

The Scottish Colours.—The first Colours granted to the Foot Guards in Scotland were those given by Charles II to his Life Guards of Foot in 1650 at Falkland Palace. They are described by Sir James Balfour, Lyon King of Arms, in "Sir James Balfour Denmilne Historical Works," Vol. IV, thus:

Colonel's	Azure. The Royal Arms, without any crown, viz.: Quarterly (i) and (iv) Scotland, (ii) England and France, (iii) Ireland.
Lieutenant-Colonel's	Azure. A Unicorn argent. The Scottish supporter of the Royal Arms.
Major's	Azure. A Lion rampant or. The English supporter of the Royal Arms.
1st Captain's	Azure. Three Fleurs-de-lis or. The "Lilies of France."
2nd Captain's	Azure. On an escutcheon or, a Lion rampant gules. The Lion of Scotland.
3rd Captain's	Azure. Three Lioncels passant guardant or. The Lions of England.
4th Captain's	Azure. A Harp or, stringed argent. The Harp of Ireland.

These badges were borne on one side of the Colours only; on the other, in great gold letters, the words "Covenant, For Religione, King and Kingdoms."

In Scotland, during the Civil War period, the Infantry Colours were, as a rule, St. Andrew's Cross covering the whole flag, in different colours from regiment to regiment, some blue, some white, and so on. Sometimes the Colonel's Colour was quite plain but with his crest, motto or other device, and sometimes it had St. Andrew's Cross in a canton next to the staff like the Lieutenant-Colonel's in England had the St. George's Cross. The Major's Colour, however, does not appear to have been distinguished by the stream blazant or "pile wavy" until after the Restoration, and even then it was not an invariable rule. The Captains' Colours were distinguished by numerals, or marks of cadency, or by "spots or several devices," but more by devices than spots. In a MS. volume in the British Museum (Harl. 1460), entitled "Colours taken from the Scots at Preston and Dunbar," many reproductions of such Colours may be seen.

In common with the other regiments of Foot Guards, the design of the Colours of the Scots Guards was changed by James II in 1685. According to the Windsor Colour Book, they then appeared thus:

Colonel's	Plain white throughout.
Lieutenant-Colonel's	The white saltire of St. Andrew on a blue field.
Major's	Same as Lieutenant-Colonel's, but with the stream blazant.
Eldest Captain's	Same as Lieutenant-Colonel's, but with the numeral "1" in silver above the centre of the Cross.

The cords and tassels of the Colonel's were of silver and gold, and the others of blue and gold.

The above would be the pattern of the last Scottish Colours of the Scots Guards.

The Union Colours.—The Union of England and Scotland occurred in 1707, the general effect on Army Colours being the placing of St. George's Cross over St. Andrew's Cross. In 1712 an issue of Colours was made to the Scots Guards, their description being:

Colonel's	Crimson.
Lieutenant-Colonel's	Union.
Major's	Union.

In the bill for making these Colours there is an item, "For painting and gilding of 18 ensigns with Emblems, Scrolls and Mottoes on both sides," which indicates that, unlike the Grenadier and Coldstream Guards, the Scots Guards had mottoes on scrolls. The emblems had a warlike character, the mottoes being explanatory of their character. The reason for the difference in the badges and emblems of the English and Scottish Guards has been stated to be that Scottish Kings did not adopt individual badges. The emblems on the Scots Guards Colours were therefore not purely Scottish in character, but rather warlike. The earliest representation of them is probably in the Windsor Colour Book.

Although only the Colonel's Colour was crimson in 1712, in 1729 both the Lieutenant-Colonel's and Major's were also of that hue with a Union in the upper canton. The Major's had the pile wavy, or stream blazant, in addition. The next record is in the Windsor Colour Book for 1768, the only major alteration from the 1751 arrangement being in the change of place of the Thistle and the Rose in the Lieutenant-Colonel's Colours.

In 1801 Colours were altered throughout the Army to agree with the new union with Ireland. Following this the next record of the Colours of the Scots Guards will be found in the Vellum Colour Book, signed by the Prince Regent in 1811.

In 1855 the Colonel's, Lieutenant-Colonel's and Major's Colours became respectively the Queen's Colour of the 1st, 2nd and 3rd Battalions, as in the Grenadier and Coldstream Guards.

An interesting historical episode is associated with the Colours of the 3rd Battalion, raised in 1899, disbanded 1906, re-raised 1914 for the Great War, and reduced again in 1919. The story is told in the two following announcements of His Majesty George V:

Buckingham Palace.

"Today I have presented to the 3rd Reserve Battalion of my Scots Guards the Colours of the 3rd Battalion, of which King Edward VII resumed charge when the Regiment was reduced by that Battalion in 1906.

(*Sgd.*) GEORGE R.I.,
Colonel-in-Chief, Scots Guards."

22nd October, 1914.

Buckingham Palace.

"I have this day resumed charge of the Colours which I presented to the Third Battalion of my Scots Guards.

(*Sgd.*) GEORGE R.I.,
Colonel-in-Chief, Scots Guards."

16th April, 1919.

As every other regiment laid up its Colours for the duration of the Great War, the 3rd Battalion Scots Guards had the

Marching off the Colours of the 2nd Bn. Scots Guards at Chelsea Barracks after duty at the Wedding of Queen Elizabeth II, 20th November, 1947.

unique distinction of being the only Regular battalion to carry a Colour at home during the war.

The present description of the Battalion Colours of the Scots Guards, as recorded in the Army List, is:

The Queen's Colours.

1st Battalion—Gules (crimson). In the centre the Royal Arms of Scotland, ensigned with the Imperial Crown. Motto, "En! Ferus Hostis." In base, the Sphinx superscribed "Egypt."

2nd Battalion—Gules (crimson). In the centre the Thistle and the Red and White Roses conjoined, issuant from the same stalk all proper, ensigned with the Imperial Crown. Motto, "Unita Fortior."

In base, the Sphinx superscribed "Egypt"; in the dexter canton, the Union.

The Regimental Colours.

The Union: In the centre, a Company badge ensigned with the Imperial Crown. In base, the Sphinx superscribed "Egypt."

The twenty-four Company badges are borne in rotation, one on the Regimental Colour of each of the Battalions.

Company Badges.

A certain amount has already been stated about these badges. As in the Grenadier and Coldstream Guards, they are borne in rotation. The complete list and date of grant is as shown in the following table, in which it will be noticed that each badge is accompanied by a motto.

Suc-cession Number	Description	By whom and when granted	
I	On an escutcheon argent the Royal Crest of Scotland—viz., on the Royal Crown proper a Lion sejeant guardant gules armed and langued azure, crowned and holding in the dexter paw a naked sword proper, pommel and hilt gold, and in the sinister the Royal Sceptre of the last, both erect in pale Motto: "In Defence"	Queen Anne	1712
II	A Hand Grenade fired proper ... ... Motto: "Terrorem affero"	Queen Anne	1712
III	A Lion rampant gules ... ... Motto: "Intrepidus"	Queen Anne	1712
IV	Pendant to a Thistle proper, the Badge of the Most Ancient Order of the Thistle Motto: "Nemo me impune lacessit"	Queen Anne	1712
V	On an escutcheon or, a mount vert, thereon a Lion passant guardant gules Motto: "Timere nescius"	Queen Anne	1712
VI	On an escutcheon, or a Griffin segreant azure Motto: "Belloque ferox"	Queen Anne	1712
VII	The Royal Badge of Queen Elizabeth I—viz., a Phoenix issuing from flames proper Motto: "Per funera vitam"	Queen Anne	1712
VIII	A Thunderbolt proper ... ... Motto: "Horror Ubique"	Queen Anne	1712
IX	On a mount vert a Cannon in fesse or, fired proper, mounted on a carriage sable Motto: "Concussae cadent urbes"	Queen Anne	1712
X	A Salamander statant in flames proper ... Motto: "Pascua nota mihi"	Queen Anne	1712
XI	On an escutcheon azure the Cross of St. Andrew argent Motto: "In hoc signo vinces"	Queen Anne	1712

Suc-cession Number	Description	By whom and when granted
XII	Military Trophies proper ... ... Motto: "Honores prae fero"	Queen Anne 1712
XIII	On an escutcheon or a mount vert, thereon a Talbot passant proper Motto: "Intaminata Fide"	Queen Anne 1712
XIV	The entire label on the Arms of His Royal Highness The Duke of Connaught Motto: "Te Duce vincimus"	Queen Victoria 1889
XV	The Galley of Lorne ... ... Motto: "Ne obliviscaris"	Queen Victoria 1889
XVI	The Union Badge of His Majesty James I— viz., the Rose and Thistle dimidiated and conjoined Motto: "Fecit eos in gentem unam"	Queen Victoria 1899
XVII	The Crest of His Royal Highness the late Prince Consort, within the collar of the Order of the Garter with the George appendant Motto: "Treu und Fest"	Queen Victoria 1900
XVIII	The Crest and Motto "Si je puis" of Lord Linlithgow Motto: "Si possim"	King Edward VII 1901
XIX	On an escutcheon azure a Unicorn rampant argent Motto: "Res non verba"	King Edward VII 1901
XX	On an escutcheon or a Lion rampant gules Motto: "Forward"	King Edward VII 1901
XXI	The Jewel of the Order of the Thistle ... Motto: "Fortis in Arduis"	King Edward VII 1901
XXII	On an escutcheon a representation of the Union Flag of Great Britain (1707) Motto: "Nil desperandum"	King Edward VII 1901
XXIII	A Thistle encircled by a representation of the collar of the Order of the Thistle with the badge appendant Motto: "Noli me tangere"	King Edward VII 1901
XXIV	On an escutcheon or a Fleur-de-lis gules ... Motto: "Pro patria"	King Edward VII 1901

THE IRISH GUARDS

Historical Note on the Origin of the Regiment.

A previous regiment of Irish Guards was perhaps the earliest regiment of "Foot Guards," having been raised in 1642 shortly before the battle of Edgehill. This regiment had a short existence, being practically destroyed at Naseby in 1645. Soon after the Restoration, Charles II formed another regiment of Irish Guards,* and gradually increased its strength to two battalions. The Colonelcy was given to James Butler, First Duke of Ormonde. The headquarters of the regiment were in Dublin, and their organization approximated to that of the 1st Guards in that they had a King's Company.

About 1689 it entered the French service and during the French Revolution it was merged into the 92nd Regiment of the Army of France, but, refusing to serve under the banner of revolution, it died out.

The present regiment was raised in 1900, under Army Order 77, which reads thus:

> "Her Majesty the Queen, having deemed it desirable to commemorate the bravery shown by the Irish Regiments in the operations in South Africa in the years 1899 and 1900, has been graciously pleased to command that an Irish Regiment of Foot Guards be formed, to be designated the 'Irish Guards.' "

Colours Generally.

Owing to the short life of the original Irish Guards and the distance of time, little is known of the Colours they bore, but from the accounts of the Great Wardrobe of the period the late Captain Balfour, Scots Guards, unearthed a bill which showed that twelve Colours were issued to them in 1662. They were of yellow taffeta with crimson and gold cords and tassels, and were painted and gilded "with severall Badges proper for that Kingdome" (viz., Ireland). The badges, therefore, then as now, would be of a distinctly Irish character, although there appears to be no record of their exact description.

Unlike the three senior regiments of Guards, the Irish Guards (also the Welsh Guards) have no State Colour, their Queen's Colour being carried on those occasions when State Colours are ordered to be borne. Like all the Guards, however, they wear their Company badges in rotation on their Regimental Colour.

---

* The Patent is dated Westminster, 23rd April, 1662.

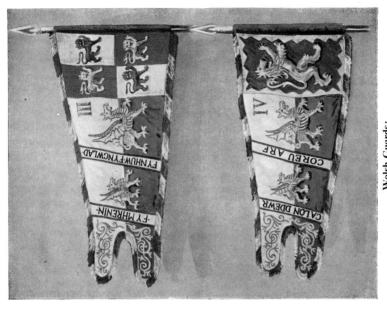

Welsh Guards:
Colours of the 3rd Company (above)
and the 4th Company (below)

Welsh Guards:
Colours of The Prince of Wales's Company (above)
and the 2nd Company (below)

Queen's Colour.

The description of the Queen's Colour is—Gules (crimson): in the centre the Royal Cypher or, within the collar of the Order of Saint Patrick with badge appendant proper, ensigned with the Imperial Crown.

This Colour (then the King's) was presented to the Regiment by King Edward VII on 30th May, 1902, on the Horse Guards Parade.

Regimental Colour.

This Colour is the Great Union bearing the Company badges in rotation. The first Regimental Colour was therefore the Great Union, bearing the badge of the 1st Company—viz., the Royal Cyphers of Queen Victoria and of King Edward VII. The cyphers are borne side by side in the centre of the St. George's Cross, that of King Edward being on the dexter side. They are ensigned with an Imperial Crown with the number of the Company in black on a gold label beneath the cyphers. This Colour was presented to the Regiment with the King's Colour mentioned above.

Company Badges.

The following is the list of Company badges as authorized on 8th November, 1901:

Company	Description
1st	The Royal Cyphers of King Edward VII and Queen Victoria or.
2nd	The Cypher of H.R.H. The Duke of Connaught or, encircled by a wreath of shamrocks vert.
3rd	The Royal Badge of Ireland (the Harp) within the circle and motto of the Most Illustrious Order of St. Patrick proper.
4th	The Badge of the Most Illustrious Order of St. Patrick proper.
5th	Two swords in saltire, the points upwards proper, pommels and hilts or, surmounted by the Union badge of Ireland (a shamrock).
6th	The Knot and two Roses as in the collar of the Most Illustrious Order of St. Patrick.
7th	Argent, a saltire gules. (The Cross of St. Patrick on a silver shield.)
8th	The Crest of Field-Marshal Earl Roberts, V.C., K.G., K.P., G.C.B., G.C.S.I., first Colonel of the Irish Guards.

G

The following eight Company badges were authorized in 1945:

Company	Description
9th	The Crest of Ireland within the collar of the Order of St. Patrick.
10th	On a six-pointed star argent a dexter Hand couped gules (from the arms of Ulster).
11th	A Sea Horse gorged with a mural crown proper (from the arms of Belfast).
12th	A Castle inflamed proper (from the arms of Dublin).
13th	An ancient Irish Crown or (from the arms of Munster).
14th	An Irish Wolfhound statant proper.
15th	A dimidiated Eagle displayed sable conjoined with a sinister arm embowed sleeve argent, the hand grasping a sword erect proper. (from the arms of Connaught).
16th	A pierced Narcissus argent (from the arms of the Earl of Cavan).

Each of the above Company badges is ensigned with an Imperial Crown, and the number of the Company in black on a gold scroll is underneath each badge.

WELSH GUARDS

Historical Note on the Origin of the Regiment.

Just as the South African War of 1899-1902 gave birth to the Irish Guards, so the Great War of 1914-18 brought into being the Welsh Guards. In the words of the late General Sir Francis Lloyd*:

"It has been the unanimous wish of the Welsh people—than whom none are more noted for their loyalty to the Crown—that the Principality should take its place among the nations of the British Isles in finding a regiment to assist in guarding the Throne.

"King George V gave expression to this sentiment, and to his own wishes, on February 6th, 1915, by commanding the Field-Marshal Earl Kitchener, K.G., then Secretary of State for War, to put His Majesty's orders into execution. Accordingly, as I was commanding the London District, I was sent for by the Field-Marshal and ordered to raise a battalion immediately. On my asking Lord Kitchener how soon he expected this to be done, he replied in his usual abrupt manner: 'In a week!' My answer was 'They shall go on guard on St. David's Day.' And they *did*!"

* In the introduction to "The History of the Welsh Guards," by Colonel Dudley Ward, D.S.O., M.C.

The official authority for creating the regiment runs as follows:

Published on the 4th March, 1915.

ROYAL WARRANT
WELSH GUARDS

GEORGE R.I.

Whereas we have deemed it expedient to authorize the formation of a Welsh Regiment of Foot Guards, to be designated the "Welsh Guards";

OUR WILL AND PLEASURE is that such regiment shall be deemed to be a corps for the purpose of the Army Act.

Given at Our Court at St. James, this 26th day of February, 1915, in the 5th year of Our Reign.

By His Majesty's Command.

KITCHENER.

(Published as Army Order 124 of 1915.)

General Lloyd had promised Lord Kitchener that the Welsh Guards would be on guard on St. David's Day—*i.e.*, just a week from the formation of the regiment—and this was fulfilled. As the King watched the parade from Buckingham Palace he saw a most unusual sight, for the Commanding Officer, Lieutenant-Colonel Murray Threipland, was doing duty as Captain of the King's Guard.* That night was the only occasion when Lord Kitchener dined "On Guard."

On 17th August, 1915, within six months of its formation, the Welsh Guards left Southampton for France, and a glance at its roll of battle honours will convey a sufficient impression of its distinguished services during the Great War.

Queen's Colour.

The description of this Colour is: Gules (crimson); in the centre a Dragon passant or, underneath a scroll with motto "Cymru am Byth."† The whole ensigned with an Imperial Crown.

---

* This is the only instance in the history of the Brigade of Guards of a Commanding Officer going on duty as Captain of the King's Guard.

† "Wales for ever."

Regimental Colour.

The Colour is the Great Union and bears the fourteen Company badges in rotation.

*Company Badges.**

The first eight badges were authorized in 1915, the ninth to the thirteenth in 1942, the fourteenth in 1946, and the fifteenth in June, 1952. Each badge is ensigned with the Imperial Crown with the number of the Company in black on a gold scroll below each badge.

Company	Description
Prince of Wales's	Gules three Lions passant in pale argent. (These arms are attributed to Gruffudd ap Cynan, King of Gwynedd (North-West Wales) and founder of the First Royal Tribe.)
No. 2	Vert three Eagles displayed in fesse or. (These arms are attributed to Owain Gwynedd, eldest son of Gruffudd ap Cynan, who succeeded his father as King of Gwynedd.)
No. 3	Quarterly or and gules four Lions passant guardant counter-charged. (The arms are said to have been borne by Llywelyn ab Iorwerth (1173-1240), Llywelyn the Great.)
No. 4	Gules a Lion rampant and a border indented or. (These arms are attributed to Rhys ap Tewdwr, King of Deheubarth (South Wales) and founder of the Second Royal Tribe.)
No. 5	Or a Lion rampant gules. (The arms are attributed to Bleddyn ap Cynfyn, King of Powys (North-East and Central Wales) and founder of the Third Royal Tribe.)
No. 6	Paley of eight argent and gules a Lion rampant sable. (The arms of the princes of Powys Fadog, the northern part of the ancient Kingdom of Powys.)
No. 7	Quarterly first and fourth argent three Boars' heads sable, tusked or and langued gules; second and third per bend sinister ermine and erminois a Lion rampant or. (The arms are attributed to Elystan Glodrudd, King of Gloucester and Hereford, and, by right of conquest, Prince of Fferlis, which is the territory between the rivers Severn and Wye.)
No. 8	Gules three Chevrons argent. (These arms are attributed to Iestyn ap Gwrgan, known as the last Prince of Glamorgan and founder of the Fifth Royal Tribe.)
No. 9	Gules a Chevron between three Lioncels rampant or. (These arms are attributed to Hwfa ap Cynddelw, Lord of Llys Llifon in Anglesey, and founder of the First Noble Tribe.)
No. 10	Sable a Chevron between three Fleurs-de-lis argent. (These arms are attributed to Collwyn ap Tango, Lord of Evionydd and Ardodwy and founder of the Fifth Noble Tribe.)
No. 11	Vert a Chevron ermine between three Wolves' Heads erased argent. (These arms are attributed to Rhirid Flaidd (Rhirid the Wolf), Lord of Penllyn, now in the county of Merioneth.)

* *Vide* "Wales and the Welsh Guards," by Major H. M. C. Jones-Mortimer, Welsh Guards.

Company	Description
No. 12	Argent a Chevron between three Ravens sable. (These arms are attributed to Sir Rhys ap Thomas, K.G., 1449-1525.)
No. 13	Sable a Lion rampant argent. (These arms are attributed to Gwaethfoed, Prince of Cardigan and Lord of Cibwr, probably the area between Caerphilly and Cardiff.)
No. 14	Argent three Boars' Heads couped sable langued gules. (These arms are attributed to Cowryd ap Cadfan, Lord of the Vale of Clwyd and founder of the tribe called Gwehelyth Ceinmerch.)
No. 15	Argent a cross fleury engrailed sable between four Cornish choughs. (These arms are recorded in the College of Arms as those of Prince Edwin of Tegengl (or Tegeingl) of Flintshire).

CHAPTER XI

HERALDRY AND STANDARDS, GUIDONS AND COLOURS

GENERAL

PERHAPS the earliest writer on the connection between heraldry and Colours was Markham, who published his "Five Decades of Epistles of Warre" in 1622. Therein he lays it down that the Colours of the Captains

"ought to bee mixt equally of two several colours, that is to say (according to the rules of Heraldry) of colour and mettal, and not colour on colour, as greene and red or black and blew, or such like, nor yet mettall on mettall as white and yellow or orangetawny white. It is then to be understood, that every Gentleman of Coat-armour (being capable to beare Colours) ought to carry them compounded of these two principall colours which are contained in his Coat-armour, being the field and the chiefe charge thereon."*

From this it may be deduced that up to the issue of the 1747 Regulations, which abolished the Colonel's control of the design of Colours, such Colours of the present army had been of the same hue as the field of the shield upon which their personal arms were marshalled. In the case of the army of the Commonwealth (1645-1660) it has already been seen that the hue of the Colours corresponded with the name of the regiment —e.g., the Red Regiment had red Colours, the Blue Regiment had blue Colours, and so on.

A departure from the strict laws of heraldry was authorized

* In English heraldry there are two metals—viz., gold (or), represented by the colour yellow, and silver (argent, abbreviated "arg"), represented by white. There are also five colours—viz. :

Blue	(azure, abbreviated az.)
Red	(gules, abbreviated gu.)
Black	(sable, abbreviated sa.)
Green	(vert)
Purple	(purpure, abbreviated purp.).

by the General Regulations and Orders for the Army of 1822, wherein it is laid down that "The Second Colour of those (regiments), which are faced with Black, is to be St. George's Cross throughout, the Union in the Upper Canton; the three other cantons Black." As St. George's Cross is red, a colour, and black is a colour, it resulted in colour on colour. However, in the Colour Vellum Books (see later) in the Office of the Inspector of Regimental Colours, the Colours of the "50th (or the West Kent) Regiment," which had black facings, are depicted with a narrow white strip (*i.e.*, a fimbriation of metal) between the red cross and the black field, thus bringing the whole design within the laws of heraldry. In the same book the Colours of the 58th (or Rutlandshire), 64th (or 2nd Stafford-shire) and 70th (or Glasgow Lowland) Regiments, all of which had black facings, are shown without the strip of white.

Honorary distinctions—*i.e.*, battle honours, badges, devices, etc., for service—originated from the "Augmentations of Honour" of heraldry. According to Boutell (*vide ante*), "Aug-mentation, or Augmentation of Honour, is a term employed to denote an addition to a Shield of Arms, especially granted by the Sovereign to commemorate some worthy or illustrious deed, and forming an integral element of the Shield as an hereditary bearing." He then illustrates this definition by quoting the case of the Duke of Norfolk. To commemorate the victory he gained at Flodden Field on 9th September, 1513, Henry VIII granted to him and his descendants, as an Aug-mentation of Honour, the Royal Shield of Scotland, having a demi lion only, which is pierced through the mouth with an arrow, to be charged upon the silver head of his shield. Another example is that of the great Duke of Wellington, who, in recognition of his illustrious services, was granted the Union Badge (without the Imperial Crown) charged upon an escut-cheon and displayed in the chief point of his shield.

In at least one instance the representation of a Regimental Colour has been granted as an augmentation to a coat of arms. During the fighting on 13th December, 1813, when Wellington was endeavouring to cross the River Nive in southern France during the Peninsular War, the brigade commanded by Major-General John Byng was opposed to very gallant and stubborn French troops at Mouguerre. In a moment of inspiration Byng seized the Regimental Colour

of the 31st Regiment (now The East Surrey Regiment) and ran
forward with it. The assault was successful and he planted the
Colour on the French position. For this exploit he received an
augmentation to his arms. He was elevated to the peerage
on 12th May, 1835, as Baron Strafford and created Earl of
Strafford in 1847. In Burke's Peerage of today this signal
award is recorded thus—"over all, in bend sinister, a representation of the Colours of the 31st Regiment. *Crest*, Out of a mural
crown an arm embowed, grasping the Colours of the 31st
Regiment, and pendant from the wrist by a riband, the gold
cross presented by Royal Command for Lord Strafford's
gallant achievements, all proper, and on an escroll, the word
' Mouguerre.' " The late Viscount Byng of Vimy, of Great War
(1914-18) fame, was a son of the second Earl and bore the arms
described above. Thus a famous Cavalryman bore an Infantry
Colour in his arms.

The first honorary distinction in the form of a badge and
motto was that granted by William III to The Royal Irish
Regiment (disbanded 1922) for their gallant conduct at the
siege of Namur in 1695. The distinction took the form of one
of the King's own badges, the Lion of Nassau, with the motto
"Virtutis Namurcensis Praemium." Another such grant was
the Sphinx, superscribed "Egypt," awarded to many regiments,
under Horse Guards letter of 6th July, 1802, which had taken
part in the successful campaign against the French in Egypt
in 1801.

The most numerous distinctions on Colours are battle
honours in the form of names of actions or campaigns. "In
the period of decadence whole words or sentences, commonly
the names of military or naval victories, are often seen in
Coats-of-Arms" (Encyclopædia Britannica). This practice is
fairly common, as may be seen in any book of the Peerage—
e.g., Lord Gough has "China," "India," "Goojerat" and
"Barrosa"; Lord Kitchener, "Khartoum"; Viscount Comber-
mere, "Salamanca."

The first grant of a distinction in the form of a name or an
action or campaign was "Emsdorff," granted to the 15th King's
Light Dragoons (later 15th Hussars) to be borne on the second
and third Guidon under the Royal Warrant of 19th December,
1768. This action was fought on 16th July, 1760, during the
Seven Years' War. The next grant was announced by Horse

Guards letter of 28th April, 1784, being the word "Gibraltar" to the 12th (Suffolk), 39th (Dorsetshire), 56th (2nd Essex) and 58th (2nd Northamptonshire) Regiments, for their service during the siege of "The Rock" from 1779 to 1783. Under various authorities between 1827 and 1836 these regiments were authorized to bear "The Castle and Key" superscribed "Gibraltar," with the motto "Montis Insignia Calpe," in place of the single word "Gibraltar." Dates were added later. Under Army Order 73 of 1909 the grant was extended to The Highland Light Infantry. Honours for Minden (fought on 1st August, 1759), the 1801 campaign in Egypt against the French, Maida (fought on 4th July, 1806) and for the Peninsular War (1808-1814) followed, and the practice became established.

THE INSPECTOR OF REGIMENTAL COLOURS

In view of the close connection between heraldry and Colours it was only logical that the official who should control the design of Colours should be an officer of the College of Arms. It has already been mentioned that, in the Royal Warrant of 1661 concerning the Colours of the Grenadier Guards, Sir Edward Walker, Garter Principal King-of-Arms, was associated with their design, and, although both he and his successors were doubtless consulted by regiments regarding Colours, it was not until 1806 that an Inspector of Regimental Colours was officially appointed.

In their Inspection Returns before 1770 many Inspecting General Officers recorded the state of the Regimental Colours, but this part of their duties does not appear to have been carried out with that thoroughness which the Horse Guards required, so that when Major-General Gage was going to inspect regiments in North America in that year, his attention was drawn to the Warrant of 19th December, 1768, which deals with Colours as well as Clothing and Appointments. Here is the Warrant of 7th March, 1770, issued to Gage:

"Whereas We have thought fit to issue Our Regulations for the Colours, Clothing and Appointments of Our several regiments of infantry, bearing date 19th December, 1768, with Our Orders that they should be duly obeyed, and put in execution, at such times as the several particulars should be furnished, careful inspection is to be made whether these Our Regulations are exactly complied with according to the intent and meaning thereof, and a report to be made accordingly.

(*Sgd.*) BARRINGTON."*

The Inspection Returns before 1770 contain references to Standards and Colours, but usually they merely recorded the number in possession of the regiment and the date of issue. Nothing was noted as to their condition. It was much the same after 1770, but one does occasionally notice such an entry as "Colours good," "Colours bad" or "Colours nearly worn out," or, as in the case of the 9th Foot (now The Royal Norfolk Regiment) for 1798, "The Colours were nothing but rags, so that no device or number could be seen on them." The Inspection Return for 1772 shows that these Colours were issued in that year.

Generally speaking, Inspecting Officers do not appear to have been much concerned with whether the devices, badges, etc., on the Colours were correctly emblazoned or otherwise; but owing to the heraldic connection of such distinctions, regiments consulted the College of Arms themselves on such matters before the Office of the Inspector of Regimental Colours was instituted.

In 1803 and 1804 the Board of Ordnance wrote to Mr. Nayler, York Herald, chiefly in regard to the delay in issuing Colours. The correspondence on the subject shows clearly that there were constant delays in the issue of Colours about this time, and this reason was advanced when advocating the creation of the appointment.

Mr. Nayler was appointed Inspector of Regimental Colours on 4th June, 1806, and in April, 1807, he sent out a circular letter to all Commanding Officers in the following terms:

"Sir,

"I am directed to request you will forthwith acquaint me whether your Regimental and Camp Colours correspond with the enclosed sketches *A*, *B*, *C*. Should there be any deviation you will have the goodness to transmit sketches of the Colours at present borne by the Regiment under your Command (for which purpose the blanks *D*, *E*, *F* are enclosed) at the same time stating the authority

---

* William, Viscount Barrington, Secretary-at-War.

Colours of the 2nd Bn. The Royal Scots.
Example of a blue Regimental Colour of a Royal Regiment.

Colours of the 2nd Bn. The East Yorkshire Regiment.
Example of a white Regimental Colour.

by which such alterations may have been made, and return them addressed to me under cover to The Right Hon. the Secretary at War."

The sketches *A, B, C* were based upon the Royal Warrant of 19th December, 1768.

By the courtesy of the late Sir Henry Farnham Burke, who was Garter King of Arms and Inspector of Regimental Colours at the time, I have been permitted to examine the replies received by Mr. Nayler, and in view of the irregularities brought to light there can be no question as to the wisdom of instituting this office.

During the period Mr. (later Sir George) Nayler held the appointment (1806-1831) the expediency of continuing the office twice occupied the attention of the authorities, and on each occasion its necessity was felt and admitted.

Originally the duties of the Inspector of Regimental Colours were confined to the Regular Army, but in 1855 they were extended to include the Militia. For a long time now his advice has been sought by almost every Colour-bearing unit throughout the British Commonwealth.

The office of the Inspector is at the College of Arms, Queen Victoria Street, London, E.C.4. The following is a list of gentlemen who have held the appointment:

Sir George Nayler ...	Garter King of Arms	Appointed 4th June, 1806. (then York Herald). Died 28th October, 1831.
Sir William Woods ...	Garter King of Arms	Appointed 11th November, 1831 (then Norfolk Herald). Died 25th July, 1842.
Sir Albert William Woods, G.C.V.O., K.C.B., K.C.M.G. (son of Sir William Woods)	Garter King of Arms	Appointed 28th July, 1842 (then Lancaster Herald). Died 7th January, 1904.
Sir Henry Farnham Burke, K.C.V.O., C.B.	Garter King of Arms	Appointed 22nd June, 1904 (then Somerset Herald). Resigned the appointment 22nd June, 1929.
Sir Gerald Woods Wollaston, K.C.B., K.C.V.O. (grandson of Sir Albert and great-grandson of Sir William Woods)	Garter King of Arms	Appointed 23rd June, 1929 (Garter King of Arms, 1930-1944. Retired as Garter, 1944, and now Norroy and Ulster King of Arms). The present Inspector of Regimental Colours.

The appointment appeared in the Army List for the first time in January, 1812, on page 104 thus: "Inspector of Regimental Colours—George Nayler, Esq., York Herald. Office—Herald's College."

It retained this form up to and including the October 1871 edition, but in the November 1871 edition the appointment is shown "Inspector of Colours."

Thus it remained until Sir Henry Farnham Burke was appointed in 1904, when it was altered in the October edition of that year to "Inspector of Regimental Colours of the British and Indian Armies."

The entry now reads as it did originally, "Inspector of Regimental Colours," and he is responsible for them throughout the military forces of the British Empire. His responsibility was first laid down in King's Regulations by Amendment No. 87 to Queen's Regulations (1940) by the insertion of a new paragraph, 19A, which reads thus:

> "The Inspector of Regimental Colours is the sole responsible authority on all details appertaining to the designs of standards, guidons and colours. It is his responsibility:
>
> (a) To arrange for the preparation of drawings of new standards, guidons and colours, for approval by the Army Council and His Majesty the King.
>
> (b) To ensure the safe custody of the approved drawings of such standards, guidons and colours, which will form the authority for the design of subsequent issues.
>
> (c) To arrange for the preparation of drawings, for the guidance of contractors, when standards, guidons and colours, are authorized to be replaced. He is solely responsible for the first inspection of the design of the standards, guidons and colours, when manufactured."

THE VELLUM COLOUR BOOKS

The most reliable evidence concerning Regimental Colours as they appeared at the commencement of the nineteenth century is contained in the painted record in the office of the Inspector of Regimental Colours.

As stated in the previous chapter, when Mr. Nayler was appointed to the office he set about his work with energy and enthusiasm, for he was anxious to assist Colonels of Regiments in the provision of Colours bearing the correct devices as authorized by the Royal Warrants of 1751 and 1768. Correspondence shuttle-cocked between his office and regiments stationed all over the world for several years. Where a regiment made a claim to a distinction for which no authority could be traced the matter was referred to the Commander-in-Chief for decision.

Gradually he succeeded in establishing what every regiment's Colour should bear, and to obviate any further doubts upon this matter he took the very wise step of having a painting made in colours of almost every Colour of the Foot Guards and Infantry of the Line. The paintings are made on vellum and occupy four books as follows:

The Foot Guards: one book.
Infantry Regiments—
From 1st (or The Royal Scots) to 33rd (or the 1st Yorkshire West Riding Regiment): one book.
From 34th (or The Cumberland Regiment) to 64th (or the 2nd Staffordshire Regiment): one book.
From 65th (or The 2nd Yorkshire North Riding Regiment) to 104th Regiment: one book.

A Royal Warrant is bound up with each book. Here is that in that of the Foot Guards:

In the name and on the behalf of His Majesty
GEORGE P.R.

George the Third by the Grace of God of the United Kingdom of Great Britain and Ireland, King Defender of the Faith, etc. To all to whom these Presents shall come Greeting. Know ye that we having been graciously pleased to approve of the Paintings of the Badges and Devices borne on the Colours of Our Three Regiments of Foot Guards, are further pleased to direct and command that no alteration therein shall on any account be permitted but by the Special Command of Us Our Heirs and Successors, and that the same having been countersigned by Our Commander-in-Chief and our Secretary at War shall be deposited in the office of Our aforesaid Commander-in-Chief under the care and custody of Our Inspector of Regimental Colours. Given at Our Court at Carlton House this eleventh day of March, 1811, in the Fifty-first year of Our Reign.

By command of His Royal Highness The Prince Regent in the name and on the behalf of His Majesty.

DAVID DUNDAS, Commander-in-Chief.
PALMERSTON.

Here is that in the other three books, except that the titles of the regiments "commencing" and "concluding" vary in each case as shown above.

GEORGE R.

George the Fourth by the Grace of God of the United Kingdom of Great Britain and Ireland, King Defender of the Faith, etc. To all to whom these presents shall come Greeting. Know ye that we having been graciously pleased to approve of the Badges, Devices and Inscriptions borne on the Colours of the several battalions of Our Regiments of Foot as the same are depicted in the Paintings hereunto annexed commencing with Our First (or Royal Scots) Regiment of Foot and concluding with Our Thirty-third (or First Yorkshire West Riding) Regiment of Foot are further pleased and direct and command that no alteration therein shall on any account be permitted but by the Special Command of Us Our Heirs and Successors, and that the same having been countersigned by Our Commander-in-Chief and Our Secretary at War shall be deposited in the Office of Our aforesaid Commander-in-Chief under the care and custody of Sir George Nayler, our Inspector of Regimental Colours, and his Successors in that office. Given at Our Court at Carlton House this eleventh day of July in the second year of Our Reign.

By His Majesty's Command,
(Sgd.) FREDERICK, Commander-in-Chief.
PALMERSTON.

Besides being of great assistance to the Inspector, this painted record must have been, and probably is now, of immense value to writers of regimental histories and seekers after truth in this matter.

One interesting minor feature which is noticeable is the difficulty of spelling "Rolica," the name of Wellington's opening battle of the Peninsular campaign, fought on 17th August, 1808. In the Vellum Book, on the Colours of the 1st Battalion Northumberland Regiment (now Fusiliers) it is spelled "Rolica," but on the Colours of the 2nd Battalion of the same regiment it is "Rolice." Again, on those of the 29th or Worcestershire Regiment it is "Roleira." It was not until the publication of Army Order 219 of 1911 that the spelling was finally fixed at "Roliça." On the shoulder-belt ornament of officers of The Rifle Brigade it was spelled "Roleia" until 1951.

Here are depicted the Colours borne by the following regiments before being made "rifle" regiments:

26th, or Cameronian Regiment
90th, or Perthshire Volunteers,
   Light Infantry.
	Later 1st and 2nd Bns.
	   The Cameronians.

60th, or Royal American
   Regiment, Light Infantry.
	Now The King's Royal
	   Rifle Corps.

83rd Regiment
86th, or Royal County Down
   Regiment.
	Later 1st and 2nd Bns.
	   The Royal Ulster
	   Rifles.

The Rifle Brigade was a rifle regiment from its formation in 1800, so never carried Colours.

The names of regiments following the numbers are the territorial titles allotted to regiments under Horse Guards letter dated 13th May, 1782, many of which disappeared entirely on the linking up of regiments under the "Cardwell System" in 1881.*

Here are some lost titles to be found in the Vellum Books:

Cambridgeshire Regiment	(30th)
Huntingdonshire Regiment	(31st)
Cumberland Regiment	(34th)
Herefordshire Regiment	(36th)
2nd Somersetshire Regiment	(40th)
Monmouthshire Light Infantry	(43rd)
South Devonshire Regiment	(46th)

* *Vide* General Order 40, of 1881.

West Norfolk Regiment   (54th)
Westmorland Regiment   (55th)
Rutlandshire Regiment   (58th)
West Suffolk Regiment   (63rd)
Glasgow Lowland Regiment   (70th)
Bucks Volunteers   (85th)
Royal County Down Regiment   ·   (86th)
Prince of Wales Tipperary Regiment (99th)

**The Colours of the Grenadier Guards being handed to the Ensigns by the
Regimental Sergeant-Major**

CHAPTER XII

THE OFFICE OF THE STANDARD- OR COLOUR-BEARER

In ancient times the selection of an ensign-bearer was a matter of considerable importance, particularly in the era prior to the introduction of weapons which could kill at a distance, such as muskets. As the quality of the musketry improved and the effective range increased, the Colours became a too obvious mark for the enemy, causing terrible casualties among the colour parties, until at last they were banished from the battle-field. At all times a peculiar and distinctive honour has been attached to the office of standard- or colour-bearer.

In the army of ancient Egypt each company had its standard-bearer, who was an officer of approved valour: the royal standards were carried by royal princes or by persons of the royal household (Dr. Lord, "Beacons Light of History").

As an indication of the dignity attaching to the post among the Carians of the fifth century B.C. it is noted that the Carian soldier who slew Cyrus the Persian, brother of Artaxerxes, was allowed the honour of carrying a golden cock at the head of the army, it being the custom of the Carians to wear that bird as a crest on their helmets.

In the Chinese "Book of War," written in the fifth century B.C.* we find that "In the teaching of war, spears are given to the short, bows and catapults to the tall; banners and standards to the strong." It required "strong" men when it is remembered that the standards were very much larger than they are now, and that whilst the spearmen and bowmen could obtain a rest the standard-bearer had to keep his flag aloft throughout the battle.

In the Roman army of the first century B.C. the standard-bearer was one of the centurion's assistants, or lieutenants. He held the same relative rank in the French army of the

---

* Translated by the late Major E. F. Calthrop, R.F.A.

fifteenth century, the English army of the sixteenth century, and the army of Gustavus Adolphus in the seventeenth century (*vide* Fortescue).

In the Norman account of the battle of Hastings we find that "The Duke called for the standard which the Pope had sent him, and he who bore it having unfolded it, the Duke took it, and called to Raoel de Conches, 'Bear my standard,' said he, 'for I would not but do you right: by right and by ancestry your line are standard-bearers.'" The same work also states, as regards the Saxon King, Harold, "The right of the men of London is to guard the King's body, to place themselves around him, and to guard his standard."

The general organization of the headquarters of a "Captaines Command" in the Middle Ages consisted of the Captain, his *locum tenens*—lieutenant—and his standard-bearer, who, with the lieutenant, appears to have done most of the rough work in the command. These persons have been given various titles at various times.

Roger Williams published his book, "A briefe Discourse of Warre," in 1590, and he has numerous references to Ensignes, Guydons and Cornets—*e.g.*, "To every severall company belongeth one Ensigne, one Guydon and one Cornet; the Ensigne over the men at Armes, the Guydon over the Archers, the Cornet over the light horsemen."

Carrying the Colours is one of those duties in which the name of the office has transferred to the person who attends it. Hence ensign a "flag" becomes ensign a "rank," and the same is seen in cornet and guidon. Before the term ensign, guidon or cornet were employed, the person who performed this office was denominated "Alferis"* and later "Ancient."

Gerat Barry, in his book written in 1634, has a chapter "Treatinge of the election and office of an Alferish of a companie of Infanterie," and the following excerpt clearly denotes that person's duties, in spite of the quaint spelling:

> "The chardge and office of an Alferis or Ansign bearer of a Companie of Infanterie is to be reputed as a Captaine leftenant in whose Choysinge, his Captaine is to have many and great considerations. . . . For as much as the

---

* From the Spanish.

ensigne is the true foundation of the Company. . . . In
occationes of fightings withe his enemy, he is to sheaw
himself dreadfull and terrible, with his sworde* in his
righte hande, and his Colours in his left, bravely displaying
the same. . . . That morninge he is to putt or display his
colours in his windows. In the assault or winning of any
towne or forte of emportance, he is not to putt his colours
in any place till the furie of the enemy be wholie van-
quished, orderlie and prudentlie accomodated and prevented, and when all the furie is paste and dulie prevented,
he shall putt in his Coloures into his lodginge, and display
the Same in the window nexte unto the street, that the
Captaine, Officeres, and Souldiers may note, and marcke
where the Colours are; to repaire unto them with speede
when ocatio offereth. And alwayes let him be verie carefull
to ordaine a good garde for the same, and that he himself
shall looke well thereunto."

The term "ancient" appears to be a corruption of "ensign,"
and Shakespeare uses it in this sense; thus

"'Tis one Iago, ancient to the general."
(*Othello*, Act II, Scene 1.)

"Sir, Ancient Pistol's below and would speak with you."
(2 *K. Henry IV*, Act II, Scene 3).

Dealing with the derivation of the word "ensign," Walton†
says:

"In the infantry the ensign corresponded to the Cornet
of Cavalry; but the Colour was not pennon-shaped,
whence the difference in the appellation of the two corresponding grades. The derivation of the word 'Cornet'
may be traced to the XVth Century, but as the infantry is
an older arm than Cavalry we must go further back for
the origin of the word 'Ensign.' I imagine it is derived
from the French 'enseigne' from the Latin for a military
standard, namely 'insignia.' Of the correctness of this
derivation we find additional corroboration in two ancient
spellings of the title. In French 'enseigne' signifies also a

---

* In the Army of the Commonwealth captains carried a pike,
lieutenants a partisan and ensigns a sword. Each regiment had ten
ensigns.
† "History of the British Standing Army."

'sign-board' and in a work published in 1627 the English word is spelt 'Hand-signe.' "

Again, in other works, as in Shakespeare, we find the word "ancient" used to signify the ensign of a company—the officer as well as the Colour—while the same word "ancient" was employed as late as Queen Anne's reign to signify a ship's flag or colour.

The following copy of an Ensign's Commission in Cromwell's day clearly indicates his duties:

"Oliver Cromwell, Esq., Captain Generall and Commander in Chiefe of the Armie and Forces raised and to be raised by authority of Parliament within ye Commonwealth of England.

"To John Wells, Ensigne

By virtue of the power and authority to me derived from ye Parliament of England, I doe hereby constitute and appointe you Ensigne of ye Compy of Foote whereof Captaine Ethilbert Morgan is Capte . . . in the regt. whereof Lieut. Genll. George Monck is Collonell.

"These are therefore to require you to make yr psent repaire unto the same compy, and taking charge thereof as Ensigne, duly to exercise the inferior officers and souldrs of the Sd Compy in arme, and to use your best care and endeavour to keep them in good ordr and discipline, commanding them to obey you as theire Ensigne, and you are likewise to observe and follow any orders and direcons as you shall from tyme to tyme receive from myself and yr superior officers of the sd regimt and army, according to the discipline of warr. Given under my hand and Seals, the 17th November, 1651.

"O. Cromwell."*

In the seventeenth century Cornets and Guidons in the Household Cavalry "commanded as Majors," *vide* Nathan Brooks's Army Lists for 1684.†

---

* Both Oliver Cromwell and General George Monck started their military careers as Ensigns.

† See also "The Story of the Household Cavalry," by Sir George Arthur, and a reproduction of Nathan Brooks's Army List on pp. 59 and 143, Vol. I, of the *Journal of the Society for Army Historical Research*.

Ward, in his book "Animadversions of Warre," published in 1639, makes the following remarks regarding the quality of the person who should carry the Colours:

"I could wish our Noble Captaines would be pleased to be more circumspect in their election of officers, and not to put undeserving fellows, of base birth and qualitie into place of command, which deserves Gentlemen of qualitie to officiate, the office of Ensigne being a place of repute and honour, doth not suite every Yeoman, Taylor, or Fidler, as I have known one Company in Essex, all these or the like Mechanick fellowes have had the honour to beare the Colours before a generous Captaine of Noble birth, whose name I forbeare to relate."

Ward appears to have had just cause for complaint in regard to the type of person which was sometimes given the honour of carrying the Colour, if the following excerpt from Shakespeare means anything:

"Ten times more dishonourable ragged than an old faced ancient."
(1st Part, *K. Henry IV*, Act IV, Scene 2.)

Venn (1672) assigns the following duties to the Ensign:

"1. He shall when the Captaine or Lieutenant be present be assistant to them, or either of them, and in their absence he hath the same authority the Captain hath.

"2. In his march he is to carry the Ensign, and to take such place as shall be assigned him, and if his Company be alone, he shall upon entering the quarter, going out of his quarter, going upon the guard, or upon the fight of an Enemy, carry his Ensign advanced and flying; and if he march with the Regiment, he and all other Ensigns of the Regiment shall do as the Colonel's Ensign doth.

"3. In fight he shall never carry his Ensign advanced and flying, without offering to use it in any kind of offence, being a sign for a Company to gather by, and therefore to be preserved, for which cause he may use his sword.

"4. If he march with other Ensignes he shall take the place as shall be assigned him.

"5. The Ensign shall never turn his face out of his order, or start from any danger, or forsake his Ensign upon pain of death."

On the question of precedence Venn says:

"The Ensign hath dignity of place according to the antiquity of his Captain: But in one particular case, it hath been judged to be greater than his captain, and lendeth place to him, as thus; no Captain can receive his antiquity from his enrollment, but from the first hour in which his Colours flew; for if two be enrolled upon one day, and the latter marcheth before the face of his enemy with his Colours flying, in this case the first hath lost his priority and the latter for ever shall preceed him."

In the matter of precedence the "General Regulations and Orders for the Army" of 1804 have an interesting instruction, viz.:

"All regiments marching with Standards or Colours have a claim to receive the Compliments from any regiments or detachments they may meet on their march, not having Standards or Colours, without reference to the Rank and Precedence of the particular Corps."

The Honourable Artillery Company in the seventeenth century appear to have been very particular regarding the persons who should carry their Colours, according to the following extracts from their orders:

"1681. None under the degree of Captain was to carry the Colours."

"1682. No officer was to carry a Partisan or Colour under the degree of Captain-Lieutenant."

"1689. None under the degree of Captain-Lieutenant or a member of the Court of Assistants was to carry a partisan or Colour."*

The conspicuity imposed upon those who carried the Colours in action rendered their office, though honourable, not particularly enviable. Lord Albemarle in his reminiscences states:

"Fifteen years after the battle a French Officer was conversing with me on the subject of Waterloo. He told me that he was an artillery officer posted in that action on the extreme left of the French line, and his orders were to

---

* *Vide* "History of the Honourable Artillery Company," by Captain G. A. Raikes.

fire upon the three British regiments, the Colours of which were respectively blue, buff and green,* proving beyond all doubt that it was against our brigade that his practice was directed."

In the autobiography of Sergeant William Laurence, 40th Regiment, referring to the Waterloo Campaign he states:

"About four o'clock I was ordered to the Colours; this although I was used to warfare as much as anyone, was a job I did not at all like, but still I went as boldly to work as I could. There had been before me that day fourteen Serjeants already killed and wounded, and the staff and colours almost cut to pieces."

The influence of Colours in steadying and encouraging troops is the reason why we find many officers of high rank carrying them in modern wars at critical moments. Thus the Archduke Charles of Austria at Aspern (1809) led his young troops to the last assault with a Colour in his hands. The venerable Marshal Schwerin was killed at the battle of Prague (1757) while carrying a regimental Colour. At the first battle of Bull Run (1861) the raw Confederate troops were rallied under a heavy fire by General Joseph Johnston, their Commander-in-Chief, who stood with a Colour in his hand until the men assembled in order.

In the cavalry it was the custom to tie the Standard to the leg of the standard-bearer. It is related that at Fontenoy Colonel Erskine, who commanded the "Greys," tied the Standard to his son's leg and said "Go, and take good care of your charge; let me not see you separate. If you return alive from the field you must produce the Standard." After the fight the young Cornet rode up to his father and showed him the Standard as tight and as fast as in the morning.

The same custom existed in the French army. At the battle of Dettingen a Sergeant of 1st The Royal Dragoons captured the Standard of the Mousquetaries Noirs. The lance was broken, the Standard stained with blood, and the Cornet who carried it was killed without falling, being buckled to his horse, and his Standard buckled to him.

---

* Mitchell's Brigade, composed of the 23rd—blue; 14th—buff; 51st—green.

Officers have always carried the Colours of the infantry, and so they did the Standards of the Cavalry until 1822, when the following order was issued from Horse Guards under date 30th November, 1822:

> "His Majesty has been pleased to command that standards in Cavalry regiments shall be carried in future by troop Serjeant-Majors, and the Commander-in-Chief desires the same may be observed accordingly.

> "H. TORRENS, Adjt. Genl."

The rank of "Colour-Sergeant" was introduced by General Order dated 6th July, 1813, in which it was stated: "It is His Royal Highness's Pleasure that the duty of attending the Colours in the field shall be at all times performed by these Serjeants."

Official directions as to who should carry the Colours do not appear in the Regulations until those of 1868, wherein it is stated: "The Colours of infantry are, whenever practicable, to be carried by the two senior ensigns." In 1870 the rank of Ensign was abolished, and its effect is found in the next Regulations concerning Colours, viz. those of 1873: "The Colours of infantry are, as a rule, to be carried by the two junior lieutenants." This was repeated in the Regulations for 1881 and 1885, but in those of 1889 it is "The Colours of infantry are, as a rule, to be carried by the two *senior second-lieutenants.*" In the next issue of Regulations (1898) an amplification was made to this as shown here:

> "Standards and guidons of cavalry will be carried by Squadron Sergeant-Majors. Colours of infantry will be carried by the two senior second-lieutenants, *but on the line of march all subaltern officers will carry them in turn.*"

The regulations have not varied on this point since 1898.

Before leaving the question of carrying the Colours, it is interesting to note that on the line of march the duty of carrying them was shared from early times, for Sir James Turner in his "Pallas Armata," written in 1670, states, in regard to the composition of a Foot Company: "Add, therefore, three Corporals to the hundred soldiers, you shall have seventeen compleat files, and one man over, whom you may appoint to help the Ensign to carry his Colours." And again: "After he (the

Ensign, 9th Foot, with Regimental Colour, and Colour-Sergeant as escort, in action, late Peninsular War period, 1812-14.

Ensign) hath marched a mile out of his quarters, he may ride and give the Colours to another to carry, which is ordinarily a Pikeman (whose Pike his companions are obliged to carry by turns) but at the sight of a General Officer or his own Colonel, the Ensign-bearer is to alight and take his Colours in his own hands. In France, in the time of Henry the Great, he was allowed to have a young fellow to assist him to carry the Colours, who for that service had half a soldier's pay."

Continued from opposite page]
of some conspicuous sign or token which the soldier might follow and, upon any defeat or dispersion of their troops, resort to. This invention was by Lycurgus carried to Sparta, and from thence transferred to the Romans, in whose armies they were accounted so sacred that they paid them a kind of divine reverence; whose superstition was likewise derived from the Egyptians, whose chief ensign was their god Apis, represented in the figure of a Bull, hierogliphically signifying strength and power."

CHAPTER XIII

CEREMONIES ASSOCIATED WITH COLOURS

PRESENTATION OF COLOURS

ALTHOUGH the ceremony of the Presentation of Colours is not mentioned in official regulations until 1867, there had always been some kind of recognized formality and many old prints are in existence illustrating the ceremony. The presentation was usually made by the wife of the Colonel of the Regiment.

The earliest instructions on the subject are to be found in "Field Exercise and Evolutions of Infantry—1867." These instructions appeared in regulations referring to the infantry up to "Infantry Training 1905," then they were transferred to "Ceremonial—1912," being re-transferred to "Infantry Training" again in 1922.

The latest instructions appear in "Manual of Ceremonial—1935," Chapter XII. A comparison between the earliest and latest instructions reveal that little change has occurred in the procedure.

THE CONSECRATION OF REGIMENTAL COLOURS

One of the most important features connected with Colours is their consecration. The ceremony of consecration was bound to be introduced very early in the employment of Standards and Colours for two reasons: firstly, because they were intimately connected with the Church; and secondly, their importance as symbols of the people and the sacrifice of human life which always attended their defence.

From the earliest times war flags, banners and standards have been intimately connected with the Church, both Christian and pagan, and the element of consecration is conveyed in some of their designs.* The Israelites, for instance, carried the

---

* Thomas Simes (1778) states: "The most learned and skilful antiquarians agree that the original use of ensigns or colours in war came from the Egyptians, who being under no regular discipline, and therefore often invaded and overcome by their neighbours, invented the carrying

[Continued on opposite page

sacred standard of the Maccabees, which bore the initial letters of the Hebrew text, "Who is like unto Thee, O God, amongst the gods" (Exodus xv. 11); the Labarum of the Emperor Constantine bore the sacred monogram of Christ; the standard of Joan of Arc (1429) bore the figure of Christ on one side, and on the other a representation of the Annunciation and the words "Ave Maria." Joan also wore a consecrated sword, marked on the blade with five crosses, which had, at her bidding, been taken for her from the shrine of St. Catherine at Fierbois. She generally bore her banner herself in battle; she said that though she loved her sword much, she loved her banner fifty times as much—and she loved to carry it because it could not kill anyone. Poor Joan! She apparently did not realize that it gave her soldiers the necessary impulse to kill.

Two of the most reliable authorities on the antiquities of the ancient Romans, Daremberg* and Adam,† state that the military flag was the symbol of the god of war—the visible sign of the invisible spirit—represented in material form by a statue in the city but in the legion by a standard. Daremberg writes:

> "Tertullian declared that the creed of the standard constituted in some form all the religion of the army, and they gave it precedence over all other gods. . . . Under the Empire the temples of Rome continued to receive some ensigns, but they must, in each camp, following the regular religious services of the temple, erect the ensigns which they have in their chapel, inviolate refuge, where was also worshipped the images of Emperors. When in camp it was the ensign which was placed first, and when a satisfactory site had been chosen, probably in the middle of the general's headquarters, they raised a chapel there, making an altar of turf on which they placed the ensign."

Adam states that the ensigns were made of wood, silver and gold

> "on which were represented the images of warlike deities, as Mars or Minerva; and, after the extinction of liberty, of the emperors or of their favourites. Hence the standards

---

* "Dictionary of the Antiquities of the Ancient Greeks and Romans," Daremberg (Library, British Museum).

† "Roman Antiquities," Alexander Adam. LL.D.

**Presentation of Colours to the 1st Bn. Coldstream Guards by H.M. King George VI
at Windsor on 3rd April, 1951, on the occasion of the presentation of new Colours
to the 1st and 2nd Battalions.**

were called 'Numina legionum,' and worshipped with religious adoration. The soldiers swore by the standards and deposited their money at them as in a sacred place."

Dr. Lord states:*

"Both religion and honour bound him (the Roman soldier) to his standards; the golden eagle which glittered in his front was the object of his fondest devotion."

Whatever may have been the attitude of mind of the Jews towards their standards, it is not difficult to comprehend that to the pagan mind "his ensign was the incarnation of his god of war," a portable or mobile god; and like so many pagan ideas which still find expression in our Christian system, this idea still persists in a modified form in our *esprit de corps*, or "creed of the regiment," symbolized in Colours, the continuity of that spirit being maintained by the consecrating of each new set of Colours.

As regards the ceremony of consecration, the Scriptures produce very meagre information on the subject, and the nearest approach to anything definite appears to be contained in "In the name of our God we will set up our banners" (Psalm xx. 5), from which it might be inferred that the Jews would hardly "set up" their banners "in the name of God" without a formal ceremony. Further, in view of the fact that they carried a standard bearing a portion of scripture (*i.e.*, the standard of the Maccabees), it is practically certain that such a standard would not have been handed over to the military leader without some formal ceremony of consecration. Josephus also informs us that "Jonathan, the high priest, levied an army out of all Judea, and attacked the citadel at Jerusalem, and besieged it; it was held by a garrison of Macedonians." Here again it might be inferred that Jonathan would certainly have consecrated or blessed the banners of the troops he had raised.

So firmly established had become this practice of consecrating war flags that many ancient writers appear to have taken it for granted that posterity would not require a special reference to it in a general history, and this no doubt accounts for the scanty references to the subject in the early part of the Christian era. Here and there, however, one is able to light on a few passages bearing on the subject. For instance, we find that in

* In "Beacon Lights of History," Vol. II, p. 251.

A.D. 800 the Patriarch of Jerusalem sent Charlemagne the keys of the city and a banner, the latter which he presumably blessed. In A.D. 1060 Pope Alexander II sent the Normans a banner "which he had blessed" and under which they fought against the Arabs for the conquest of Sicily.

Our national flag—the Great Union—has a very close connection with the Church, in that it is composed of the crosses of the three national saints. The red Cross of St. George, the English national saint, was the flag under which we fought our early battles from the fourteenth century. Speaking of the period about 1366, Fortescue says: "Every man wore his red cross of St. George on a white surcoat and on his shield, a badge which henceforth became distinctive of the English soldiers for two centuries." In the Golden Legend we read "The Blyssed and Holy Martyr Saynt George is patron of this realme of England, and the crye of men of Warre."

Shakespeare has several references to the Cross of St. George as a battle flag:

> "Sound drums and trumpets, boldly and cheerfully,
> God and St. George ! Richard and Victory."
>
> *(King Richard II.)*

Again at the siege of Harfleur:

> "The game's afoot.
> Follow your spirit, and upon this charge
> Cry, God for Harry, England and St. George."
>
> *(King Henry V.)*

On the union with Scotland the cross of the patron saint of that country was incorporated into our national flag, and again in 1801 the cross of the patron saint of Ireland was added.

French early history provides much evidence on this aspect of the subject. The ancient Kings of France bore the blue hood of St. Martin upon their standards. The Chape de St. Martin was originally in the keeping of the monks of the abbey of Marmoutier, and the right to take it into battle with them was claimed by the Counts of Anjou. Clovis bore it against Alaric in 507, for victory was promised him by a verse of the Psalms which the choir were chanting when his envoy entered the Church of St. Martin at Tours. Charlemagne fought under it at the battle of Narbonne, and it frequently led the French to victory.

Before the Norman Conquest of England in 1066, William

of Normandy submitted his case against Harold to the Pope, and Sir Edward Creasey tells us* that

> "after a formal examination of William's complaints by the Pope (Alexander II) and the cardinals it was solemnly adjudged at Rome that England belonged to the Norman Duke; and a banner was sent from the Holy See which the Pope himself had consecrated and blessed for the invasion of the island. . . . All the adventurous spirits under Christendom flocked to the Holy Banner."

Many years before Hastings, however, the Turks had been making trouble in the Holy Land, but nothing appears to have been done on the Christian side until Pope Urban II declared a "sacred war" against them in 1095.

> "Every man stimulates the passion of his neighbours. All vie in their contributions. The knights especially are enthusiastic, for they can continue their accustomed life without penance, and yet obtain the forgiveness of their sins. Religious fears are turned at first into the channel of penance; and penance is made easy by the indulgence of martial passions. Every recruit wore a red cross, and was called croise—cross-bearer—whence the name of the holy war" (Dr. Lord).

Grose says† that in "England holy or sacred banners were frequently carried into the field by the monks or other ecclesiastics, in order to inspire a confidence in the troops, who were taught to believe that the Saint, whose banner was then displayed, would interest himself on their behalf." Thus, at the battle of the Standard, 1138, the banners of St. Peter of York, St. John of Beverley and St. Wilfrid of Ripon were erected on a wagon and moved in the midst of the army: the standard of St. Cuthbert was carried with the army of Edward I into Scotland, and with that of the Earl of Surrey to the battle of Flodden Field.

It is also thought by some authorities that, on the Continent in the fourteenth century, the act of consecration was sometimes performed by the King or Prince, who simply took the furled banner from the knight and unfurled it, making a few suitable remarks.

* In "Fifteen Decisive Battles of the World" (Battle of Hastings).
† In "Military Antiquities."

An instance of such a ceremony is recorded by Froissart in his "Chronicles," Chapter CCXXXVII, in connection with the battle of Najara in 1367 (3rd April), thus:

> "Then Sir John Chandos brought his banner rolled up together to the Prince (of Wales) and said, 'Sir, behold here is my banner: I require you to display it abroad and give me leave this day to raise it ; for, Sir, I thank God and you, I have land and heritage sufficient to maintain it withal.' Then the Prince and King Don Peter took the banner between their hands and spread it abroad, the which was of silver, a sharp pile gules, and delivered it to him and said, 'Sir John, behold here your banner, God send you joy and honour thereof.' Then Sir John Chandos bore his banner to his own company, and said, 'Sirs, behold here my own banner and yours, keep it as your own.' And they took it, and were right joyful."

William Maskell, in his "Monumenta Ritualia Ecclesiæ Anglicanæ," states that the practice of consecrating Regimental Colours is "very ancient," and among *Benedictiones diversæ* gives the text of a *Vexillorum processionalium, vel militarium benedicto*, which, from the style of Latin employed, fixes the services about the thirteenth or fourteenth century.* The ceremony was performed by no one inferior to a bishop.

Authorities are of opinion that Shakespeare wrote the first part of King Henry VI between 1588 and 1596, in which we find Talbot invoking the Almighty to bless "our Colours":

> "God and St. George, Talbot and England's right,
> Prosper our Colours in this dangerous fight."
> (Act IV, Scene 2, last two lines.)

This appears to be the nearest Shakespeare gets to consecration of Colours, and, although he makes Titus Andronicus say "I consecrate my sword, my chariot" (Act I, Scene 2), he tantalizingly makes no reference to his ensign.

That some form of ceremony of consecration existed in the sixteenth century we have the evidence of Sir John Smithe in his "Instructions, Observations and Orders Mylitaire," composed in 1591 and published in 1595. In that section of his book "concerning Ensignes and Ensignebearers" Sir John

---

* Reproduced as Appendix G.

I

states: "which said displaying of the Prince's standard ought to be performed with certen notable respects, praires and ceremonies; which because I do not certenlie know them all, I omitte." It is a pity Sir John's memory was not stronger on this aspect of ensigns, for then we might have known the details of this ancient ceremony. However, he confirms for us that "certen notable respects," prayers, etc., were observed in the sixteenth century.

Barry (1634), "Treatinge of the election and office of Captaine of a companie of Infanterie," writes, "After choysinge his officers as aforesaid, before he marches with the same, he is firste to cause the Colores to be blest, and afterwards deliver the same to the Alferis (ensign)." This is one of those rare pieces of evidence on the subject which has come out of the early seventeenth century and illustrates the continuity of the practice.

In the Museum of the Royal United Service Institution there is a picture of the ceremony of the Consecration of Colours presented by Lady Dundas to the 3rd Regiment of Royal East India Volunteers in 1799.

On 27th January, 1808, new Colours were presented to the 76th Regiment (2nd Battalion The West Riding Regiment)* at Jersey. The Regimental Record states: "After divine service the regiment again formed in the great square where the new Colours were placed on drums, opposite the centre, and consecrated by the Dean in the usual manner." Unfortunately, no details of the "usual manner" are given, but it is obvious that the practice of consecrating the Colours was of long standing in the Regular Army.

The matter of the consecration of Colours appears to have been raised in official quarters in 1830, at which time the Rev. Dr. Dakins, Principal Chaplain to the Forces, stated:

> "No regulations, in my recollection, ever did exist for the performance of that ceremony. The custom was prevalent, but the manner varied; in some instances the Colours were presented on the Field, laid on a table in a marquee, and consecrated by an appropriate prayer. On other occasions the Colours were taken to a Church, and deposited during Divine Service upon the altar. Religion

---

* *Vide* "Historical Record of the 76th Regiment," Hayden.

and Loyalty were indissoluble ties. The feeling was good, and it prevailed. Hence arose the consecration of Colours. No form having been enacted, there is one that might be observed in strict conformity with the Canons of our Church. The service should be short and impressive, and, in my view of it suited to the solemnity.

"I would take it from the Communion Service:

"1st, The Lord's Prayer.

"2nd, The Collect that follows.

"3rd, One of the Two Collects for the King.

"4th, The Prayer for the whole State of Christ's Church militant here on earth. (This is a beautiful and most comprehensive prayer.)

"5th, One of the Collects at the end of the Communion Service.

"6th, The Blessing.

"This form would, as it appears to me, be quite sufficient if the ceremony were performed in the Field.

"In the Church there can be no departure from the performance of the whole of the Service: if the Minister should choose to introduce an appropriate Prayer, that act will depend upon his own discretion."

The following interesting paragraph, which throws light on an old custom, is taken from Cannon's "Historical Records of the 5th Foot (Northumberland Fusiliers)." On 14th December, 1836, new Colours were presented to the regiment, so

"On the following Sunday the Colours were, according to custom on such occasions, taken with the regiment to Church, when the duty of soldiers, both as men and Christians, was inculcated by the Chaplain to the Forces in the most impressive manner."

William Maskell, in his work already cited, quotes "prayers used at the Consecration of Regimental Standards and Colours" from "a printed form for the use of the Reformed Church of England, London, 1838," which no doubt was the outcome of Dr. Dakin's suggestion.

The earliest reference to the consecration of Colours found in the official regulations is in Queen's Regulations for 1867, and then only in connection with "Presentation of Colours."

Section 21, para. 8, reads: "The Consecration will then proceed. (A form of prayer for this ceremony may be procured at the Chaplain-General's Office.) After the consecration," etc.

The earliest official instructions regarding the service of "Consecration of Colours" are found in Queen's Regulations for 1899, para. 40 of which states:

> "The Consecration of Colours will be performed by Chaplains to the Forces or by officiating clergymen in accordance with an authorized Form of Prayer, copies of which may be obtained from the Under-Secretary of State, War Office; 'Form A' is for general use, and 'Form B' is for special use when Colours are consecrated by a Roman Catholic priest. General Officers Commanding will ensure that no departure from the procedure laid down in either of these forms of prayer takes place.
>
> "When the Officer Commanding an Irish Battalion is desirous of having the consecration of its new Colours performed in accordance with Form B, that Order of Service will be used. General Officers Commanding may, however, authorize members of different denominations to officiate at the ceremony, in which case all or parts of Forms A and B may be used, but nothing is to be added to either Form of Prayer."

This regulation was unaltered in the 1901, 1904 and 1908 editions, but the following amendment was contained in those for 1912:

> "In the case of Scottish Battalions 'Form C' will be used if the ceremony takes place in Scotland, and also elsewhere if the majority of the men are Presbyterians."

The 1912 (Reprint 1914) King's Regulations added nothing to the foregoing, but in those for 1923 we find a slightly different wording, thus:

> "The Consecration of Colours will be performed by Chaplains to the Forces, or officiating Chaplains in accordance with an authorized Form of Prayer, copies of which may be obtained from the Secretary, The War Office. Form A is for general use. When the majority of the men of the unit are Roman Catholics the consecration of its new Colours will be performed by a Roman Catholic

Service of Consecration at the Presentation of Colours to the 1st Bn. The Green Howards by H.R.H. The Princess Royal at Catterick Camp, 27th July, 1938.

H.R.H. The Princess Royal addressing the parade after presenting Colours to the 1st Bn. The Green Howards, Catterick Camp, 27th July, 1938.

priest and the Order of Service in Form B will be used. In the case of Scottish Battalions Form C will be used."

The remainder of the paragraph is unchanged.

It will be noticed that nothing has so far been officially laid down for the consecration of Cavalry Standards and Guidons. It is curious that these never received the same veneration as Infantry Colours. In fact, when His Majesty King George V presented new Standards to the Household Cavalry on 24th June, 1927, an adaptation of the Service for the consecration of Infantry Colours was employed.

In the 1928 edition of the King's Regulations, however, "Standards" are now included for the first time in the orders regarding consecration.

LODGING AND TROOPING THE COLOUR

One of the most popular military spectacles is that of the ceremony of "Trooping the Colour." The annual event on the Horse Guards Parade, London, on the occasion of the Sovereign's birthday, and similar ceremonies in garrison towns or stations overseas by regiments commemorating some notable episode in their history, the presentation of new Colours and the laying up of old ones, all tend to keep fresh in the mind of the public a piece of ritual that can be definitely traced to the sixteenth century, and doubtless was observed long before.

Perhaps the earliest writer on this subject was Sir John Smithe, who wrote his "Instructions, Observations and Orders Mylitarie" in 1591, but did not publish them until 1595. Writing of the Ensign-bearer he states:

> "When he commeth neare to the place where he shall lodge . . . he then being on foot, must himself with great respect and reverance take and carrie the Standard, be it imperial or royal, and place it in his lodging under a strong and verie convenient guarde of soldiers, and so likewise in the morning upon the occasion of dislodging, he himselfe, being stronglie accompanied, ought to take the Standard into his own hands, and to march and take his place according to the direction of the Prince or his Lieutenant General."

Here the lodging and dislodging were ceremoniously carried

out by a "strong" and "verie convenient guarde," and as Sir John was writing as the result of experience, this ritual must have been observed for some years previous to 1591.

Markham (1622) says that the Ensign-bearer may have the pick of the billets, thus: "He shall never lodge or dislodge them but with a guard. . . . He may in garrison challenge the first and principall lodging." Other pre-Restoration military writers confirm the practice of lodging and dislodging with a guard.

One of the earliest military writers of the present Standing Army was Captain Thomas Venn, who published in 1672 his "Military Observations or Tacticks put into Practice for the Exercise of Horse and Foot; The Original of Ensignes; The Postures of their Colours." The matter of his work, however, refers to a period thirty years earlier, for he states in one paragraph, "It was in the years 1641 and 1642 that I minded any of these military actions." Nevertheless, subsequent writers must be grateful to him for putting on record the details of the ceremony observed in the first part of the seventeenth century, the relevant extracts of which are given here:

"The Ensigne hath this Dignity to have a Guard ever about it, which no other Officer hath; neither is it to be disinlodged, or unlodged, without a special guard attending upon it both of Musquetteers and Pikes; (And so for a Cornet with his own Squadron of Horse). Also in the Field if it be in particular discipline or otherwise upon a Alt, or stand, at such time as the Army or Company are to refresh themselves with victuals or other rest, in this case the Ensigne shall by no means lay his Colours upon the ground, or put them in unworthy or base hands, but he shall first furle and fold them up and set the butt end on the ground supported with the Serjeants Holbearts (holbards) and the Ensigne himself shall not go from the view thereof, unless he shall leave a sufficient guard for them."

Venn then gives the method by which the ceremony was performed:

"And lastly when the Ensign returns from the Field and is to be lodged; in former times the Lieutenant had the Vanguard; but that I shall not insist upon, because I have observed it to be left off by able souldiers.

"The Captain leading them out of the field, and coming near the place intended to lodge his Colours, converts the ranks of Musquetteers of both divisions to the right and left outwards and joyns them; and being so fixed, the body of Pikes stand in the reer, and the Ensign in the head of them, the Captain before the Colours, with the Drums and Serjeants guarding the Colours on each side, and the Lieutenant behind, the Ensign bearer, and all being advanced, shall troop up with the Colours furl'd to his lodging or quarters; and as he approacheth thereto, he shall with a bow to his Captain carry in his Colours; then the word shall be given to all the Musquetteers to make ready; that being done they shall present, and upon the beat of Drum, or other word of command, give one intire volley; and then command every officer to go to their quarters, and to be in readiness upon the next summons, either by Drum or Command."

Apparently there was not always time to perform all the movements of the ceremony detailed above, so Venn mentions how it was done in an abbreviated form:

"It may fall out that time will not permit this large circumstance; then the whole Company being drawn up in a body shall troop up to the place where the Ensign shall quarter, to see the Colours safely lodg'd, which being effected, the Musquetteers shall with one intire volley discharge their musquets and so depart to their respective quarters; commanding all upon the next summons to be in readiness."

Passing from unofficial statements to official Regulations, an early record of the ceremony is contained in "The Duke of Cumberland's Standing Orders for the Army, 1755,"* paras. 21, 22, 25 and 28 of which are reproduced here:

Para. 21. "If there be a guard which mounts with Colours, the Captain is then to send for them *in form.* The Ensign advancing his Espontoon, posts himself at the head of the detachment, which is to go for the Colours, and the Captain (having ordered the said detachment to poize and rest their firelocks on the left arm) orders him

---

* See *Journal of the Society for Army Historical Research*, Vol. V, pp. 192-3.

to march, the Drummers beating a 'Troop.'* When the Ensign comes to the place where the Colours are, he orders the detachment to fix their bayonets and present their arms, the Drummers beating a 'Point of War.' As soon as the Colours are handed out to the Ensign, he then orders them to rest their bayonets on the left arm, and troops his detachment to the parade; when he comes to one of the flanks of the Parade, he is to face his Detachment to the right or left, the men marching between the ranks, and the Ensign in front of the line of officers (each of whom are to pay the proper respect to the Colours by pulling off their hats as they pass) till he comes to the centre of his Guard. The Detachment being come to their ground, the Captain orders them to unfix their bayonets and shoulder."

Para. 22. "When the Colours come near the Parade the Town Major orders the whole to rest their firelocks continuing in that posture, and the Drummers of the several guards beating a 'March' till the Ensign with the Colours has taken his post, when the Major orders the whole to shoulder. The Town Major having acquainted the Field Officer of the Day that all is completed, and received his orders for the guards to march, he proceeds and gives directions for each guard to march off. If the Parade is narrow the Town Major will order the ranks to close, before the guards march off."

Para. 25. "The Captain is, every evening, to order the Ensign to lodge the Colours *regularly* in the Guard Room; the Serjeants with their halberts advanced accompanying him, and the guard, resting their firelocks, but the drums not to beat. In the morning the Colours are to be brought to the head of the guard *in like manner*."

Para. 28. "All guards to be Troop'd back regularly to the Parade, and there dismiss'd, except guards which mount with Colours, which guards are to be marched

---

* In his "Treatise of Military Discipline," published in 1762, "Lieut.-General Humphrey Bland, Esq." shows how the word "Trooping" became associated with guards, where he states: "The Officer of the old guard is to order his men to rest their firelocks . . . and then march off, the Drummer beating a Troop, for which reason, when a guard dismounts, it is called 'Trooping off a guard'."

back to the Parade, and after the Colours are *regularly* lodged are to be dismissed there when the detachment is returned."

The above paragraphs show that at that time there was a clear connection between guard mounting and Trooping the Colour, a fact which has given rise to the erroneous assumption that Trooping the Colour arose out of guard mounting in 1755, whereas, as already shown, Trooping, or Lodging, the Colour was a ceremony performed at least as early as 1591.

Para. 21 mentioned "the Drummers beating a Troop"; this was a piece of drum music, and gradually the expression "Trooping" supplanted that of "Lodging" in reference to this ceremony. The latter term was current in the Brigade of Foot Guards as late as 1810, as shown by the following extract from the Guards Brigade Orders by H.R.H. The Duke of Gloucester, dated 4th May, 1792:

"H.R.H. the Duke of Gloucester orders that when the Colours of the King's Guard are lodged at Retreat beating and the Dismounting they are always to be Trooped." (Reissued in Guards Brigade Orders, 28th November, 1810.)

The above-quoted Standing Orders of 1755 became the basis of "General Orders," which in turn evolved into "King's (or Queen's) Regulations." Gradually the details of the ceremony of Trooping were modified to meet the conditions (weapons and drill) of the times, and the present instructions will be found in "Manual of Ceremonial, 1935," Chapter XII, which bear many resemblances to those of the eighteenth century.

The ceremony that takes place on the Horse Guards Parade annually on the Sovereign's birthday is a part of the Guard-mounting parade for that day.

DISPOSAL OF OLD COLOURS AND THE CEREMONY OF "LAYING-UP"

In view of the reverential attitude adopted towards Colours, it is not surprising to find that, on their retirement from service, they are placed in sacred edifices or other public buildings, or in the care of those who will preserve them with due regard to their symbolic significance and historic associations. The fact that Colours were consecrated would give them an element of sacredness which could not be wholly ignored when their disposal was under consideration.

The Roman Standards were guarded with religious veneration in the temples of the metropolis, and our present custom accords generally with this.

Chaucer provides us with a fourteenth-century reference to this custom in "The Canterbury Tales," where he makes the knight in "The Knighte's Tale" say "In thy temple I wol (will) my banner honge (hang)."

In the days before the Standing Army each leader of a body of troops provided his own standard, guidon or ensign, and this very naturally was retained by him after a campaign or when it was no longer serviceable.* Long after the inauguration of the Standing Army the Colonel of the Regiment provided the Colours, and when these were retired he disposed of them on behalf of his regiment. He sometimes kept them himself, hence we find a number of very old Regimental Colours in the hands of families as well as in churches. It was not until 1855 that the State provided the Colours for Line regiments, but even as late as 1881 we find this instruction: "Unserviceable Colours, Standards or Guidons will, when replaced, be disposed of as the Officer Commanding the Regiment may deem fit" (Clothing Regulations, 1881, para. 520). This is an indication that, though the State provided the Colours, they had not yet any wish to interfere with the ancient right of the Colonel to dispose of his Colours.

An interesting sidelight on this custom is to be found in a pamphlet (in German) entitled "The Hanoverian Colours in the National Museum of the City of Hanover," by Dr. Wilhelm Pessler, Director of the National Museum.† It appears that

---

* Ward (1639): "After any Company is cashired, if the Ensigne hath behaved himselfe honourably, the Chaptaine ought to bestow the Colours on him as a favour."

Venn (1672): "If any man shall recover the lost Ensign and bring it away flying, etc., no matter how low in condition the man is, if the Captain upon any after considerations bestow those Colours upon some other man, it is disgrace both to the Captain and his Ensign, for he doth injury to Vertue and discourage Valour."

† I wish to acknowledge my indebtedness to Dr. Pessler for this pamphlet and other useful information he has sent me for the preparation of this work.—T. J. E.

the Colours of the British-German Legion were presented to the Regiment by the late Duke of Cambridge. In the year 1867 they were in the Garrison Church, Hanover, but as this building was required to house homeless refugees the Colours were temporarily placed in the Town Hall. It was finally decided to place them in the Market Church, but before doing so the sanction of H.R.H. was sought because "the Duke of Cambridge had a right to their disposal."

As late as 1896 the old Standards of the 1st King's Dragoon Guards were returned to the late Emperor of Austria, who was Colonel of the Regiment. Fine collections of old Colours are now to be seen in the Royal Hospital, Chelsea, and the museum of the Royal United Service Institution, Whitehall, London.

The early Colours were disposed of in various ways. The First or Colonel's Standard of the 8th Horse (later 7th Dragoon Guards, now 4th/7th Royal Dragoon Guards), carried by Cornet Richardson, whose exploit at Dettingen is related on page 23, was presented to him as a mark of appreciation of his gallant conduct.

At the surrender of Saratoga (1777) Colonel Hill, of the 9th Regiment, stripped the Colours off their staves and secreted them in his baggage. When the regiment returned to England he presented them to George III. The King did not retain them, but handed them back to Hill, in whose family they remained until deposited in the Chapel at Sandhurst.

The *Journal of the Society for Army Historical Research*** contains the following interesting information dealing with the disposal of Colours:

"BURNING OF THE COLOURS OF THE SECOND BATTALION,
KING'S REGIMENT (8TH FOOT)

"This took place at Portsmouth in 1816 prior to the disbandment of the Battalion. The Colours were brought to the Officers' Mess Room at the conclusion of dinner. The destruction and burning are described in the following words:

"Every officer now seized the dessert knife that lay before him, and in less time it might have been imagined possible, the Colours were stripped from their poles and cut up with a rapidity that left no time for remonstrance nor interposition; a very small portion fell to my share, as I was one of the last

---

* See Vol. III (1924).

who came in for the spoil, but such as it is I have religiously preserved it, and I believe it is the only thing in the shape of a relic that I have ever been able to keep so long.

" 'And the poles? What shall we do with the poles?' observed the young officer of Grenadiers who had first introduced the subject of the Colours, and while the excitement was now at its height.

" 'They shall be my charge,' returned Captain S. 'You may rely upon it that the agents shall see as little of them as of the Colours themselves, and if the one are out of all risk of being used as substitutes for brooms, the others shall never serve them as broom handles.'

"He then, after hacking them first with a large carving knife, broke the poles across his knee in pieces of about three feet long, and these, together with the fragments of colour and tassel which still adhered to them, were consigned to the fire that was blazing in one corner of the mess-room. We watched their rapid destruction with anxiety but in silence, and when they were wholly consumed, Captain S. desired one of the waiters to bring in a small vessel for the purpose of receiving the ashes. These having been as carefully separated as could be from the grosser and less sacred particles with which they had unavoidably been mixed up were then carried into the barrack-yard, in the centre of which a grave had been dug for their reception. Into this they were carefully emptied, and when properly covered a prayer was read over them by the enthusiastic Captain, who, moreover, in his capacity of officer of the day gave orders to the sergeant of the barrack-guard to plant a sentinel over them, and to continue that duty until the morning. In the course of half-an-hour he again made his appearance in the mess-room, assuring us with a solemnity of manner that at any other moment we should have considered farcical, but which was then in perfect unison with our own feelings, that all our apprehensions might now cease, as every vestige of the Colours of the King's Regiment had now disappeared altogether. This intelligence we hailed with all that wild enthusiasm which might be supposed to result from partial inebriation and powerful excitement of feeling, and when at a late hour we separated for our several barrack rooms it was with a sullen satisfaction at what we had done, and without a care or reflection of what was to ensue on the morrow."

Colour of the 9th Soudanese Regiment.

This regiment was raised in May, 1884, and disbanded on 30th June, 1930. During the Nile Campaign of 1884-5 the 1st Bn. The Queen's Own Cameron Highlanders and the 9th Soudanese served together at the defence of Kosha in 1885 and a close friendship grew up between the two regiments. As a consequence of this The Camerons presented the 9th Soudanese with the Colour shown in the photograph above, which they carried during the whole of their existence, and on disbandment they returned it to The Cameron Highlanders.

The battle honours on the Colour are "Nile, 1884-85," "Kosha," "Ginnis," "Sarras," "Gemmeiza," "Toski," "Argin," "Firket," "Hafir," "Sudan, 1897," "Abu Hamed," "The Atbara," "Khartoum," "Gedid," "Sudan, 1899," "Nyam-Nyam."

When the 37th Regiment of Madras Native Infantry (grena-diers) was disbanded in 1882 its Commandant, Colonel H. C. Z. Claridge, was allowed to retain possession of its Colours. He brought them to England and gave instructions that they should be buried in his grave. He died at Ryde, Isle of Wight, on 3rd January, 1899, and his funeral was delayed until the Colours could be fetched from London and buried with him.

Syke's "Local Records of Newcastle," under date of 31st May, 1763, page 111, states: "The old Colours of the 25th Regiment of Foot (Lord George Lenox's) quartered in Newcastle, being so much wounded in Germany, and par-ticularly at the glorious and ever memorable Battle of Minden (1st August, 1759) were buried with military honours." The incident is also mentioned in "Lowland Scots Regiments," where—page 200—it is stated that the Colours "had been carried at Fontenoy, Culloden, Roucoux, Val, Minden, Wer-burg, Campan, Fellinghausen and Wilhelmstal." There is no record as to where they were buried.

The records of The Green Howards show that when Lieutenant-Colonel Alexander Milne died at Demerara on 5th November, 1827, the Colours of the Regiment were buried with him, this being his last dying request.

In 1828 the King's Colour of the old 4th King's Own was presented to an officer of that regiment—Captain Mason—as a wedding present, his bride being the daughter of the Colonel of the Regiment.

As recently as 25th May, 1927, a letter appeared in *The Times* from the late General Sir H. Smith-Dorrien, Colonel of The Sherwood Foresters, requesting information regarding the whereabouts of an old set of Regimental Colours, the first set carried by the 2nd Battalion raised in 1823. The Colours were presented at Malta in 1825. In reply to this a letter appeared in the same journal two days later from a Mr. Stanhope Kennedy, who said that no doubt the Colours General Smith-Dorrien was concerned about had shared the same fate as those of the old 25th (King's Own Scottish Borderers) in the later fifties. It appeared that after new Colours had been presented the old ones were cut up and distributed among the officers as relics. "My father (then a Captain in the 25th)," writes Mr. Kennedy, "had a large and good fragment mounted

[*Photo: Graphic*

The Old Colours of the 3rd Bn. Coldstream Guards entering Exeter Cathedral, 2nd September, 1950.

and framed under glass, showing the silk thistles and part of the motto."

The Colours of the Prince of Wales' Own Fencible Infantry (disbanded 1802) were retained by Sir William Johnston, who raised the Corps. In due course they passed to his great grandson, Brigadier-General J. J. Collyer, C.B., C.M.G., D.S.O., who has presented them to the Officers' Mess of the Depot, The West Yorkshire Regiment (Prince of Wales's Own).

As previously stated, since 1855, when the State, as distinct from the Colonels, commenced to provide Colours, they (*i.e.*, the State-provided Colours) have been "laid-up" in churches or some other public building. The "Laying-up" Ceremony is as impressive as that of consecration.

It was not until 1898 that instructions were issued to the effect that they remained the property of the State when replaced on retirement from service. As already shown, as late as 1881 the Regulations provided that "Unserviceable Colours, Standards or Guidons will, when replaced, be disposed of as

[*Photo: Graphic*

General Sir Charles Loyd, Colonel of the Regiment, handing over the old Colours of the 3rd Bn. Coldstream Guards to the Cathedral Authorities in Exeter, 2nd September, 1950.

K

[Photo: *Gale & Polden Ltd.*

Colours of the 1st, 2nd, 1st/4th, 2nd/4th, 5th, 7th, and 11th Battalions The Royal Hampshire Regiment at Aldershot on 11th September, 1945, on the occasion of the Presentation of the Freedom of the Borough to the Regiment.

the Officer Commanding the Regiment may deem fit." Here are the first instructions on the subject, taken from the Clothing Regulations of that year (1898):

"When Standards, Guidons or Colours are replaced they remain the property of the State, and should be deposited in some church or other public building. If this is not practicable, officers Commanding will submit through the usual channel proposals for their disposal. No one is entitled to sell old Standards, Guidons or Colours or to deal in them in any way."

All subsequent instructions on this subject have been in the same terms, but the following sentence was added in the 1926 issue of Part I, Clothing Regulations: "In no circumstances may these articles be allowed to pass into the possession of any individual."

The present instructions will be found in King's Regulations (Reprint 1945), para. 940, the first sub-para. of which reads as follows:

"Old Standards, Guidons and Colours remain the property of the State. After replacement, they will be laid up in a church or other public building (a regimental museum *which is normally open to the general public* is regarded as a public building); they will not be otherwise disposed of without War Office sanction. *In no circumstances will they be sold or allowed to pass into the possession of an individual.* . . . If the donor of any standard, guidon or colour has at the time of presentation made any stipulation regarding its disposal that would conflict with the foregoing instructions the matter will be referred to the War Office."

Official Forms of Service for the Laying-up of Colours, etc., have been drawn up for use.

It was formerly the practice that laid-up Colours could not be removed from their resting-place and taken back into service. This, however, has now been modified and the laid-up Colours of disbanded or amalgamated battalions may be re-taken into service by those battalions should they be resuscitated and provided the Colours are deemed serviceable. This is not to be confused with the practice of depositing Colours for safe custody, such as on mobilization.

CHAPTER XIV

COLOURS OF VARIOUS FORCES

MILITIA AND SPECIAL RESERVE

ALTHOUGH there is no Militia now, the old Militia regiments had Colours from the time they were raised. This force was under the administration of the Home Office until 1852, and it was not until the following year that Colours are mentioned in the "Regulations for the Militia." Paragraph 107 therein reads: "Colours will be provided by the Ordnance or they may be provided under directions of the Colonel, and the contract price will be allowed by the Ordnance." In 1854 the "contract price" was limited to £20 per pair of Colours. The 1868 Regulations laid down that the Colours were to last thirty years and that £15 would be allowed "for a single Colour with belt and case and twice that sum for a pair." When new Colours were required application had to be made to the War Office for designs. Gradually the control of Militia Colours was brought into line as far as possible with those of Regular battalions, the process being continued when the Militia changed its name to Special Reserve in 1908. They were, however, not allowed to bear the honorary distinctions that had been granted to the Regular battalions of their respective regiments: in this respect they were restricted to battle honours, etc., which had been granted to them as Militia. This regulation was modified by Army Order 251 of 1910, which allowed the distinctions granted to Line battalions being borne and those granted as Militia to lapse. Apparently some Special Reserve (late Militia) battalions preferred to carry their old Militia distinctions only, and a War Office letter of 23rd February, 1911, gave all battalions the option, as a temporary measure, of carrying only the Militia honours or those of the Line battalions. When new Colours were presented the distinctions of the Line battalions were to be emblazoned thereon and the Militia distinctions to lapse for ever.

Colours of the 19th London Regiment (St. Pancras).
The Regiment now forms part of the Royal Regiment of Artillery.

Colours of The Gold Coast Regiment, Royal West African Frontier Force.

SERVICE BATTALIONS

During the Great War of 1914-18 numerous Service Battalions were raised to augment Infantry Regiments. In 1919 it was authorized that those Service Battalions (other than those of Rifle Regiments, but including Yeomanry Regiments which had adopted an Infantry role) which had served overseas would each be provided with a silk Union Flag. These flags were not consecrated, neither were they maintained at public expense. When these Service Battalions were disbanded soon after the War their Union Flags were laid-up in a manner similar to Colours.

COLOURS OF THE VOLUNTEER FORCE, TERRITORIAL FORCE AND TERRITORIAL ARMY

Volunteers were raised for the Napoleonic War under Acts of 1794 and 1804, but this force ceased to exist about 1815. Their Colours are referred to in "The British Soldiers' Guide and Volunteer Self-Instructor" (1803). Mention is also made of them in "The Orderly Book of Captain Daniel Hebb's Company in the Loveden Volunteers (Lincolnshire), 1803-8." (See *Journal of the Society for Army Historical Research*, Vol. IV (1925).) One of the Orders, under date, Stubton, 12th January, 1804, reads:

> "Whenever the landing of the enemy, or any extraordinary alarm shall render it necessary to call out the Regiment, if it happens in the day-time, the Regimental Colours will be hoisted on the Tower of Hough, and Stubton churches, and if in the night, the Bells of many of the churches in the hundred will be ordered to be rung, besides which, in either case, messengers will be despatched in different directions."

In 1859, when an invasion by the French under Napoleon III was feared, another Volunteer Force came into being, which has found continuity of existence in the Territorial Force of 1908 and the Territorial Army of 1921 and still persists.

The first reference to Colours of this Force appeared in "Drill and Rifle Instruction for Volunteer Rifle Corps" (1859). Article 101 stated that "Neither Standards nor Colours are to be carried by Corps on parade, as the Volunteer Force is

composed of Arms to which their use is not appropriate."
This followed the practice in the Regular Army wherein Rifles
do not carry Colours. This rule obtained until the Volunteer
Force became the Territorial Force in 1908, and, although no
reference is made to Standards, Guidons and Colours in the
Territorial Force Regulations of that year, War Office Circular
Memorandum No. 100 of 3rd September, 1908, authorized:

Yeomanry   Each regiment styled or dressed as "Dragoons"
            may be permitted to carry a Guidon.
Infantry   Each Infantry battalion that does not bear the
            title "Rifles" or "Rifle Brigade," or is not
            dressed in the uniform or does not wear the
            appointments of a Rifle Regiment, may carry
            two Colours, King's and Regimental.

The Guidons or Colours were not provided from Army
funds, but in other respects they conformed generally to the
practice in the Regular Army in regard to design, etc. They
have, however, been provided from public funds since 1947. As
to the distinctions to be borne upon them, it was laid down that
"None of the devices, mottoes and distinctions authorized for
a Regular regiment will be borne upon the Colours of an
Infantry Battalion of the Territorial Force which, though
affiliated to it, does not bear its title." Such a regulation
prevented the complete unification of all parts of a regiment,
Regular, Special Reserve and Territorial Force, but during the
Great War of 1914-18, Army Order 298 of 1917 stated:

   "In consideration of the services of the Territorial Force
   during the War, His Majesty the King has been pleased
   to approve of units of the Territorial Force being permitted
   to wear on their badges the mottoes and honours worn on
   the badges of the corps, regiment or department of which
   they form part."

This foreshadowed a complete unification of all parts of a
regiment or corps which was enhanced by the change of title
of the Territorial Force to Territorial Army in 1921. Three
years later the Territorial Army Regulations in respect to
Colours were practically identical with those of the Regular
Army, thus making unification complete.

Since the conclusion of the Great War of 1914-18 numerous
units of the Territorial Army have been converted from their

original arms to other arms. Such units which, in their previous arm, were entitled to carry Guidons or Colours may still carry them in certain circumstances.

This practice is entirely opposed to the history and meaning of Colours and reduces them to mere ornaments. As already shown, when Dragoons were converted to Hussars or Lancers they ceased to carry Guidons, and when Infantry Regiments were converted to Rifle Regiments they ceased to carry Colours. This historic connection between Regiments and Guidons and Colours is now weakened by Royal Artillery units, converted from Yeomanry or Infantry, carrying Guidons or Colours, as though they were still Cavalry or Infantry. Further, it may be argued that if some Royal Artillery carry Colours, why not all? It is a proud tradition of the R.A. that their guns are their Colours, but this is now somewhat modified by silken Colours being flown by some of their units.

The Cheshire Regiment wearing oak leaves in their head-dress marching past with wreaths on the heads of the Colour-pikes.

COLOURS OF THE MILITARY FORCES OF THE
BRITISH COMMONWEALTH

The regulations governing the design, etc., of Standards, Guidons and Colours of the Military Forces of the countries of the British Commonwealth and Colonies conform generally to those laid down for the British Army. This was also the case of the Indian Army before India was constituted two separate Dominions (India and Pakistan) on 15th August, 1947: since that date Pakistan has continued to adhere to the British Army regulations, but the army of the new India laid up its King's Colours in the National Defence Academy at Dehra Dun on 23rd November, 1950. A description of the laying-up ceremony is given in Appendix "H," p. 226.

The main distinguishing feature of the Commonwealth Colours is in the central wreath which, instead of being the Union wreath of roses, thistles and shamrocks, is composed of leaves of a national tree, plant, etc.

In the Canadian Army this central wreath is composed of autumnal maple leaves.

The Guidon- and Colour-bearing units of the Australian Army have at least two features peculiar to themselves, in that the central wreath is composed of wattle leaves and berries, and the central device includes a "Regimental Patch" reminiscent of the patch worn on the uniform during the Great War of 1914-18.

The distinguishing feature in the Colours of regiments of New Zealand is the introduction of the fern-leaf wreath. Otherwise the design approximates that of the Colours of regiments of the United Kingdom.

In South Africa the central wreath is composed of protea.

Before 1947 the composition of Indian Army Colours, etc., appears to have been originally somewhat unregulated, but following in their main features those of the British Army. Latterly, however, the regulations for the British Army have been followed more closely. For instance, illustrations of the Colours of the early part of the nineteenth century show the central wreath composed of various leaves, whereas those presented in recent years have the approved Union wreath.

An old Standard of The Poona Horse consists of a centre-piece sewn on separately, on which is embroidered a circle of

Guidon of 4th Light Horse Regiment in Australia.

Guidon of The Otago Mounted Rifles of New Zealand.

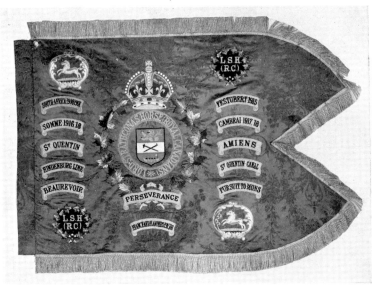

Guidon of Lord Strathcona's Horse (Royal Canadians).

Regimental Colour of 2nd South African Infantry.

Regimental Colour of Northern Rhodesia Police as carried before conversion to The Northern Rhodesia Regiment.

leaves enclosing a monogram, ensigned by an old pattern crown (twelve battle honours are also sewn on); whereas a modern Standard of this regiment follows the rules as to design of British Cavalry, and include the Union wreath, title circle, modern crown, White Horse of Hanover in first and fourth corners, and rose, thistle and shamrock in second and third corners.

The Colour of the late 2nd/2nd Bombay Pioneers, disbanded in 1932, was quite unique and was associated with a fine episode in the history of the regiment. As the 3rd Regiment of Infantry it was raised for service in the First Afghan War of 1839-42, and in February, 1841, occupied Kelat-i-Ghilzie, where the defences were in a bad state of disrepair. An overwhelming force of Ghilzais attacked the place, and though it was repelled it maintained an investment which cut off the regiment from the outside world. Supplies of every description

Queen's Colour of The Northern Rhodesia Regiment.

gradually whittled away, and during the winter the temperature fell to 40 degrees below freezing point. With the advent of milder weather the enemy drew its throttling cordon tighter round the fort and from well-sited trenches harassed the garrison with telling fire. A relief force was eventually sent to it, and as soon as the enemy had news of this it increased its pressure. On 21st May, 1842, the Ghilzais assaulted in two strong columns against the weakened regiment, making a determined attack to capture the place by storm. Three times they placed ladders against the wall in readiness to mount, but each time Captain Craigie's men repulsed them with considerable loss, and they finally withdrew, leaving the ground covered with their dead and five standards. The relief force arrived the next day. To commemorate this gallant service the following Order was published by the Government of India:

Regimental Colour of The Northern Rhodesia Regiment. A white Colour with the red Cross of St. George.

"The Regiment of Bengal Irregular Infantry, lately known as the 3rd Regiment of Infantry in the service of Shah Shuja, shall, in consideration of the valour, discipline and fortitude manifested by that regiment on many occasions and especially in the defence of Kelat-i-Ghilzie, continue embodied under its present Commandant, Captain Craigie, and be brought on the strength of the Bengal Army as an extra regiment and be denominated the 'Regiment of Kelat-i-Ghilzie.'

"To every officer, N.C.O. and private will be presented a silver medal bearing a mural Crown with the superscription of 'Kelat-i-Ghilzie' and on the reverse the word 'Invicta—1842.' The Regimental Colour of the Regiment of Kelat-i-Ghilzie will be composed of the three colours of the Military Ribbon of India and in the centre there will be inscribed the words 'Kelat-i-Ghilzie.' "

The colours of the Military Medal Ribbon of India are red, yellow and blue, and the Regimental Colour is composed of those colours arranged horizontally with red at the top.

This fine regiment remained on the establishment of the Indian Army until 1932, when it was disbanded as the 2nd/2nd Bombay Pioneers.

[*Photo: "Soldier" Magazine*

The Truncheon of the 2nd K.E.O. Gurkha Rifles

A Substitute for Colours: Grant of Honorary Truncheon
to 2nd King Edward VII's Own Gurkha Rifles

(The Sirmoor Rifles)

This unique honorary distinction was granted to the Sirmoor
Battalion (the predecessors of the 2nd King Edward's Own
Gurkha Rifles) for their service at Delhi during the Indian
Mutiny. The particular services for which the award was made
are stated in the "History of the 2nd King Edward's Own
Goorkha Rifles (The Sirmoor Rifles)," by Colonel L. W.
Shakespear, as follows:

> "The Sirmoor Battalion, which formed part of the main
> picquet (Hindoo Rao's House),* was never once relieved
> during the siege, and was assisted by the 60th Rifles and
> the Guides Corps, with detachments of other infantry
> regiments. It sustained and defeated 26 separate attacks
> on the Ridge, and, moreover, made two attacks on the
> enemy's position at Kissenganj.

> "The Sirmoor Battalion was the only regiment of the
> whole force which was exposed to constant fire, Hindoo
> Rao's house being within perfect range of nearly all the
> enemy's guns, and was riddled through and through with
> shot and shell. For a period of three months and eight
> days this Regiment was under fire morning, noon and
> night."

For this service the Regiment was accorded the honour of
carrying a third Colour, *vide* the following extract from a
General Order by the Commander-in-Chief, No. 379 of 1858:

> "In acknowledgment of the distinguished services of the
> Sirmoor Rifles before Delhi, the Right Honourable the
> Governor-General in Council is pleased to confer on that
> Regiment the privilege of carrying Colours similar to those
> of line regiments, as well as an honorary Colour, on which
> the word 'Delhi' shall be inscribed in Persian, Hindi and
> English.

> "His Lordship further sanctions the appointment of one
> Colour-havildar per Company in this Regiment, and of
> one extra jemadar to carry the honorary Colour.

---

* A very exposed position well in advance of the main line.

"The regiment will henceforth be designated 'The Sir-moor Rifle Regiment.' "

The Sirmoor Battalion had carried Colours ever since it was raised, but apparently without the necessary official sanction, so that the above-quoted General Order gave them covering authority for the continuance of the custom. Unfortunately, however, with the honour of being converted into a Rifle Regiment, they had to cease carrying Colours to conform to the practice in the British service. Now the question arose regarding the third Colour, and Colonel Reid, the Commanding Officer in 1859, suggested the grant of a Truncheon, and this was agreed to by the India Office on 31st August, 1859.

Colonel Shakespear says that "This Truncheon was devised and sent out by Queen Victoria." It was presented to the Regiment, on behalf of the Queen, by General Sir Hugh Rose, the Commander-in-Chief in India, on 30th November, 1863, at Lahore.

The description of the Truncheon is: It stands about six feet high, is of bronze, and is surmounted by a crown in silver, supported by three Gurkha soldiers in bronze. On a ring of silver below the figures are inscribed in silver letters the words "Main Picquet, Hindoo Rao's House, Delhi, 1857." Below this ring is a representation in bronze of the Delhi Gate of the Palace of the Moguls, with two kookeries, the Gurkha national weapon, under it in silver. Below the Gate is another silver ring on which is inscribed on three sides "Sirmoor Rifles" in silver letters. On a third silver ring just above the upper end of the staff, which is of bronze, the words "Main Picquet, Hindoo Rao's House, Delhi, 1857," are again inscribed in the Nagri character. There is a fourth plain ring of silver which connects the bronze staff with the upper portion of the Truncheon (see illustration on page 142).

The Truncheon is accorded the same honours as those normally paid to a Queen's Colour, is carried on parade by a Jemadar with an escort of two havildars and two naicks as Colour party, and all recruits touch and salute it as an additional ceremony to the ordinary one of "swearing in" on enlistment.

The Truncheon was made in England by Messrs. Hunt and Roskell, of Old Bond Street, London, W.

The King's Colour of the Royal Navy,
as carried during the reign of King George VI, and which was Trooped and carried
off parade on 22nd May, 1952, when H.R.H. The Duchess of Kent presented the
Portsmouth Command with a new Queen's Colour.

Head of Colour Pike.

The Brigade of Gurkhas was formed on the British Establishment on 1st January, 1948 (A.O. 147/1947), and under Army Order 135/1950 King George VI was graciously pleased to approve that the dignities and compliments appropriate to a King's Colour of Infantry that were accorded to the Truncheon when the 2nd King Edward VII's Own Gurkha Rifles was part of the Indian Army shall continue to be accorded now that the regiment is part of the British Army.

ROYAL NAVY

The Queen's Colour

In 1925 King George V approved for use by the Royal Navy of Colours corresponding to the King's Colours carried by Military Forces.* They consist of a silk White Ensign with a Crown and Royal Cypher superimposed, 3 feet 9 inches by 3 feet, with red, white and blue silk cord and gold tassels, carried on an ash staff, surmounted by a gilt badge consisting of the Admiralty anchor on a three-faced shield with Crown superimposed.

A Queen's Colour is held in each of the following Commands:

(*a*) One in each Home Port, kept at the Royal Naval Barracks.

(*b*) One in each of the following Commands, kept on board the Flagship of the respective Commanders-in-Chief: Home Fleet, Mediterranean Station, East Indies Station, South Atlantic Station, American and West Indies Station.

(*c*) Two in each of the following: Royal Canadian Navy —one for Halifax and one for Esquimalt; Royal Australian Navy—one for the Flagship of Her Majesty's Australian Fleet and one for Flinders Naval Depot.

(*d*) One in the Royal New Zealand Navy.

The Queen's Colour is paraded on shore on the following occasions, namely:

(*a*) By a Guard of Honour mounted for Her Majesty The Queen, Her Majesty Queen Elizabeth The Queen Mother, Her Majesty Queen Mary, His Royal High-

---

* The Royal Navy do not carry any Colour comparable with a Regimental, or Second, Colour.

L

ness The Duke of Edinburgh, or for any other member of the Royal Family.

(b) By a Guard of Honour mounted for a Foreign Sovereign or for the President of a Republican State.

(c) At parades to celebrate the birthday of Her Majesty.

(d) On such important ceremonial occasions as may be ordered by the Admiralty; or at Malta and Gibraltar by the Naval Commander-in-Chief, Mediterranean; or in the fully self-governing countries of the Commonwealth on occasions of important ceremonial when the Governor-General or President of the Republic of India is present, as may be directed by the Naval Commander-in-Chief, after consultation with the authorities of the country concerned.

The Queen's Colour is not paraded on occasions other than the foregoing and is not paraded on board ship or in foreign territory.

The Queen's Colour is only lowered to Her Majesty The Queen, Her Majesty Queen Elizabeth The Queen Mother, Her Majesty Queen Mary, His Royal Highness The Duke of Edinburgh, other members of the Royal Family, Foreign Sovereigns, Presidents of Republican States, members of Foreign Reigning and Royal Families, Governors-General, Governors, High Commissioners, Lieutenant-Governors, Captains-General or Special Royal Commissioners acting on behalf of the Sovereign, within their jurisdiction.

The Colour is carried by a Sub-Lieutenant or Lieutenant, the Colour Party consisting of one Chief Petty Officer and two Petty Officers (in seamen's dress) or Leading Seamen. The Colour officer wears a sword; the Chief Petty Officer is armed with a drawn cutlass and the two Petty Officers, or Leading Seamen, with rifles and fixed bayonets. The bayonets are provided with short sheaths to slip on the points to avoid tearing the Colour.

When uncased the Queen's Colour is at all times saluted with the highest honours. Guards of Honour actually mounted, or engaged in their duties, salute the Queen's Colour when uncased. Salutes to the Colours are not acknowledged.

When the Queen's Colour is paraded on the occasion of a funeral it is draped with a black bow. The Colour is not draped when paraded for any other reason.

Colours of the Lord High Admiral's Regiment, 1664~89.

THE COLONEL'S COLOUR.

THE LIEUTENANT-COLONEL'S COLOUR.

THE MAJOR'S AND THE
COMPANIES' COLOUR.

COLOUR OF CAPT. CHARLES
MIDDLETON'S COMPANY IN THE
VIRGINIA EXPEDITION OF 1676.

ROYAL MARINES

In common with other regiments the original Marine Regiments carried Colours appropriate to the period in which they existed. The present Royal Marines were formed in 1755, when fifty companies were raised by the Admiralty and organized into three Divisions at Chatham, Portsmouth and Plymouth respectively. King's and Regimental Colours were furnished to each Division soon after raising. A fourth Division was formed at Woolwich in 1805 and disbanded in 1869.

In 1947 the "Divisions" were renamed "Groups." These Groups consist of a Group Headquarters and several units.

At present there are only two Groups, those at Portsmouth

and Plymouth: the Group at Chatham was withdrawn in August, 1950, and its Colours laid up. (See below for the details of the laying-up.)

In addition to the Colours carried by the Royal Marines at Portsmouth and Plymouth, the 40th, 42nd and 45th Commandos, Royal Marines, each carry a stand.

The descriptions of the Colours carried are as follows:

ROYAL MARINES BARRACKS, EASTNEY

The Queen's Colour

The Union Flag, in the centre of which is a foul anchor with the Imperial Cypher interlaced: above, the Imperial Crown surmounted by a scroll inscribed "Gibraltar"; below, the globe within a laurel wreath, and below the wreath a scroll inscribed with the corps motto "Per Mare Per Terram."

The Regimental Colour

The Colour is dark blue with a small Union Flag in the canton nearest the top of the Colour pike. The badges, etc., are the same as on the Queen's Colour, except that the foul anchor is interlaced with the Royal Cypher of George IV—G.R. IV—and in the corners (except that bearing the small Union Flag) is the Imperial Cypher.

ROYAL MARINES BARRACKS, PLYMOUTH

Both the Queen's and the Regimental Colours are as for those at the Royal Marines Barracks, Eastney, except that the Royal Cypher of King George VI replaced the Imperial Cypher of King George V.

ROYAL MARINES COMMANDOS

The Colours are similar to those held by the Royal Marines Barracks, Plymouth, but as the first Colours to be presented to the Corps in this reign, they differ in bearing the Royal Cypher of Queen Elizabeth II. Moreover, the Regimental Colours bear the numerical designation of the Commandos to which they were presented. Their cords and tassels are also distinctive, the gold thread being interlaced, in the case of 40 Commando with light blue, of 42 Commando with white,

Colours of the Portsmouth Division, Royal Marines, presented by H.R.H. The Prince of Wales, at Portsmouth, 3rd December, 1931.

and 45 Commando with red. These are the distinguishing colours of the lanyards worn by the officers and men of those units.

Other Details

(*a*) All Colour pikes are topped with the Royal Crest, as in the case of Army Colours. The Royal Marines Colours have no fringe. Their size is 3 ft. 9 in. by 3 ft. and the Colour pike is 7 ft. 10½ in.

(*b*) Significance of the Globe, Foul Anchor and battle honour "Gibraltar." On 26th September, 1827, new Colours were presented to the Chatham Division by H.R.H. The Duke of Clarence, on behalf of King George IV, who concluded his address in the following terms.

> "His Majesty has selected for the Royal Marines a Device to which their achievements have entitled them and which by his permission I this day present to you—a Badge which you have so honourably earned. From the difficulty of selecting any particular place to inscribe on these Standards, Your Sovereign has been pleased to adopt the Great Globe itself as the most proper and distinctive badge. He has also directed that his own name shall be added to that peculiar badge the Anchor which is your distinctive bearing, in order that it may be known hereafter that George IV had conferred on you the honourable and well-earned badge this day presented to you. The motto, peculiarly your own, 'Per Mare Per Terram' has been allowed to remain and surmounting the entire is the word 'Gibraltar' in commemoration of the important national services you performed there."

The date of the adoption of the motto is not known, but it was worn on a badge at the battle of Bunker's Hill in 1775 during the American War of Independence.

The laurel wreath surrounding the Globe is said to have been granted for services at the capture of Belle Isle in 1761.

The Colours carried at present were presented as below:

Portsmouth In 1931 by H.R.H. the Duke of Kent. The previous stand was presented by Queen Victoria in 1894.

Plymouth On 1st August, 1951, by H.R.H. the Duke of Edinburgh. The previous stand was presented by H.R.H. the Duke of Saxe-Coburgh and Gotha in 1896.

Commandos On 29th November, 1952, by H.R.H. The Duke of Edinburgh at Malta G.C. This is only the second occasion that Colours have been presented to a Royal Marines unit outside the United Kingdom. The first occasion was when Colours were presented to the 1st Battalion R.M. by the British Envoy at a parade in Roscio Square, Lisbon, on 17th December, 1810.

The Colours of the Royal Marines were carried in action at Belle Isle 1761, America 1775-76, Spain 1810-12, America 1813-15, and Japan 1864.

As regards the carrying of Colours, their escort, compliments paid to and by Colours, the Royal Marines follow the Army practice.

LAYING-UP OF COLOURS

Chatham

The Colours of the Chatham Group were laid up in Rochester Cathedral on Sunday, 28th May, 1950, and were accepted by the Dean of Rochester into the safe-keeping of the Cathedral. This impressive ceremony was witnessed by Representatives of the Board of Admiralty, the Chaplain of the Fleet, Commander-in-Chief The Nore, Commanding Officers of local units, Representatives of The East Surrey Regiment which had many and long associations with the Chatham Group, Representatives of the United State Marine Corps and local Civic Dignitaries.

Plymouth

As mentioned above, new Colours were presented to the Plymouth Group in August, 1951. The old Colours will be laid up in the King's Chapel, Gibraltar, in accordance with a scheme by which all regiments and corps associated with the siege and capture of Gibraltar are presenting Colours or some furnishings to the King's Chapel. "Gibraltar" is the only battle honour borne on the Colours of the Royal Marines and it refers to the capture of "The Rock" in 1704-05.

ROYAL MILITARY ACADEMY SANDHURST

The first set of Colours to be presented to the Royal Military College, Sandhurst, was on 15th August, 1813, the presentation being made by Queen Charlotte, Consort of George III. Her Majesty was supported by H.R.H. The Prince Regent and the Duke of York, and they were received by the Governor, Lieutenant-General Sir Alexander Hope, K.B. These Colours bore the motto "Vires Acquirit Eundo," which was the College motto until 1946 on amalgamation with the Royal Military Academy, Woolwich, when it was altered to "Serve to Lead." A medallion was issued a few years after the presentation to commemorate the ceremony, and this bore the motto "Vires Acquirit Eundo."

The next set of Colours was presented by William IV, accompanied by Queen Adelaide, with the Duke of Wellington in attendance, on 14th September, 1835. Colours were also presented during the reign of Queen Victoria. Later presentations were made by King George V on 10th May, 1913, and H.R.H. The Duke of Connaught on 8th June, 1933.

The latest presentation was made on 14th June, 1947, by King George VI, who was accompanied by Her Majesty Queen Elizabeth, (the Queen Mother), Her Majesty The Queen (then H.R.H. Princess Elizabeth) and H.R.H. Princess Margaret. This is the first set of Colours to be presented since the amalgamation: their description is:

Queen's Colour.—The Great Union, in the centre a circle inscribed in gold "Royal Military Academy Sandhurst" ensigned with the Imperial Crown.

Regimental Colour.—Blue, the Academy being "Royal": in the centre a circle inscribed "Royal Military Academy Sandhurst," and within the circle the Royal Cypher, the whole ensigned with the Imperial Crown and enclosed in the Union Wreath: below the Wreath a scroll inscribed with the motto "Serve to Lead." Other scrolls are inscribed "Royal Military Academy 1741-1946" and "Royal Military College 1799-1946," the latter being near the Colour pike.

The Colour pikes of both Colours are surmounted with the Royal Crest, identically the same as for Infantry Colours, and both Colours have fringes and tassels.

Before the amalgamation in 1946 the College motto "Vires

Presentation of Colours to the Royal Military Academy Sandhurst, by
H.M. King George VI, 14th June, 1947.

Acquirit Eundo" was borne on the Colours, but "Serve to Lead" is now the motto of the Academy, and this is also borne in the Cadets' cap-badge.

The Colours are carried on all ceremonial parades, including Guards of Honour furnished by the Academy. They are carried by Officer Cadet Sergeants. The compliments paid by and to the Colours are the same as for Infantry Colours.

The King George Vth Banner

On 7th November, 1918, King George V presented a banner to the Royal Military College, and it was His Majesty's wish that it should be known as "King George Vth's Banner" and be carried by the Champion Company of the College. This banner is regarded as a Colour and is accorded the same compliments. It is carried on all ceremonial parades under arms, and when not carried it is hung in the dining-hall opposite the tables of the Champion Company. It is carried by a non-commissioned officer of this Company and on parade is escorted by "The Banner Escort," consisting of two Gentlemen Cadets below the rank of Sergeant. It is lowered to the reigning Sovereign only. An extra Colour belt is provided for it, see p. 41.

The following extract from the Court Circular gives the details of the presentation of this unique banner:

Extract from the Court Circular dated Buckingham Palace,
7th November, 1918

The King presented the "King George Vth's Banner" (to be carried by the Champion Company of the Royal Military College) to a Guard of Honour of Gentlemen Cadets from the Royal Military College in the Forecourt of the Palace this morning.

The Queen and Princess Mary were present and witnessed the Parade.

The Guard of Honour under the Command of Under Officer J. O. Doyle received His Majesty with a Royal Salute.*

The King, accompanied by Field-Marshal the Duke of Connaught, then inspected the Guard of Honour.

The Drums having been piled in the centre of the Forecourt,

---

* H.R.H. The Duke of Gloucester, then Prince Henry, was a Gentleman Cadet at Sandhurst and was a member of the Guard of Honour.

the Banner was placed upon the drums, and His Majesty addressed the Gentlemen Cadets as follows:

"A short time ago your Commandant, in order to encourage competition both in military exercises and sports, instituted a Champion Company at the Royal Military College. This struck me as such an excellent idea for promoting efficiency and *esprit de corps*, and I wished to be in some way associated with it, and I decided to present a Banner to be always carried by the Champion Company on parade.

"I have now much pleasure in handing my Banner to this splendid Guard of Honour, representing all the Companies of the Battalion.

"I hope it will be looked upon as an emblem of honour, and that the contests for its possession will help to foster those chivalrous and sporting instincts so characteristic of the British Race."

Under Officer the Earl of Brecknock made the following reply:

"May it please Your Majesty, as Under Officer of the present Champion Company, I have been deputed by my comrades at the Royal Military College humbly to express our gratitude for Your Majesty's gracious gift of 'King George Vth Banner.' This Banner will be in the custody of the Champion Company, Royal Military College.

"To earn the proud distinction of bearing and safeguarding this Banner will never be forgotten by us or our successors. 'King George Vth Banner' is the emblem to remind us of the undying loyalty and devotion the Gentlemen Cadets of the Royal Military College will always owe and feel to Your Majesty's Throne and Person.

"We are very justly proud of the interest Your Majesty is graciously pleased to take in the Royal Military College, of which we are all determined to do our best to prove ourselves in some degree worthy."

The Banner was then handed to the King by Colonel H. T. Paley (Assistant Commandant, Royal Military College), His Majesty returning it to the Ensign Under Officer the Earl of Brecknock, who received it from the King on bended knee. The Banner was then trooped.

The Guard of Honour then left the Forecourt, marching past His Majesty in fours.

The old Colours of the Royal Military College, presented by H.M. King George V, at Sandhurst, on 10th May, 1913.

The King was attended by the Equerries-in-Waiting, and the following were present on Parade: General Sir Henry Wilson (Chief of the Imperial General Staff) and the Military Members of the Army Council, Major-General Geoffrey Fielding (General Officer Commanding London District), Major-General L. A. M. Stopford (Commandant, Royal Military College), Major North Dalrymple Hamilton, Scots Guards (Adjutant), and the Company Commanders of the Royal Military College.

ROYAL AIR FORCE

In December, 1947, King George VI approved the award of Colours, for carrying on ceremonial occasions, to the following:

(a) The Royal Air Force in the United Kingdom.

(b) The Royal Air Force College at Cranwell, Lincolnshire.

(c) No. 1 School of Technical Training, Royal Air Force, at Halton, Buckinghamshire.

Formal approval for all of these Colours was given by His Majesty on 6th July, 1949.

On 20th June, 1950, His Majesty approved a design of "The Standard" to be borne by R.A.F. squadrons which fulfil certain conditions.

In August, 1952, Queen Elizabeth II approved the award of a Queen's Colour to the Royal Air Force Regiment.

Queen's Colours

Royal Air Force in the United Kingdom.—This Colour is of silk in R.A.F. light blue, square in shape, being 3 ft. 9 in. wide and 3 ft. 9 in. on the staff, excluding the fringe, which is of light blue and silver; it has blue and silver tassels. The Colour is carried on a staff 8 ft. 6 in. long, surmounted by a Crown. The design is in the form of the R.A.F. Ensign—that is, a small Union in the canton near the head of the staff, and in the bottom right canton the R.A.F. roundel of red, white and blue concentric circles; but, in addition, it has the Royal Cypher in the centre.

The Colour was presented on behalf of King George VI by Her Majesty The Queen, then H.R.H. The Princess Elizabeth, in Hyde Park, London, on 26th May, 1951. Her Majesty read the following address on behalf of The King:

"I am very glad to present my Colour today to the Royal Air Force in the United Kingdom. Your Service was formed during the reign of my father, King George V, and I myself have had the closest ties with the Royal Air Force since its formation in 1918. I have watched with the keenest admiration how it has grown up from those early days to prove in every way worthy of its place alongside the older Services.

"During the dark days of 1940, when my people stood alone to defend the cause of freedom, the Royal Air Force played the foremost part in turning the tide which led to ultimate victory. Your duties at all times call for high qualities of endurance and skill, to which must be added the dash and zest of youth.

"The courage and determination which have marked your achievements in war have been matched in their quiet heroism by many feats of daring and enterprise that your Service has been called upon to perform in times of peace.

"The great traditions of the Royal Air Force have been established through unflinching devotion to duty, and I am deeply conscious of the many gallant young lives which have been laid down, not only in conflict with the enemy, but in facing the many hazards which are in the very nature of your ordinary duties.

"I now hand over this King's Colour, confident that you will honour it as the emblem of your achievements and the shrine of your Service traditions. Let it be a reminder to you of the devotion and sacrifices of your predecessors and a symbol of the trust which I repose in the Royal Air Force."

The Colour was carried by Flying Officer D. Mullarkey, the Colour Escort being Flight Sergeants S. C. Orrell and J. E. W. Tonks. It was consecrated by the Rev. Canon L. Wright, K.H.C., Chaplain-in-Chief, Royal Air Force.

Royal Air Force College, Cranwell.—This Colour is of silk in Royal Air Force light blue, square in shape, being 3 ft. 9 in. wide and 3 ft. 9 in. on the staff, excluding the fringe, which is of silver. It is carried on a staff 8 ft. 6 in. long, surmounted by a Crown. As to design: it has a wreath of laurel in silver running

The King's Colour
for the Royal Air Force in the United Kingdom

Presented in Hyde Park, London, on 26th May, 1951, by Her Majesty The Queen
(then Princess Elizabeth) to a representative detachment of the Royal Air Force.

the whole length of the periphery, the College Crest within a white circle inscribed with the words "Royal Air Force College Cranwell" in gold and ensigned by the Crown, in the centre.

Normally, only badges are borne on Colours, but in this instance a crest is carried in the centre of the Cranwell Queen's Colour. The crest was granted to the R.A.F. College, as part of a Grant of Arms, by Letters Patent of 19th December, 1929. The crest is the figure of Daedalus proper shown, as usual for crests, on a wreath, and serves the dual purposes of signifying the flying man of Greek mythology and H.M.S. *Daedalus*, which was the name of the Royal Naval Air Service station at Cranwell during the Great War of 1914-18.

The Colour was presented by King George VI at the College on 6th July, 1948, and in presenting it His Majesty said:

"I am very glad to be here today to see you on parade and to present to you this new Colour, the first ever to be borne by the Royal Air Force. I want to tell you what it stands for before it is carried back to its place in the centre of your parade.

"First, it is the King's Colour, and therefore the symbol of the loyalty which you owe to your country.

"Secondly, as the Colour of your Service, it enshrines the history, embodies the traditions and represents the ideals of the Royal Air Force.

"Finally, it belongs to this College and commemorates the leaders who have gone out from Cranwell, and especially those who have laid down their lives.

"Just as this Colour has been consecrated, so, too, you yourselves in saluting it are dedicating yourselves to the service of all that it represents. Look upon it, then, as your standard of honour and uphold it by your loyal and unstinting service.

"You are now at the beginning of your careers in the Royal Air Force. Yours is a calling both arduous and daring. It will demand courage, initiative and a readiness to meet danger in a spirit of adventure. It will demand, also, what for many is more difficult to achieve—the zealous and conscientious performance of your daily tasks and duties.

"The way to the stars is not easy, and it is only by application, hard work and devotion to duty that you will reach the heights. By its daring, for its efficiency and through sacrifice, the Royal Air Force has won renown throughout the world. It has proved

Presented by H.M. King George VI at Cranwell on 6th July, 1948.

itself our shield and spearhead in war. It stands today as a guardian of peace.

"I am glad to honour the Royal Air Force and you by giving you this Colour. I commit it to your faithful keeping, in the sure confidence that you will hand it on with added honours to your successors."

The Colour was carried by Flight Cadet Sergeant H. A. Caillard, the Colour Escort being Flight Cadet Sergeant E. D. Finch and Flight Cadet Corporal D. J. Muff. It was consecrated by the Right Rev. J. A. Jagoe, C.B., C.B.E., M.A., B.D., Chaplain-in-Chief, Royal Air Force.

The Cranwell Queen's Colour is carried on all ceremonial parades and church parades, and for Guards of Honour to members of the Royal Family or reigning foreign royalty. It is carried by a Flight Cadet Sergeant of the Queen's Squadron (Senior Term) nominated by the Commandant of the College.

The Colour is lowered to Her Majesty The Queen, Queen Elizabeth The Queen Mother, and Queen Mary, to direct descendants of the Royal Family and to reigning foreign royalty.

The normal salutes are paid to the Colour by armed parties, individuals, etc.

The R.A.F. College was formed at Cranwell, Lincolnshire, in February, 1920.

No. 1 School of Technical Training, Royal Air Force, Halton.
—The Queen's Colour of this School is similar in design to that of the R.A.F. College, Cranwell, with the exception that in the centre it has the badge of the School, namely, a beech tree on a mound, within the standard frame for R.A.F. badges, a reference to the fact that a beech wood overlooks the establishment.

The Colour was presented by Her Majesty Queen Elizabeth II on 25th July, 1952, and presenting it Her Majesty said:

"Air Commodore Weston, Officers, Staff and Apprentices of No. 1 School of Technical Training:

"I am very glad to be here today to present your new Colour.

"As you know, your School was founded in the reign of King George V, my grandfather, and it owes its existence to the foresight and inspiration of Lord Trenchard, who is here with us now.

"It was clear then, as it still is, that the Royal Air Force

Queen's Colour for No. 1 School of Technical Training, Royal Air Force.

must be able to place the same reliance on the technical skill of its tradesmen as on the gallantry of its pilots and the experience and imagination of its commanders. Halton was the first school to be started for this purpose, and today, it gives you not only technical skill but a spirit which is acclaimed wherever the Royal Air Force serves in defence of our Country and our Commonwealth.

"It is right, therefore, that Halton should be the first Apprentice School to earn the award of a Colour, and I am sure that you will always remember this occasion, as I shall, as a great day for yourselves and for your Service.

"Your traditions have been well and firmly established by those who have gone before you. For they have made their mark and have justified the confidence which the Royal Air Force has always placed in them, while many of their number have given their lives in carrying out their duties. From what I have been told and, even more, from what I have seen on this parade, I am sure that you will be very worthy successors to their example of honour, service and sacrifice.

"I congratulate you on your drill and on the smartness of your turn-out, which are proof of your keenness and your quality, and I give you your Colour in the knowledge that while you are here you will guard it well. Let it also be a reminder to you of the trust that I place in the Royal Air Force. During your future service you will, I know, strive to the utmost to be worthy of that trust and to maintain the unsullied standards of which this Colour is a symbol."

The Colour Bearer was Sergeant Apprentice F. M. A. Hines, the Colour Escort being Sergeant Apprentice C. R. Grant and Sergeant Apprentice R. A. Grant, who are twin brothers. It was consecrated by the Rev. Canon L. Wright, C.B.E., Q.H.C., Chaplain-in-Chief, Royal Air Force.

The Halton Queen's Colour is carried on all ceremonial parades and church parades, and for Guards of Honour to Members of the Royal Family or reigning foreign royalty. It is carried by a Sergeant Apprentice nominated by the Commandant of the School.

The Colour is lowered to Her Majesty the Queen and other Members of the Royal Family and to reigning foreign royalty.

The normal salutes are paid to the Colour by armed parties, individuals, etc.

No. 1 School of Technical Training was founded at Halton in March, 1920.

Royal Air Force Regiment.—The Queen's Colour is in silk of Royal Air Force blue, fringed and tasselled with blue and white, in the centre the Royal Cypher (E.R. II), in the canton the Union, in the fourth quarter the badge of the Royal Air Force Regiment, *i.e.*, two rifles in saltire enfiled by an Astral Crown.

The details as to salutes to and by the Colour are the same as for other R.A.F. Colours.

M

The Queen's Colour
of the Royal Air Force Regiment

The Colour was approved to mark the tenth anniversary of the forming of the Regiment.

The Standard

The Standard consists of a rectangular silk flag in Royal Air Force light blue, measuring 2 ft. 8 in. on the staff and 4 ft. in the fly. It has a border composed of roses, thistles and shamrocks, and in the centre is the officially approved Squadron Badge, with white scrolls on each side as required, inscribed with the

ROYAL AIR FORCE SQUADRON STANDARD

Approved design for Standards for Squadrons of the Royal Air Force.

battle honours of the unit. The Standard is fringed and
tasselled in gold and blue.

The staff is 8 ft. 1 in. in length and is surmounted by an Eagle
in gold with wings elevated.

Responsible Authority for R.A.F. Colours, etc.

The responsible authority for all matters of design of R.A.F.
Colours and Standards is J. D. Heaton-Armstrong, M.V.O.,
Chester Herald and Inspector of R.A.F. Badges at the College
of Arms, who was appointed in April, 1935. He is also Inspector
of Badges for the Royal Canadian Air Force, Royal Australian
Air Force, Royal New Zealand Air Force, Royal Pakistan Air
Force, and the South African Air Force, and is also responsible
for the Colours of some of these forces.

LA MARTINIERE SCHOOL FLAG

In June, 1857, during the Indian Mutiny, Sir Henry Lawrence ordered the staff and boys of La Martiniere College at Lucknow to leave the college and enter the Residency. This was done, and from 30th June to 22nd November, 1857, when Lucknow was relieved by Sir Colin Campbell, they formed part of the defensive garrison. They were entrusted with the defence of a post which was named "The Martiniere Post": it faced one of the rebel's strongest positions only a few yards away. They kept their post intact throughout the long siege, though on 10th August, 1857, they had a providential escape, for an enemy mine, intended to blow them to atoms, exploded just wide of the position. The explosion was followed up by a determined assault, but the boys and staff held their ground and repelled the enemy with heavy loss. Most of the boys defended the post, while the younger ones acted as hospital orderlies, nurses, cooks, punka-coolies for the sick and wounded, and performed similar duties.

The oldest boy was only fifteen years of age, and the youngest

Flag presented to La Martiniere College in recognition of its distinguished service during the Indian Mutiny.

nine and a half years. Despite the awful conditions of the siege, being under constant gun and musket fire, terrible heat, stench from decaying dead rebels which gave every facility to cholera, smallpox, etc., the casualties among the boys were remarkably small: two died and two were wounded. One master was also wounded.

The Martiniere Contingent were awarded the Mutiny Medal and bar. In commemoration of this service the local Auxiliary Force, which included two platoons from the College, was granted as its badge a representation of the Residency Tower with a scroll beneath inscribed "Defence of Lucknow, 1857" and a commemorative marble slab inscribed "The Martiniere Post" placed in the defended position.

A further honour was accorded the College by being presented with a flag by His Excellency the Viceroy, to be carried on ceremonial occasions. It is emblazoned with the College badge and a representation of the Residency with "Defence of Lucknow, 1857" inscribed below. This is a unique distinction, for the College is the only school throughout the Empire to bear a battle honour.*

---

* I am indebted to the Principal of the College, W. E. Andrews, Esq., E.D., M.A. (Oxon), F.R.G.S., for the material upon which this account is based. The College was founded for European and Anglo-Indian boys by Major-General Claude Martin, of the Honourable East India Company, who died in 1800.

Dipping the Colour in Salute: 1st Bn. Welsh Guards at the Trooping the Colour Parade on the Horse Guards, 1949.

CHAPTER XV

MISCELLANEOUS

LOWERING (OR VAILING) COLOURS IN SALUTE

THE lowering, or vailing as it was formerly called, of Regimental Colours as part of a salute is a custom of ancient origin, and is regarded as saluting in a most respectful manner with the highest honours.

An early reference to this custom is made by Sir John Smithe in his "Instructions, Observations and Orders Mylitarie," published in 1591, wherein he states:

"Also if any Ensigne bearer or Ensigne bearers in their band or bandes, happen to march by an Emperour or King, or by the Lieutenant-Generall, they ought to carrie them displayed and advaunced, and when they come almost over against such a Prince or his Lieutenant-Generall, they ought to pull downe their ensignes lower and bow downe forward the point and taffeta of their ensign or ensignes, not directlie towards the prince, or Lieutenant-Generall, but directly towards the waie that they are marching; and at the same instant, they ought also to bow something forward their heads and bodies, in token of respect and reverence."

In "Five Decades of Epistles of Warre," which Francis Markham published in 1622, he lays down how Colours should be borne at a funeral thus:

"To conclude then with the Office of this Ensigne-bearer; and when any of his Company die, he shall at the buriall traile his Colours after the body to doo honour to the Funerall, but when the body is in the ground, hee shall then tosse them up and display them."

Gerat Barry, in his "Discourse of Military Discipline" (1634), deals with another aspect of this subject:

"In occation of framinge of squadrones incounteres or assaultes with the enemy, he is to carry his Coloures

167

displayed, and passinge be (by) the Captain Generall, he is to advance it bowinge the point some whate down wardes, but if he pass by the Kinge or Prince he is to bowe almoste to the grounde one of his knees, a difference from the generall, and in passinge by the Blessed Sacramente he is to kneele on both knees, and with the Coloures to the grounde showinge great reverence unto the same, and all his Company in like manner, and their armes laied on the grounde till the Blessed Sacramente pass."

Robert Ward, in his "Animadversions of Warre" (1639), wrote:

"When an army is drawne into Batalia, the Ensigne ought to stand out before the front of it some five paces, and if the Generall, or some other chiefe Officer of the Field passe by, he is gently to vaile his Coloures holding the butte end of his staffe at his girlested. . . . If a King or great Prince passeth by, the Ensigne is to vaile his Coloures close to the ground with his knee bending, in token of alegiance and submission."

This custom of lowering Colours in salute was officially recognized in the earliest form of King's Regulations, *i.e.*, the "General Regulations and Orders for His Majesty's Forces" dated 12th April, 1786, wherein it is laid down:

"This General Salute is to be considered as a Part of the Exercise, and no compliment to the Reviewing General, let his Rank be what it will; the Ensigns therefore who carry the Colours are to drop them, at the same time the Colonel and other officers drop their swords, in performing the last motion of the salute; keeping them down till the Signal is given from the Right as before, for the officers to bring back their arms to their former position."

In the Regulations of 1799 the language becomes more formal and reads thus:

"All armies salute crowned heads in the most respectful manner, Colours and Standards dropping and officers saluting. . . . A Field Marshal is to be saluted with the Colours and Standards of all the forces, except the Horse and Foot Guards, and excepting when any of the Royal Family shall be present; but in case a Field Marshal is

Colonel of any regiment, or Troop of Horse or Foot Guards, he is to be saluted by the Colours or Standards of the Regiment or Troop he commands."

All the subsequent regulations to those of 1837 have the same instructions, but in that year, owing to the recent accession of Queen Victoria, a definite instruction was added: "The Queen, and other Members of the Royal Family are to be saluted by Standards and Colours dropping; Officers saluting; and Bands playing 'God Save the Queen.'" The Queen was married to Prince Albert in 1840, and in the next Queen's Regulations, those of 1844, this is noted thus: "The Queen Dowager, His Royal Highness The Prince Consort of the Reigning Sovereign, and other Members of the Royal Family," etc.

The Queen's Regulations of 1868 are framed upon the modern model, as will be seen from paragraph 54, which reads as follows: "Her Majesty's forces are on all occasions to receive the Sovereign with the highest honours, viz., with a 'Royal Salute'; standards and colours lowered," followed by the usual instructions regarding members of the Royal Family, foreign sovereigns and field-marshals. All later editions of Queen's or King's Regulations repeat the same instructions regarding the lowering of Colours and Standards, but amplified to include various Royal personages—i.e., the Queen Mother, the Prince of Wales—as well as Viceroys, High Commissioners, Governors, etc., as representative of the Sovereign.

In the sixteenth and seventeenth centuries, when Colours were vailed, lowered or trailed they actually touched the ground even in wet weather, but now to prevent Colours from becoming soiled they are rolled loosely round the Colour pike if the ground is wet or dirty.

Draping of Colours

When Colours are carried at funerals of those entitled to this mark of respect, they are draped with crepe attached to the head of the Colour pike. After the body has been interred the crepe is removed. In former times the Colour was "trailed."

It is customary for Standards, Guidons and Colours carried at funerals to be draped with black crepe. The usual method is to tie the crepe in a large bow just below the head of the Standard or Guidon lance or Colour pike, and to allow the ends to hang down to about the bottom of the flap.

On the death of a Sovereign the draping is carried out for a specified period. When King George VI died on February 6th, 1952, the Colours, when carried on parade, were ordered to be draped until 15th February, 1952, inclusive.

COLOURS NOT NOW CARRIED ON ACTIVE SERVICE

The disaster which befell the 1st Battalion 24th Foot (now The South Wales Borderers) during the Zulu War occurred on 22nd January, 1879, and in their gallant endeavour to save the Queen's Colour from capture by the enemy Lieutenants Melvill and Coghill lost their lives. Although the heroic defence of Rorke's Drift, immediately following the disaster, did something towards mitigating its effect upon public feeling, it gave rise to the question of the necessity of taking Colours into action in modern wars. This question was voiced by Sir Alexander Gordon in the House of Commons on 12th August, 1880, when he asked Mr. Childers, Secretary of State for War, "Whether, before the next Session, he will consider the propriety of discontinuing the antiquated institution of 'Colours of a Regiment,' and thus place Regiments clothed in red on a similar footing with those clothed in green?" Mr. Childers promised to consult his military advisers.

It is possible that the War Office had the matter under consideration already, but whether or not, it was clear that it must now be brought to a head and a decision reached. In any case, General C. H. Ellice, the Adjutant-General to the Forces, drew up a Memorandum in July, 1881, in which he refers to "From the replies received"; and Mr. Childers, the Secretary of State for War, stated in the House of Commons on 29th July, 1881, that "The Commander-in-Chief sent to all General Officers and Colonels Commanding battalions in the United Kingdom a Circular inviting their opinion as to the expediency of retaining one or both Regimental Colours, and, should they be retained, as to the expediency of taking them with the regiment on active service." (See Hansard for 29th July, 1881, column 121.) These two references show that the question was being actively pursued in the War Office.

Draped Colours as carried following the death of King George VI.

Sir Alexander Gordon exhibited some persistence by a further question to Mr. Childers in the House on 3rd February, 1881, in which he asked, with reference to the Secretary of State's reply on 12th August, 1880, "Whether he had during the Recess considered the propriety of placing regiments clothed in red on the same footing as those clothed in green, with respect to Regimental Colours, by discontinuing the use of such impedimenta?"

Whatever vagueness there may have been in Sir Alexander's language, there was certainly none in a question on the same subject, and addressed to Mr. Childers on the same day, asked by Admiral Egerton: "Whether he will take steps to enquire if, under the existing circumstances of military warfare, and in view of the great risk to and loss of valuable lives attending the practice of carrying Regimental Colours into action, it may not be desirable to modify the rules of the service regarding it?" Mr. Childers replied to both questions that inquiries were being made but were not yet complete.

Admiral Egerton's question may have been inspired by the death of Lieutenant L. Baillie of the old 58th Foot (The Northamptonshire Regiment) during the action at Laings Nek on 28th January, 1881, during the Boer War. Baillie was wounded when carrying the Regimental Colour, and he himself was carried out of action by Lieutenant A. R. Hill (later Hill-Walker). They were under very heavy fire from the enemy, and Baillie was again wounded, this time mortally. Hill-Walker was awarded the Victoria Cross for his great courage and bravery on this occasion. This was the last time that Regimental Colours were carried in action.*

---

* It is on record, however, that Princess Patricia's Canadian Light Infantry carried a Regimental Colour in France during the Great War, 1914-1918. The Colour was presented to the Regiment by Princess Patricia on 23rd August, 1914, and accompanied the regiment to France on 20th December, 1914, returning with it to England on 8th February, 1919. Its usual position was at Battalion Headquarters, but it flew on the front line trenches on 8th May, 1915, being hit by shrapnel and bullets, when it gave much inspiration to the regiment, enabling it to hold out against great odds. On the march in France it was carried by an officer with proper escort, and respect and compliments were paid to it by all troops. This Colour was decorated by Princess Patricia on 21st February, 1919, with a laurel wreath bearing the inscription: "To the P.P.C.L.I. from the Colonel-in-Chief, Patricia, in recognition of their heroic services in the Great War, 1914-18." (*Journal of the Society for Army Historical Research*, Vol. XIV, Autumn, 1935, p. 185.)

Mr. Childers gave a complete reply to these questions on
29th July, 1881, a part of which has already been quoted above:
he continued: "To this Circular 83 answers have been received,
and after carefully weighing them the Duke of Cambridge has
decided upon, and I have approved, a General Order, which
will recite that 'In consequence of the altered formation of
attack and the extended range of fire, Regimental Colours shall
not in future be taken with the battalions on active service.
When, however, a battalion goes abroad in the ordinary course
of relief, they will accompany the battalion, but be left with
the depot which has to be formed on such occasions if the
regiment goes on active service. Except in this respect no
change will be made, both Colours being retained as affording
a record of the services of the regiment and furnishing to the
young soldier a history of its gallant deeds. At reviews and
occasions of ceremony, they will be usually taken with the
battalion.'" (Hansard, 29th July, 1881, column 121.)

Although a General Order is mentioned in Mr. Childers's
reply, in fact a Horse Guards letter dated 17th January, 1882,
was published instead. Both the Secretary of State's reply and
the letter followed closely the Memorandum drawn up by the
Adjutant-General in July, 1881.

BRAVE DEEDS AROUND THE COLOURS

THE BUFFS AT ALBUHERA

Gallantry of Ensigns Thomas and Walsh and Lieutenant Latham

The battle of Albuhera, fought on 16th May, 1811, during
the Peninsular War, was one of the most desperate of the
whole campaign, the casualties on both sides being considerable. Many acts of bravery were performed in the British
ranks, and in his admirable history of The Buffs Captain
C. R. B. Knight has recorded very lucidly the valiant conduct
of Ensign Edward Thomas, a boy barely sixteen, Ensign Charles
Walsh and Lieutenant Matthew Latham in endeavouring to
protect the Regimental Colours from the enemy. The following
account of this epic struggle is taken from Captain Knight's
history.

The circumstances of the death or wounding of officers of

the Regiment, in the majority of cases, are naturally unknown. Captain Gordon mentions that Colonel Stewart had his horse shot under him, but at what period of the action he does not say. There are, however, some notable instances in which details can be recorded. In the savage onslaught of the Polish and French cavalry a most determined effort was made by the enemy horsemen to capture the Colours of the Regiment. Round the Colour party collected a surging mass of cavalry-men which the escort had no chance of keeping at bay. In a few seconds the three sergeants were overwhelmed and cut down, and a lancer had seized the pike of the Regimental Colour, carried by Ensign Edward Thomas, a boy barely sixteen years old. "Only with my life," cried Thomas, when called upon to surrender his charge, whereupon he was immediately struck down, mortally wounded, and the Colour was captured. Of this brave young officer the Earl of Londonderry writes:*

> "Though young in years, and holding but an inferior rank in his profession, his name will be recorded in the list of those of whom England has just cause to be proud; and his example will doubtless be followed by others, as often as the chances of war may leave them only a choice between death and dishonour."

The same writer also reproduces a letter from Captain Stevens of The Buffs, who writing of Thomas says:†

> "He rallied my company after I was wounded and taken prisoner, crying out, 'Rally on me, men, I will be your pivot.' . . . He was buried with all the care possible by a sergeant and a private, and only two survivors of my company, which consisted of sixty-three men when taken into action."

Round Ensign Charles Walsh, who was carrying the King's Colour, there was a similar scene. The pike of the Colour had been broken by a cannon shot, and Walsh was making des-perate efforts to escape with the Colour and to gain the pro-tection of such men as were still standing near him. Lieutenant Matthew Latham, who was close at hand, seeing that Walsh was wounded and that he was about to be taken prisoner,

---

* "Narrative of the Peninsular War," Vol. II, p. 139.
† *ibid.*, p. 317.

rushed forward and seized the Colour from him. Latham, in turn, was now beset by French and Polish horsemen, from whom for a time he was able to defend himself with his sword. At last, however, a French hussar seized the remaining piece of the Colour pike, and made a cut at him, inflicting a terrible wound which took off his nose and the side of his face. Quite undaunted, Latham continued to use his sword with effect until another blow severed his left arm. Dropping his sword, he now seized the Colour with his right hand and still continued to struggle with his opponents, crying out that only with his life would he surrender the Colour; until at last he was thrown down, trampled on and pierced with lances. So many men were then around him, however, every man striving to gain the coveted trophy for himself, that each man impeded the efforts of his neighbour to kill the now desperately wounded Latham. So intent were all of them on the capture of their intended prize that they failed to notice the approach of the squadrons of the 4th Dragoons by which they were quickly scattered, and Latham was thus allowed his last few moments of conscious-ness in which to tear the Colour from the pike and to conceal it in the breast of his coat, where after the battle it was found, by whom it is not known, under his apparently lifeless body.

There are several stories of the fight for the Colours of The Buffs at Albuhera. Captain Gordon, who was on the spot, writing immediately after the battle, says: "Our Colours, which were taken and retaken three times, are now in our possession fixed on two halberts."* Soult, in his despatch, claims to have a Colour of The Buffs in his hands; it is evidently the Regimental Colour to which the marshal refers, and he was probably unaware of the fact that, thanks to the gallantry of Sergeant William Gough of the 1st Battalion 7th Royal Fusiliers, this Colour had been recovered during the successful advance of the Fusilier brigade. This is a point which has hitherto never been made clear, for Sergeant Gough is usually credited with the discovery of the King's Colour under the unconscious Latham. That this non-commissioned officer actually recaptured the lost Regimental Colour during the course of the action is proved beyond dispute by the

---

* Captain Gordon's letter.

following letter written by the officer commanding the 1st Battalion Royal Fusiliers:

"CAMP, ALBUERA,

"18*th May*, 1811.

"Sir,

"When the 1st Battalion of the Fusiliers under my command drove the enemy from the heights they were desired to obtain the possession of the guns which our artillery on the left had been obliged to abandon, together with the regimental colour of the Buffs, which fell into our hands, Sergeant Gough got possession of the colour, and I am requested by the regiment to say, if this is meant to be the subject of an official report to Field Marshal Beresford, that they do not wish to obtain, and will willingly forego any credit to be acquired at the expense of brave soldiers who discharged their duty to the utmost.

"I have, &c., &c.,

"MERVIN NOOTH, Major,

"Commanding 1st Battalion Fusiliers.*

"MAJOR PEARSON,
   "Commanding Fusilier Brigade."

After Albuhera, commanding officers were authorized to recommend one sergeant each for promotion to the rank of ensign. The Royal Fusiliers selected for this distinction Sergeant William Gough, who was appointed to the 2nd West India Regiment. From The Buffs, Sergeant William Grey was appointed ensign in the 58th (2nd Northamptonshire) Regiment; the act of gallantry which earned him his promotion is, however, not recorded.†

---

* See "Historical Records of the Royal Regiment of Fusiliers," by W. Wheater, p. 108; also speech of the Rt. Honble. Spencer Perceval in the House of Commons on 7th June, 1811 (Hansard, Vol. 20, p. 523). The letter quoted above was found, after his death, among the papers of Sir William Stewart, the commander of the 2nd Division. Major Pearson of the 23rd (Royal Welch Fusiliers) was the senior surviving officer of the Fusilier Brigade. The guns referred to were those of the battery, which had moved forward to support Colbourne's brigade.

† "Historical Records of the Royal Regiment of Fusiliers," p. 108, and MSS. History of the Regiment.

Strange to relate, Latham was still alive when he was found at the close of the action. He was taken to a convent in Albuhera, where his wounds were dressed and the stump of his arm amputated. When on the road to recovery he was sent home to England, where the Prince Regent, having heard of the manner in which he had incurred his wounds, took a personal interest in him and generously defrayed the cost of an operation to repair the terrible scars on his face. This operation was performed by the celebrated surgeon, Joseph Constantine Carpue, who was assisted by Assistant Surgeon Morrison of The Buffs.*

It was a few days after the battle of Albuhera before the true facts of Latham's gallantry became known. His wounds having made him unrecognizable, it was not unnatural that the finders of the King's Colour should have imagined that the senseless body under which it lay was that of Ensign Walsh, who had originally carried it, and to him at first was given the credit for its preservation. When Walsh, who had been taken prisoner after he was wounded, escaped from the French, he reported the circumstances of Latham's conduct. The facts, nevertheless, were not known in England for some time,† and consequently, in moving a vote of thanks for the battle of Albuhera in the House of Commons on 7th June, 1811, the Chancellor of the Exchequer, the Right Honourable Spencer Perceval, whilst paying generous tribute to the gallantry of Ensign Thomas, gave credit for the protection of the King's Colour to Ensign Walsh.‡

As a token of their admiration of Lieutenant Latham's heroic conduct, the officers of The Buffs subscribed the sum of £100 for the purchase of a gold medal on which was depicted the scene of his gallant act. Royal permission was given for Latham to wear this medal, which was duly presented to him by the officer commanding the 2nd Battalion, Major Morris, on behalf of the officers of the Regiment, at a full strength

---

* Memorandum added to Cannon's History in the W.O. Library.

† In October, 1841, a memorandum was added to Cannon's History, giving an account of the gallantry of Latham. This memorandum, however, is inaccurate in that it ascribes the finding of the King's Colour to the Royal Fusiliers. It makes no mention of the fact that Sergeant Gough recaptured the Regimental Colour.

‡ Hansard, Vol. 20, p. 523.

N

parade held at Reading on 12th August, 1813. Official recognition of his gallantry came to Latham in February, 1813, in the form of a commission as captain in the Canadian Fencible Infantry, from which corps in May, 1814, he exchanged back into The Buffs. He retired from the Army in April, 1820, receiving a pension of £100 a year and a further bonus of £70 a year on account of his wounds.*

THE 24TH FOOT (THE SOUTH WALES BORDERERS) AT ISANDHLWANA AND RORKE'S DRIFT

Britain annexed the Transvaal in 1877, but for some years previous to this the Boers had had trouble with the Zulus regarding the line of the border. These disputes continued under the new ownership, and matters were soon brought to a head by the ambitious Zulu king, Cetewayo, whose high-handed actions left no doubt as to his intentions. Towards the end of 1878 the British Government decided to send an expedition against him, appointing General Thesiger (afterwards Lord Chelmsford), then commanding in Natal, Commander-in-Chief of the field force. It was divided into five columns, that under the command of Colonel R. T. Glyn of the 24th being concerned with the events about to be related.

On 10th January, 1879, Glyn's column was at Rorke's Drift on the Buffalo river, but moved to Isandhlwana, ten miles away, on 20th January. Two days later a portion of the column, consisting of six companies of the 2nd Battalion 24th Foot, moved out in support of a reconnoitring party, leaving in the camp at Isandhlwana five companies of the 1st Battalion 24th Foot and one company 2nd Battalion 24th Foot, some Mounted Infantry and Native Contingents. Just as these troops were preparing for dinner firing was heard coming from the direction of the company occupying a position in advance, north of the camp. Half an hour later the main army of the Zulus, estimated by the late General Sir Horace Smith-Dorrien (who was present as subaltern) to be thirty times as strong as the British column, was seen advancing. When the Zulus got within 200 yards of the camp the Native Contingents fled, thus leaving a dangerous gap in an already weak line. Nevertheless, the handful of British troops stood firm, firing into the enormous

---

* Memorandum attached to Cannon's History.

mass of the enemy which was hemming it in on all sides. With certain death staring them in the face they sold their lives dearly, and only a few escaped from the disaster. It is from the evidence of these few that the immortal episode of saving the Queen's Colour of the 1st Battalion 24th Foot has been obtained.

It appears that on the fatal day, 22nd January, 1879, when Lieutenant-Colonel H. B. Pulleine, commanding 1st Battalion 24th Foot, saw that all was lost, he said to his Adjutant, Lieutenant T. Melvill, "You, as senior subaltern, will take the Colour and make your way from here." He mounted his horse and took the route to the Buffalo river, which was very bad going, all rocks and boulders, and three or four miles from the camp to Fugitives' Drift. When he passed Sir Horace Smith-Dorrien he had the Colour across the front of his saddle. Melvill was joined by Lieutenant Coghill, also mounted, who had been sent away from Isandhlwana owing to having an injured knee. By reason of the difficulty of getting along, some fleet-footed Zulus were able to approach within effective range of the two young officers and kept up a fairly steady fire on them.

On reaching the Buffalo river, Melvill and Coghill plunged their horses in and made for the far bank. Coghill reached it safely, but Melvill's horse had been shot and he himself was in difficulties. The current was very strong and had torn the Colour from his grasp, and it was carried away. On seeing this Coghill immediately plunged his horse into the torrent again and went to his comrade's assistance. Unfortunately, his horse too was shot and killed.

However, he reached Melvill, and with difficulty both officers reached the far bank exhausted. Whilst resting for a few moments they were surprised by some Zulus who had crossed the river at another point and were soon done to death.

Both officers were awarded the Victoria Cross posthumously. On 4th February, 1879, Lieutenant-Colonel W. Black (later Lieutenant-Colonel Sir Wilsone Black, K.C.B.) of the 2nd Battalion 24th Foot took out a search party from Rorke's Drift and found the bodies of Melvill and Coghill. A further search discovered the Queen's Colour wedged between boulders at the bottom of the Buffalo river. It was brought in and handed over to Colonel Glyn. The officers were buried where they had fallen, and a marble cross was later placed over their grave.

From Isandhlwana the victorious Zulus raced on to Rorke's Drift on the Natal side of the Buffalo river. The garrison here was only one company of the 2nd Battalion 24th Foot, 80 strong, together with a small complement from other corps, making a total of 139, of whom 35 were sick in hospital. Lieutenant G. Bromhead was in command of the company, and Lieutenant J. M. Chard, R.E., as senior officer present, was in command of the post.

At 4.30 p.m. between 500 and 600 Zulus attacked from the south, and although met with well-aimed fire from which they suffered severely they pressed on to within eighty yards of the defenders. The main body of the Zulus soon followed and at once made a series of assaults, gradually forcing the troops back on to their last line of defence. The hospital was set on fire by the enemy, and when they attacked it they were fought most stubbornly from room to room. As darkness came on the post was completely surrounded, and after several assaults had been gallantly repulsed the little band closed in towards the middle of the line. The light from the burning hospital came to their aid, and, making every round tell, created considerable casualties among the densely packed enemy. Desultory firing continued all night, but when dawn broke not a Zulu was to be seen, except great piles of enemy dead all round the post, estimated at 400.

When news of this epic stand reached England it did something towards alleviating the anguish created by the disaster at Isandhlwana. Both Chard and Bromhead were awarded the Victoria Cross. Surgeon Reynolds of the Army Medical Department displayed outstanding courage and devotion to duty throughout the action, and he too was awarded the V.C., and the coveted distinction was awarded to six others of the 24th Foot.

When the 1st Battalion 24th Foot came home in 1880, the Queen expressed a wish to see the rescued Queen's Colour, and it was taken to Osborne, Isle of Wight, under escort, where Her Majesty placed a wreath of immortelles on the staff. The original wreath was preserved in a glass case in the Officers' Mess of the 1st Battalion until the historic Colour was laid up in the Regimental Memorial Chapel in Brecon Cathedral in April, 1934, when it, too, was laid up at the foot of the Colour. The case bears the following inscription:

Colours of the 2nd/24th Foot, later 2nd Bn. The South Wales Borderers, with the silver wreath of Immortelles on the head of the pike on the Queen's Colour.

Colours of the 2nd Bn. Seaforth Highlanders, with the Assaye Colour in the centre.

THIS WREATH

WAS PLACED ON THE

QUEEN'S COLOUR OF THE 1st BATTALION 24th REGIMENT

BY

HER MAJESTY QUEEN VICTORIA

TO COMMEMORATE THE DEVOTED GALLANTRY OF

LIEUT. AND ADJUTANT T. MELVILL AND LIEUT. N. J. A. COGHILL

WHO GAVE THEIR LIVES TO SAVE THE COLOUR FROM
THE HANDS OF THE ENEMY ON 22ND JANUARY, 1879,
AND IN RECOGNITION OF THE NOBLE DEFENCE OF
RORKE'S DRIFT.

AS A LASTING MEMORIAL OF HER GRACIOUS ACT,

A FACSIMILE OF THE WREATH IN SILVER WAS
COMMANDED TO BE BORNE ON THE

QUEEN'S COLOUR OF BOTH BATTALIONS OF THE REGIMENT.

AUTHORITY DATED 15TH DECEMBER, 1880.

QUEEN AND COUNTRY

The "Authority dated 15th December, 1880," is a letter from the Horse Guards, signed by "C. H. Ellice, Adjutant-General," to Major-General Radcliffe, commanding at Colchester, stating as in the inscription.

The silver wreaths are affixed to the Colour poles immediately below the Royal Crest and are held in position by a firm pin, being removed for cleaning. When the Colours are cased the wreaths remain on the poles, the cases being specially made to fit over them.

The wreath of immortelles forms part of the clothing badge of The South Wales Borderers, and it also forms the centre badge on the Regimental Colour, where it encloses the Roman numeral "XXIV" (see p. 206).

The remnant of the rescued Queen's Colour was mounted on silk and proudly carried by the 1st Battalion The South Wales Borderers until 1934, when it was laid up with the Regimental Colour in the Havard Chapel of Brecon Cathedral. Both Colours had been in service since 1866.

THE ROYAL WELSH FUSILIERS IN CRIMEAN WAR

Extract from "The Invasion of the Crimea," by A. W. King-lake, Vol. II, p. 332:

"Then a small child-like youth ran forward before the throng, carrying a colour. This was young Anstruther. He carried the Queen's colour of the Royal Welsh.* Fresh from the games of English school life, he ran fast; for, heading all who strove to keep up with him, he gained the redoubt, and dug the butt end of the flagstaff into the parapet, and there for a moment he stood, holding it tight and taking breath. Then he was shot dead; but his small hands still clasping the flag-staff, drew it down along with him, and the crimson silk lay covering the boy with its folds; but only for a moment, because William Evans, a swift-footed soldier, ran forward, gathered up the flag, and raising it proudly made claim to the Great Redoubt on behalf of the 'Royal Welsh.' The colours floating high in the air, and seen by our people far and near, kindled in them a raging love for the ground where it stood. Breathless men found speech. Codrington, still in the front, uncovered his head, waved his cap, for a sign to his people, and then, riding straight at one of the embrasures, leapt his gray Arab into the breastwork. There were some eager and swift-footed soldiers who sprang the parapet nearly at the same moment; more followed. At the same instant Norcott's riflemen came

---

* "Afterwards, there being a punctilio which governs those matters in our service, William Evans delivered the colour to his superior, Corporal Soulbey, and Corporal Soulbey delivered it to Sergeant Luke O'Connor. Sergeant Luke O'Connor, though he soon got badly wounded, would not part with the honour of carrying the cherished standard, and he bore it all the rest of the day."

Luke O'Connor had a remarkable career. He was born in 1831 and enlisted into The Royal Welsh Fusiliers in 1849, being promoted to Sergeant the following year. At the Battle of the Alma on 20th September, 1854, during the Crimean War, he was seriously wounded when escorting the Colours. Lieut. Anstruther, who was carrying a Colour, fell mortally wounded but, in spite of his own wounds, O'Connor snatched the Colour from the ground and carried it himself throughout the remainder of the action, although strongly urged to go to the rear and have his wound attended to. For his gallant conduct on this occasion he received a Commission as Ensign into his own regiment. For subsequent conspicuous bravery during the war he was awarded the Victoria Cross. He became Major-General in 1887 and awarded the K.C.B. in 1913. Sir Luke was appointed Colonel of the Regiment in June, 1914, and died on 1st February, 1915.

running in from the east, and the swiftest of them bounded into the work at its right flank. The enemy's still-lingering skirmishes began to fall back, and descended—some of them slowly—into the dip where their battalions were massed. Our soldiery were up; and in a minute they flooded in over the parapet, hurrahing, jumping over, hurrahing, a joyful English crowd."

Extract from "The Invasion of the Crimea," by A. W. Kinglake, Chapter XVI, p. 427:

"Meanwhile General Codrington had been labouring to bring together the remnant of his brigade. Sergeant O'Connor of the 23rd still bore the colour which he had been carrying with loving care through the worst stress of the fight. The missing colour of the 7th Fusileers, now committed to the honour of the 23rd, was borne by Captain Pearson. Around these two standards Codrington rallied such men as he could gather, and made them open and form line two deep. The body thus formed numbered about 300 men, and Codrington was going to move it forward and place it on the left of the Grenadier Guards, in order to fill up a part of the chasm which had been wrought in the Household Brigade by the discomfiture of its centre battalion."*

29TH (WORCESTERSHIRE) REGIMENT AT ALBUHERA

In the desperate fighting at Albuhera numerous deeds of extraordinary valour were performed by members of every rank of the British Service. Nor was the honour of this distinction confined to hardened veterans, for boys of only a few months' service made a considerable contribution towards those deeds of heroism for which the Peninsular Campaign was noted. The 29th Foot provided two examples of such lads. Ensign Edward Furnace was an Irish boy only seventeen years old. He had the honourable duty of carrying one of the Colours at Albuhera, and as such he was a mark for the concentrated fire of the French. He received a severe wound and ought to have retired from the front line to have it dressed, but rather than let another assume his dangerous duty he refused to leave the field. However, he soon received another wound which proved fatal, thus cutting short a brave and honourable career. The

---

* "The Scots Fusileer Guards." See p. 423.

conduct of Ensign Richard Vance has also left an indelible mark on the history of the 29th by his conspicuous heroism at the same battle. He had only been gazetted to a commission a few months previously, but had acquired a keen sense of duty. He was a witness of the severe attacks upon his regiment and the danger it was in of losing its Colours by capture by the enemy. This he determined would not happen, and stripping the Regimental Colour from off its pole he placed it inside his tunic. He had hardly done so when he was killed. The battle continued to sway over his dead body, until eventually the French were driven off, when the Colour was found safe inside his coat.

<h2 style="text-align:center">THE 57TH (MIDDLESEX) REGIMENT AT ALBUHERA</h2>

It was at Albuhera that The Middlesex Regiment gained their immortal soubriquet of "The Die Hards." Early in the fighting most of the officers had become casualties, including Ensigns Jackson and Veitch, who were carrying the Colours. The Regimental Colour was riddled by a score of bullets, and the staff of the King's Colour had been smashed by almost as many. Colonel William Inglis at the head of the 57th had been a target for French marksmen from the outset and, although his horse was shot under him, he continued on foot quite undismayed. Fresh officers came forward and carried the Colours, upon which the dwindling regiment closed in, and at last the gallant Inglis received a severe wound as he stood in front of the Colours. He refused to be moved to have the wound dressed, but as the enemy attacks grew fiercer he lay on the ground and encouraged those around him by shouting "Die hard, 57th, die hard." The remnant responded magnificently and withstood all that the French sent against it until the enemy was driven from the field.

<h2 style="text-align:center">THE DUKE OF CORNWALL'S LIGHT INFANTRY</h2>

Soldier refuses to leave his Colours and dies on guard

Sir Edward John Poynter's famous picture entitled "Faithful unto Death" depicts a Roman soldier standing on guard during the destruction of Pompeii by an eruption of Mount Vesuvius in A.D. 79. The sentinel stands quite unmoved at his post

Colours of the 2nd Bn. The Worcestershire Regiment, presented by H.R.H. The Duke of Gloucester, K.G., G.C.V.O. at Plymouth, 1st June, 1930.

Example of a green Regimental Colour.

among the scenes of terror all round him, calmly awaiting his fate. A modern parallel to this inspiring example of a fine sense of duty will be found in Major-General Samuel Dalrymple's report on the terrible effects of an earthquake and hurricane that visited the island of Dominica in the Leeward Islands, British West Indies, on 9th September, 1806.

The opening paragraphs of the Report read as follows:—

"I discharge a painful duty in Communicating to you the baneful effects of an earthquake and hurricane which desolated this Island on the night of the 9th Inst. and by which the Garrison has suffered in Common with the Inhabitants of the Colony, several valuable lives being lost to the Service, and a very considerable proportion of The Troops suffering severely by fractions, and contusions, as will more fully appear by a reference to the report of Casualties hereunto subjoined.

"About 9 O'Clock on the Evening of the 9th a tremendous storm accompanied by torrents of rain, lightning & darkness commenced, and continued without intermission untill 3 O'Clock the following Morning. The Garrison of Morne Bruce consisting of the 46th Regt.* and Light Company of the 3rd West Indies Regt. had retired to rest, and were Consequently unprepared for any effort of self preservation. The Barracks were instantly torn to pieces over their heads, and razed to the Ground and many of the roofs and timbers precipitated with irresistable fury to the distance of nearly a mile around, and affecting to relate, the Hospital was the first building to suffer, such of the Troops as were not buried or entangled in the ruins. The sick, wounded, and dying remained, tho' mostly naked, exposed to the hostile elements during the whole of that disasterous Night, clinging to each other and to the Ground, in constant danger of being swept over the precipice which almost surrounds the post, and in momentarily expectation of perishing by showers of ponderous fragments of Wood and Stones from the contiguous ruins.

"Providentially the Officers of the 46th Regt. had a party of friends at their Mess, and the tempestousness of the Evening detained them longer than usual, they were seasonably apprised of their perilous situation, and by Clinging to each other effected a retreat to a place of more security, a ditch full of

---

* Later 2nd Bn. The Duke of Cornwall's Light Infantry.

mud and Water at a little distance, the bank of which afforded considerable protection from the ruins wherewith they were furiously assailed from all directions, and which were scattered with incredible impetuosity for a mile around. Most of the Officers' quarters were totally destroyed, not a vestige of some of them remaining."

The Report goes on to describe the terrible disaster, and sandwiched in between descriptions of the awful effect of the visitation on the various aspects of life on the island will be found in this paragraph:

"I trust I shall be excused in mentioning a trait of heroic fortitude evinced by a Soldier of this Regiment who unfortunately lost his life on this melancholy occasion by adhering to a sense of duty superior to the powerful incentive of self-preservation. This poor fellow was posted sentinel over the Colours, and altho' repeatedly apprised of his perilous situation, resolutely refused to abandon his Charge, & was buried, together with it, under the ruins of Major Payne's House. He was, however, dug out and had the satisfaction to know before he expired that the Colours were recovered. This too was one of the brave men who so effectually opposed the French in the Attack upon the Colony last year, and tho' very badly wounded on that occasion refused to leave his Company."

It is a pity that this brave man's name was not mentioned in the Report, but it is clear that his resolution not to forsake his Colours was not born of ignorance or mulish stubbornness, but of an elevated sense of duty towards the emblem of the spirit of his regiment, for, as shown by the last sentence of the above-quoted paragraph, his bravery was consistent wherever there was danger.

Heroism is not confined to any class, and regimental *esprit de corps* is sustained by the acts of all ranks without distinction.

THE 44TH FOOT (THE ESSEX REGIMENT) IN THE FIRST AFGHAN WAR

Lieutenant Thomas Alexander Souter saves the Regimental Colour

During the first Afghan War (1839-42) the 44th, later 1st Battalion The Essex Regiment, suffered severely at the hands of an overwhelming force of the enemy. On 13th January,

1842, a handful of survivors had reached Gundamuck, where they were confronted by a considerable body of enemy horse and foot. The senior officer of the little band indicated that he wished to see the Afghan commander, and was conducted to him. Whilst he was gone on this mission the Afghan soldiery endeavoured to plunder the worn-out British and snatch away the rifles out of their hands. On seeing this an officer shouted "Here is treachery," and heated words ensued, which soon led to an exchange of blows. The offending Afghans were driven away, and a general action was started which lasted about two hours. The heroic few put up a gallant fight against tremendous odds whilst their numbers dwindled away by casualties. At last all of their ammunition was exhausted and only twenty were left, standing defiantly against a howling, fanatical mob. Suddenly the Afghans rushed in with their knives, and an awful scene of massacre followed from which only a few escaped with their lives.

When things looked desperate Lieutenant Souter stripped the Regimental Colour from its pole and wrapped it round his body under his posteen (a sheepskin coat). Lieutenant Cumberland took the Queen's Colour, but not being able to button his coat over it handed it to Colour-Sergeant Patrick Carey of the Grenadier Company, who also wrapped it round his body under his posteen. Carey was killed, and it was not possible to recover the Queen's Colour before it fell into enemy hands.

Souter was severely wounded and taken prisoner, and whilst in captivity near Lughman, in the hills about Jellalabad, he wrote to his wife and gave details of how he saved the Regimental Colour. Here is his letter:

"In the conflict my posteen flew open and exposed the colour. They thought I was some great man, looking so flash. I was seized by two fellows (after my sword had dropped from my hand by a severe cut in the shoulder, and my pistols had missed fire); they hurried me from the spot to a distance, took my clothes off me except my trousers and cap, led me away to a village by command of some horsemen that were on the road, and I was made over to the head man of the village, who treated me well, and had my wound attended to. Here I remained a month, seeing occasionally a couple of men of my regiment who were detained in an adjoining village. At the end of a month I was handed over to Akbar Khan, and joined

the ladies and the other officers at Lughman. I lost everything
I possessed. My wound, which is from my right shoulder a
long way down my blade bone, is an ugly one, but it is quite
healed. The cut was made through a sheepskin posteen under
which the colour was concealed, lying over my right shoulder,
that thick Petersham coat I used to wear at Kurnaul, a flannel
and shirt. My sword fell from my hand, and the pistol I had
in my left hand missed fire. I threw it then upon the ground,
and gave myself up to be butchered. The man I tried to shoot
seized me, assisted by his son-in-law, and dragged me down
the hill; then took my clothes, the colour, and my money.
I was eventually walked off to a village two miles away. This
same man and his son-in-law, whose names are Meer Jann,
came afterwards to the village where I was, with my telescope,
to get me to show them how to use it. Afterwards the son-in-
law and I became thick; he brought me back the colour
(though divested of the tassels and most of the tinsel) one day,
to my agreeable surprise."

The rescued Colour was laid up in Alverstoke Church,
Hampshire, at a most impressive ceremony.

Defence of the Colours

An instance of the attachment shown by our troops to the
Colours occurred after the battle of Corunna, 16th January,
1809. It was night. The Regimental Colour of the Fiftieth
(General Napier's own regiment) was missing; a cry arose that
it had been lost. The soldiers were furious; Sir Henry Fane,
with a loud and angry voice, called out: "No, no! The Fiftieth
cannot have lost their colours!" They were not lost. "Two
gallant Ensigns—Stewart a Scotchman, and Moore an Irish-
man, had been slain as they bore the banners charging through
the village of El Vina: two colour-sergeants, whose names I
cannot recollect, seizing the prostrate colours, bravely continued the charge, carrying them through the battle. When the
fight was done, an officer received one of the standards from
the sergeant. It was now dark, and he allowed his alarm for
the safety of the colours to overpower his better judgment; he
forgot both their use and their honour, and had gone to the
rear, intending to embark with them, though the regiment was
still in its position. The stray colour was found, and the

soldiers were pacified; but this officer never could remove the feeling which his well-meaning but ill-judged caution had produced against him. The anecdote shows the sentiments entertained by British troops for their colours; sentiments pervading all ranks from the general to the drummer. Sir Henry Fane's words, thus loudly expressed, rendered him a favourite with the Fiftieth Regiment ever after. When colours are worn out they ought not to be thrown away. I understand that the Fiftieth, having been lately made a royal regiment, received a blue standard, and the silk of the old colours was burned with much ceremony. The wood of the spear was made into a snuff-box; and its lid encloses the ashes of that black banner, which had so often waved amidst the white curling smoke of battle. On the box are engraved the names of those who fell bearing the colours in combat." (From "The British Soldier," by Stocqueler, p. 77.)

POSITION OF COLOURS WHEN NOT CARRIED

When Colours are placed in Officers' Mess Rooms or other rooms for safe custody they should be placed on walls as follows, it being assumed that one is facing the wall: both Colours should be held erect, the Queen's Colour on the left and the Regimental Colour on the right: cross the Colours, the Queen's passing in front of (*i.e.*, nearer to the onlooker) the Regimental. The result is that the flag of the Queen's will then be on the right, as when being carried.

When Colours are placed on a pile of drums, the same result as placing them on walls is obtained by simply crossing them, the Queen's Colour being in front.

APPENDICES

REGULATION for the uniform CLOATHING of the MARCHING REGIMENTS of Foot, their COLOURS, DRUMS, BELLS OF ARMS, and CAMP COLOURS, 1747.

No Colonel to put his Arms, Crest, Device or Livery on any part of the Appointments of the Regiment under his command.

No part of the Cloathing or Ornaments of the Regiments to be altered, after the following Regulations are put into execution but by His Majesty's permission.

Colours   The KINGS or FIRST COLOUR of every Regiment or Battalion is to be the GREAT UNION.

The SECOND COLOUR to be the colour of the Faceing of the Regiment with the Union in the upper canton, except those Regiments which are faced with White or Red, whose Second Colour is to be the Red Cross of St. George on a White ground and the Union in the upper canton. In the centre of each Colour is to be painted or embroidered in gold Roman characters the number of the Rank of the Regiment within a Wreath of Roses and Thistles on the same stalk; except the Regiments which have Royal Badges or particular ancient Badges allowed them; in these the number of the Rank of the Regiment is to be towards the upper corner. The Length of the Pike and the Colour itself to be of the same size as those of the Royal Regiments of Foot Guards. The Cords and Tassels of all Colours to be crimson and Gold.

Drummers Coats   The Drummers of all the Royal Regiments are allowed to wear the Royal Livery vizt. Red, lined, faced and lapelled on the breast with Blue: The Drummers of all other Regiments are to be cloathed with the colour of the Faceing of the Regiment, lined, faced and lapelled with Red, and laced in such manner as the Colonel shall think fit for distinction sake, the Lace however being of the colour of that on the Soldiers Coats.

Grenadier Caps   The Front of the Grenadier Caps to be of the same colour with the Faceing of the Regiment with the Kings Cypher and crown over it embroidered in colours: the little Flapp to be of Red with the White Horse and motto over Nec Aspera Terrent; the back part of the Cap to be red and the Turnup to be the Colour of the Front with the number of the regiment in the middle.

The Royal Regiments and the six old Corps differ from the above rule as here specified.

Bells of Arms   THE BELLS OF ARMS to have THE KINGS CYPHER AND CROWN, and the number of the Regiment under it, painted on a ground of the same colour as the Faceings of the Regiment.

Drums   The Drums to be painted in the same manner.

Camp Colours   The Camp Colours to be of the colour of the Regiment, with the Rank of the Regiment upon them.

BADGES OR DEVICES allowed to be worn by particular corps.

1st Regiment, or Royal Scots

In the centre of their Colours The Kings Cypher within the Circle of St. Andrew and Crown over it: in the three corners of their SECOND COLOUR the Thistle and Crown. On the Grenadier Caps the same Device as in the centre of their Colours: White Horse and motto on the Flapp. The same Device on the Bells of Arms and Drums, with the Rank of the Regiment underneath.

2nd Regiment, or The Queen's Own Royal Regiment

In the centre of each Colour The Queen's Cypher on a red ground within the Garter and Crown: in the three corners of their Second Colours a Lamb, being their Ancient Badge. On the Grenadier Caps The Queen's Cypher, as in the Colours: White Horse and Motto on the Flapp. The Queen's Cypher on the Drums and Bells of Arms.

3rd Regiment, or The Buffs

In the centre of their Colours The Green Dragon, and in the three corners of their Second Colour the Rose and Crown. On the Grenadier Caps the Dragon: White Horse and Motto on the Flapp. The same Badge on their Drums and Bells of Arms.

4th Regiment, or The King's Own Royal Regiment

In the centre of their Colours, The King's Cypher with the Garter and Crown over it: in the three corners of their Second Colour the Lyon of England. On the Grenadier Caps, the King's Cypher as on the Colours; White Horse and Motto on the Flapp. The same Badge on their Drums and Bells of Arms with the rank of the Regiment underneath.

5th Regiment

In the centre of their Colours St. George killing the Dragon, being their ancient Badge; and in the three corners of their Second Colour the Rose and Crown. On their Grenadier Caps St. George as on the Colours and White Horse on the Flapp. The same Badge of St. George on their Drums and Bells of Arms.

6th Regiment

In the centre of their Colours The Antelope, being their ancient Badge; and the Rose and Crown in the three Corners of their Second Colours. On the Grenadier Caps the Antelope, as on the Colours; White Horse and Motto on the Flapp. The same Badge on their Drums and Bells of Arms.

7th Regiment, or The Royal English Fuziliers

In the centre of their Colours The Rose within the Garter and Crown over it; the White Horse in the three Corners of the Second Colours. On the Grenadier Caps the Rose, as on the Colours: White Horse and Motto on the Flapp. The same Badge of the Rose on their Drums and Bells of Arms; Rank of the Regiment underneath.

8th Regiment, or The King's Regiment

In the centre of their Colours The White Horse on a red ground within the Garter and Crown. The King's Cypher and Crown in the three

corners of their Second Colours. Motto Nec Aspera Terrent. On their
Grenadier Caps The White Horse, as on the Colours: The White Horse
and Motto on the Flapp. The same Device of the White Horse on their
Drums and Bells of Arms, with the Rank of the Regiment underneath.

18TH REGIMENT, OR THE ROYAL IRISH

In the centre of the Colours The Harp and Crown on a blue Field, and
in the three corners of their Second Colours The Lyon of Nassau, being
part of King William's arms. Motto Virtutis Namurcensis Praemium.
On their Grenadier Caps The Harp, as on the Colours: White Horse
and Motto on the Flapp. The same Badge of the Harp and Crown on
their Drums and Bells of Arms with the Rank of the Regiment underneath.

21ST REGIMENT, OR THE ROYAL NORTH BRITISH FUZILIERS

In the center of their Colours The Thistle within the Circle, and Motto
of St. Andrew; Crown over it; in the three corners of their Second
Colours The King's Cypher and Crown. On their Grenadier Caps The
Thistle, as on the Colours; White Horse and Motto on the Flapp. The
same Badge of the Thistle on their Drums and Bells of Arms; Rank of
the Regiment underneath.

23RD REGIMENT, OR THE ROYAL WELCH FUZILIERS

In the center of their Colours The Three Feathers issuing out of the
Prince's Coronet, with the motto Ich Dien, being the Badge of the Princi-
pality of Wales; in the three corners of the Second Colour, The Feathers,
Rising Sun and Red Dragon, being the ancient Badges of Edward the
Black Prince. On the Grenadier Caps The Three Feathers as on the
Colours. White Horse and Motto on the Flapp. The same Device of
the Feathers on their Drums and Bells of Arms with the Rank of the
Regiment underneath.

27TH, OR THE INNISKILLING REGIMENT

Allowed to wear in the centre of their Colours a Castle with three
Turrets, in a Blue field, and the name INNISKILLING over it. On the
Grenadier Caps the Castle, as on their Colours; White Horse and Motto
on the Flapp. The same Badge of the Castle on their Drums and Bells of
Arms with the rank of the Regiment underneath.

41ST REGIMENT, OR THE ROYAL INVALIDES

In the centre of their colours the Rose and Thistle conjoyn'd within the
Garter and Crown. In the three corners of the Second Colour The King's
Cypher and Crown. On the Grenadier Caps The Rose and Thistle, as on
the Colours; White Horse on the Flapp. The same badge of the Rose and
Thistle on the Drums and Bells of Arms.

All the Marine Regiments to wear in the center of their Colours a Ship
with the Sails furled and the rank of the Regiment underneath. Their
Caps, Bells of Arms and Drums, to be according to the general Regulations of the Marching Regiments.

The Grenadiers of the two Highland Regiments are allowed to wear
Bear Skin Fur Caps with the King's Cypher and Crown, on a red ground,
in the Flapp.

O

Appendix "B."

PRO/WO/26/21

ROYAL WARRANT 1st JULY, 1751.

Regulations for the Colours, Cloathing, &c. of the Marching Regiments of Foot and for the Uniform Cloathing of Cavalry, their Standards, Guidons, Banners, &c.

OUR WILL AND PLEASURE IS That the following Regulations for the Colours, Cloathing &c., of our Marching Regiments of Foot, and for the Uniform Cloathing of Our Cavalry, their Standards, Guidons, Banners, &c. be duly observed and put in execution (at such times as these particulars are, or shall be furnished), viz.

Regulations for the Colours, Cloathing, &c., of the Marching Regiments of Foot.

No Colonel to put his Arms, Crest, Device or Livery, on any part of the Appointments of the Regiment under his Command.

No part of the Cloathing, or Ornaments of the Regiments to be alter'd after the following Regulations are put in execution, but by Us or Our Captain Generals Permission.

Colours.

The King's, or First Colour of every Regiment, is to be the great Union throughout.

The Second Colour, to be the Colour of the Facing of the Regiment with the Union in the upper Canton, except those Regiments which are faced with Red or White, whose Second Colour is to be the Red Cross of St. George in a White Field, and the Union in the upper Canton.

In the centre of each Colour is to be painted, or embroidered in Gold Roman Characters, the Number of the Rank of the Regiment within a Wreath of Roses & Thistles, on the same stalk, except those Regiments which are allowed to wear any Royal Devices, or ancient badges, on whose Colours the Rank of the Regiment is to be painted towards the Upper Corner.

The size of the Colours and the length of the Pike to be the same as those of the Royal Regiments of Foot Guards.

The Cords and Tassels of all Colours to be Crimson and Gold mixed.

Camp Colours.

The Camp Colours to be square, and of the colour of the facing of the Regiment, with the number of the Regiment upon them.

Devices and Badges of the Royal Regiments and of the six old Corps.

1st Regiment or The Royal Regiment.

In the centre of their Colours, the King's Cypher, within the Circle of St. Andrew and Crown over it, in the three Corners of the Second Colour, the Thistle and Crown. The Distinction of the Colours of the Second Battalion, is a flaming Ray of Gold descending from the upper Corner of each Colour towards the Centre.

2nd Regiment or The Queen's Royal Regiment.   In the Centre of each Colour the Queen's Cypher on a Red Ground, within the Garter, and Crown over it. In the three Corners of the Second Colour, the Lamb being the ancient Badge of the Regiment.

3rd Regiment or The Buffs.   In the Centre of their Colours, the Dragon being their ancient Badge, and the Rose and Crown in the three Corners of their Second Colour.

4th Regiment or The King's Own Royal Regiment.   In the Centre of their Colours, the King's Cypher on a Red Ground within the Garter, and Crown over it. In the three corners of their Second Colour the Lyon of England being their ancient badge.

5th Regiment.   In the centre of their Colours, St. George Killing the Dragon being their ancient Badge and in the three corners of their Second Colour the Rose and Crown.

6th Regiment.   In the centre of their Colours, the Antelope being their Ancient Badge and in the three corners of their Second Colour, the Rose and Crown.

7th Regiment or The Royal Fuzileers.   In the centre of their Colours, the Rose within the Garter, and the Crown over it, the White Horse in the Corners of the Second Colour.

8th Regiment or The King's Regiment.   In the centre of their Colours the White Horse on a Red Ground within the Garter, and Crown over it. In the three Corners of the Second Colour, the King's Cypher and Crown.

18th Regiment or The Royal Irish.   In the centre of their Colours, the Harp in a Blue Field, and the Crown over it, and in the three corners of their Second Colour, the Lyon of Nassau, King William the Third's Arms.

21st Regiment or The Royal North British Fusrs.   In the Centre of their Colours, the Thistle within the circle of St. Andrew, and Crown over it and in the three Corners of the Second Colour, the King's Cypher and Crown.

23rd Regiment or The Royal Welch Fusrs.   In the centre of their Colours, the Device of the Prince of Wales, viz., Three Feathers issuing out of the Prince's Coronet. In the three corners of the Second Colour, the Badges of Edward the Black Prince, viz., Rising Sun, Red Dragon, and the three Feathers in the Coronet, Motto Ich Dien.

27th Regiment or The Inniskilling Regiment.   Allowed to wear in the centre of their Colours a Castle with three turrets, St. George's Colours flying in a blue field and the name Inniskilling over it.

41st Regiment or The Invalides.   In the centre of their Colours, the Rose & Thistle on a Red Ground within the Garter. In the three corners of the Second Colour, the King's Cypher and Crown.

Highland Regiment.   The Grenadiers of the Highland Regiment are allowed to wear Bear Skin-Fur Caps, with the King's Cypher and Crown over it, on a Red Ground, in the Turn-up, on Flap.

*General View of the Facings of the several Marching Regiments
of Foot.*

Rank and Title of the Regiment	Distinctions in the same Colour	Names of the present Colonels
Facings: Blue		
1st or the Royal Regt. ...		Lt.-Gen. St. Clair
4th or The King's Own Regt.		Col. Rich
7th or The Royal Fusiliers ...		Col. Mostyn
8th or The King's Regt. ...		Lt.-Gen. Wolfe
18th or the Royal Irish ...		Col. Folliot
21st or The R. North Brit. Fusiliers		Lt.-Gen. Campbell
23rd or The Royal Welch Fusiliers		Lt.-Gen. Huske
41st or The Invalides		Col. Wardour
Facings: Green		
2nd or The Queen's Royal Regt.	Sea Green	Maj.-Gen. Fowke
5th Regiment	Gosling Green	Lt.-Gen. Irvine
11th Regiment	Full Green	Col. Bocland
19th Regiment	Yellowish Green	Col. Lord George Beauclerk
24th Regiment (lined with white)	Willow Green	Col. Earl of Ancram
36th Regiment		Col. Lord Robert Manners
39th Regiment		Brig. Richbell
45th Regiment	Deep Green	Col. Warburton
49th Regiment	Full Green	Col. Trelawny
Facings: Buff		
3rd Regt. or The Buffs ...		Col. Howard
14th Regiment		Col. Herbert
22nd Regiment	Pale Buff	Brigr. O'Farrell
27th or The Inniskilling Regiment		Lt.-Gen. Blakeney
31st Regiment		Col. Holmes
40th Regiment		Col. Cornwallis
42nd Regiment		Col. Lord John Murray
48th Regiment		Col. Earl of Home
Facings: White		
17th Regiment	Greyish White	Lt.-Gen. Wynward
32nd Regiment		Col. Leighton
43rd Regiment		Col. Kennedy
47th Regiment		Col. Lascelles

Rank and Title of the Regiment	Distinctions in the same Colour	Names of the present Colonels
Facings: Red		
33rd Regt. (white lining) ...		Lt.-Gen. Johnson
Facings: Orange		
35th Regiment		Lt.-Gen. Otway
Facings: Yellow		
6th Regiment	Deep Yellow	Lt.-Gen. Guise
9th Regiment		Col. Waldgrave
10th Regiment	Bright Yellow	Col. Pole
12th Regiment		Lt.-Gen. Skelton
13th Regiment	Philemot Yellow	Lt.-Gen. Pulteney
15th Regiment		Col. Jorden
16th Regiment		Lt.-Gen. Handasyde
20th Regiment	Pale Yellow	Col. Lord Visct. Bury
25th Regiment	Deep Yellow	Col. Earl of Panmure
26th Regiment	Pale Yellow	Lt.-Gen. Anstruther
28th Regiment	Bright Yellow	Lt.-Gen. Bragg
29th Regiment		Col. Hopson
30th Regiment	Pale Yellow	Col. Earl of Loudon
34th Regiment	Bright Yellow	Col. Conway
37th Regiment		Col. Dejean
38th Regiment		Col. Duroure
44th Regiment		Col. Sir Peter Halket, Bt.
46th Regiment		Col. Murray
Facings: Red with blue coats		
R. Regt. of Artillery		Col. Belford

Abstract of the foregoing.

With Blue	8 Regiments
Green	9 ,,
Buff	8 ,,
Yellow	18 ,,
White	4 ,,
Red	1 Regiment
Orange	1 ,,
Blue with Red	1 ,,
In all	50

Regulation for the Uniform Cloathing of the Cavalry, their Standards, Guidons, Banners, Housings, and Holster-Caps, Drums, Bells of Arms, and Camp Colours.

Standards and Guidons.

The Standards and Guidons of the Dragoon Guards, and the Standards of the Regiments of Horse, to be of Damask embroidered and fringed with Gold or Silver, the Guidons of the Regts. of Dragoons to be of silk, the tassels and cords of the whole to be of crimson silk and gold mixed, the size of the guidons and standards, and the length of the lance to be the same as those of the Horse and Horse Grenadier Guards.

The King's, or First Standard, or Guidon of each Regiment, to be crimson with the Rose and Thistle conjoined, and Crown over them, in the centre His Majesty's Motto, Dieu et mon Droit, underneath, the White Horse in a Compartment, in the first and fourth corner, and the rank of the Regiment, in gold or silver characters, on a ground of the same colour as the facing of the Regiment in a compartment in the second and third corners.

The second and third Standard or Guidon of each Corps to be of the Colour of the facing of the Regiment, with the Badge of the Regiment in the centre, or the rank of the Regiment in gold or silver Roman Characters on a crimson ground, within a wreath of Roses and Thistles on the same stalk, the motto of the Regiment underneath, the White Horse on a Red Ground to be in the first and fourth compartments, and the Rose and Thistle conjoined upon a red ground in the second and third compartments.

The Distinction of the Third Standard or Guidon to be a figure on a circular ground of red underneath the Motto.

Those Corps which have any particular Badge are to carry it in the centre of their Second and Third Standard or Guidon, with the rank of the Regiment on a red ground, within a small wreath of roses and thistles in the Second and Third Corners.

Banners.

The Banners of the Kettle Drums and Trumpets to be the colour of the facing of the regiment with the badge of the regiment, or its rank, in the centre of the banner of the Kettle Drums, as on the Second Standard, the King's Cypher and Crown to be on the Banners of the Trumpets with the rank of the Regiment in Figures underneath.

Camp Colours.

The Camp Colours to be of the colour of the facing of the regiment with the rank of the regiment in the centre, those of the Horse to be square, and those of the Dragoon Guards, or Dragoons to be swallow-tailed.

General view of the Differences and Distinctions in the several Corps of Cavalry in the Clothing, Drummers' Clothing, Horse Furniture and Standards.

REGIMENTS	STANDARDS AND GUIDONS			
Ranks and Titles of the several Corps of Dragoon Guards, Horse, Dragoons and Light Dragoons	Colour of the Second and Third Standard or Guidon	Embroidery on the three standards	Fringe on the three Standards or Guidons	Badge, or Device on the Second and Third Standard or Guidon
Facings: Blue				
1st or King's Regt. of Dragoon Guards	Blue	Gold	Gold	King's Cypher within the Garter and Crown.
1st Horse (i) ...	Pale Blue	Gold and Silver	Gold and Silver	Rank of the Regt. I. H.
1st or Royal Dragoons	Blue	Gold	Gold	Crest of England within the Garter.
2nd or Royal North British Dragoons (ii)	Blue	Gold and Silver	Gold and Silver	Thistle within the circle of St. Andrew.*
3rd or The King's Own Regt. of Dragoons	Light Blue	Gold	Gold	White Horse within the Garter.†
5th or R. Irish Dragoons (iii)	Blue	Gold and Silver	Gold and Silver	Harp and Crown.
Facings: Yellow				
3rd Regt. of Horse or The Carabineers (iv)	Pale Yellow	Gold	Gold	Rank of the Regt. III. H.
6th or the Inniskilling Dragoons (v)	Full Yellow	Silver	Silver and Blue	Castle of Inniskilling.
8th Regt. of Dragoons (vi)	Yellow	Silver	Silver and Yellow	Rank of the Regt. VIII. D.
10th Regt. of Dragoons (vii)	Deep Yellow	Silver	Silver and Green	Rank of the Regt. X. D.
14th Regt. of Dragoons (viii)	Lemon Colour	Silver	Silver and Red	Rank of the Regt. XIV. D.
Facings : Buff and Black				
2nd or Queen's Regt. of Dragoon Gds.	Buff Colour	Gold	Gold	Queen's Cypher within the Garter.
4th Regt. of Horse (ix)	Black	Gold	Gold and Silver	Rank of the Regt. IV. H.
9th Regt. of Dragoons (x)	Buff Colour	Silver	Silver and Blue	Rank of the Regt. IX. D.
11th Regt. of Dragoons (xi)	Buff Colour	Silver	Silver and Green	Rank of the Regt. XI. D.

* Motto on the Second and Third Standard or Guidon: "Nemo me impune lacessit."

† Motto on the Second and Third Standard or Guidon: "Nec aspera terrent."

REGIMENTS	STANDARDS AND GUIDONS			
Ranks and Titles of the several Corps of Dragoon Guards, Horse, Dragoons and Light Dragoons	Colour of the Second and Third Standard or Guidon	Embroidery on the three standards	Fringe on the three Standards or Guidons	Badge, or Device on the Second and Third Standard or Guidon
Facings: White				
3rd Regt. of Dragoon Gds.	White	Gold and Silver	Gold and Silver	Rank of the Regt. III. D.G.
7th or The Queen's Regt. of Dragoons (xii)	White	Gold	Gold	Queen's Cypher within the Garter.
12th Regt. of Dragoons (xiii)	White	Silver	Silver and Green	Rank of the Regt. XII. D.
Facings: Green				
2nd Regt. of Horse (xiv)	Full Green	Gold	Gold	Rank of the Regt. II. H.*
4th Regt. of Dragoons (xv)	Green	Silver	Silver and Blue	Rank of the Regt. IV. D.
13th Regt. of Dragoons (xvi)	Light Green	Silver	Silver and Yellow	Rank of the Regt. XIII. D.

Given at Our Court at Kensington this 1st day of July, 1751, in the Twenty-fifth year of Our Reign.

By His Majesty's Command.

(*Sgd*) H. FOX.

Present Titles.

(i) 4th/7th Dragoon Guards (formerly 4th Dragoon Guards).
(ii) The Royal Scots Greys (2nd Dragoons).
(iii) 16th/5th Lancers (formerly 5th Lancers).
(iv) 3rd Carabiniers.
(v) 5th Royal Inniskilling Dragoon Guards (formerly The Inniskilling (6th Dragoons).)
(vi) 8th Hussars.
(vii) 10th Hussars.
(viii) 14th/20th Hussars.
(ix) 4th/7th Royal Dragoon Guards (formerly 7th Dragoon Guards).
(x) 9th Lancers.
(xi) 11th Hussars.
(xii) 7th Hussars.
(xiii) 12th Lancers.
(xiv) 5th Royal Inniskilling Dragoon Guards (formerly 5th Dragoon Guards).
(xv) 4th Hussars.
(xvi) 13th/18th Hussars (formerly 13th Hussars).

---

* Motto on the Second and Third Standard or Guidon: "Vestigia Nulla retrorsum"

Appendix "C."

BADGES ON STANDARDS AND GUIDONS
AND IN THE CASE OF INFANTRY ON REGIMENTAL COLOURS

In the case of Rifle Regiments the badges are those on the appointments

Centre Badges are shown in **bold type.**

Also, in the case of Hussars, Lancers and Rifles, Badges borne on Drum Banners, Appointments, etc.

REGIMENT OR CORPS	BADGES, WITH NOTES CONCERNING THEM
The Life Guards	The Royal Arms.
Royal Horse Guards ...	The Royal Arms.
1st King's Dragoon Guards	**The Royal Cypher within the Garter.**
The Queen's Bays ...	**The Cypher of Queen Caroline within the Garter.** Motto—"Pro Rege et Patria." The regiment was designated "The Queen's Own Royal Regiment of Horse" in 1727 in honour of Caroline of Anspach, Consort of George II.
3rd Carabiniers (Prince of Wales's Dragoon Guards)	**Two Carbines in saltire surmounted by the Plume of the Prince of Wales.** The Rising Sun in the second corner and the Red Dragon in the third corner. The two carbines refer to the main regimental title, while the other badges refer to the secondary title: they were badges of the Black Prince.
4th/7th Royal Dragoon Guards	This regiment was formed in 1922 by amalgamating the 4th Royal Irish Dragoon Guards and the 7th Dragoon Guards (Princess Royal's) and a Standard of each regiment is still carried. 4th Dragoon Guards: The Harp and Crown and the Star of the Order of St. Patrick. 7th Dragoon Guards: **The Coronet of Her Late Majesty the Empress and Queen Frederick of Germany and Prussia as Princess Royal of Great Britain and Ireland.** The regiment was granted "Princess Royal's" in 1788 on conversion from Horse to Dragoon Guards.
5th Royal Inniskilling Dragoon Guards	**The Monogram " V.D.G."** In the first and fourth corners the White Horse of Hanover on a green ground, in the second and third corners the Castle of Inniskilling with St. George's Colours, and the word "Inniskilling" on a primrose ground. Motto—"Vestigia nulla retrorsum." The regiment was formed in 1922 by amalgamating the 5th Dragoon Guards and the Inniskilling Dragoons. The latter regiment was formed in 1689 from the defenders of Enniskillen against the forces of the deposed King James II, hence the Castle of Inniskilling in the badge.
1st The Royal Dragoons	**The Crest of England within the Garter.** Motto—"Spectemur agendo." An Eagle. During the battle of Waterloo on 18th June, 1815, the regiment captured an Eagle Standard from the French 105th Infantry Regiment.

REGIMENT OR CORPS	BADGES, WITH NOTES CONCERNING THEM
The Royal Scots Greys ...	**The Thistle within the Circle and Motto of the Order of the Thistle.** Motto—"Second to none." An Eagle. During the battle of Waterloo on 18th June, 1815, the regiment captured an Eagle Standard from the French 45th Infantry Regiment.
3rd The King's Own Hussars	The White Horse of Hanover within the Garter, with the motto "Nec aspera terrent."
4th Queen's Own Hussars	Motto—"Mente et Manu."
7th Queen's Own Hussars	The letters "Q.O." interlaced within the Garter. The regiment became "The Queen's Own Dragoons" in 1727 on the accession of George II: it was previously designated "The Princess of Wales's Dragoons."
8th King's Royal Irish Hussars	The Harp and Crown. Motto—"Pristinæ virtutis memores." The regiment was raised in Ireland by William III in 1693 from among "Known Protestants."
9th Queen's Royal Hussars	The Cypher of Queen Adelaide reversed and interlaced within the Garter. The regiment was designated "Queen's Royal" in 1830 in honour of Queen Adelaide, Consort of William IV.
10th Royal Hussars (Prince of Wales's Own)	The Plume of the Prince of Wales, the Rising Sun, and the Red Dragon. The regiment was designated "The Prince of Wales's" in 1783, hence the badges of the Prince of Wales.
11th Hussars (Prince Albert's Own)	The Crest and Motto of the late Prince Consort· Sphinx superscribed "Egypt." In 1840 the Regiment was designated 11th Light Dragoons, but early in that year it escorted Prince Albert from Dover to Canterbury when he came to England for his marriage to Queen Victoria. To commemorate this event the regiment was converted to Hussars and had conferred upon it the title "11th (or Prince Albert's Own) Hussars" (*London Gazette*, 13th March, 1840), and later adopted the crest and motto of the Prince as its badge. A portion of the regiment served in the 1801 campaign in Egypt under Sir Ralph Abercromby, in recognition of which it was granted the badge of the Sphinx superscribed "Egypt."
12th Royal Lancers (Prince of Wales's)	The Plume of the Prince of Wales, the Rising Sun, and the Red Dragon. The Sphinx superscribed "Egypt." The regiment was granted the title "The Prince of Wales's" in 1774, hence the badges of the Prince of Wales. It served in the Egyptian Campaign of 1801 under Sir Ralph Abercromby, for which it was granted the badge of the Sphinx superscribed "Egypt."
13th/18th Royal Hussars	Two mottoes: 13th Hussars—"Viret in Æternum." 18th Hussars—"Pro Rege, pro Lege, pro Patria conamur."

REGIMENT OR CORPS	BADGES, WITH NOTES CONCERNING THEM
14th/20th King's Hussars	Formed in 1922 by the amalgamation of the 14th and 20th Hussars. 14th Hussars—The Royal Crest within the Garter. The regiment was granted the title "Kings" in 1830, hence the Royal Crest and Garter. 20th Hussars—
15th/19th The King's Royal Hussars	Formed in 1922 by the amalgamation of the 15th and 19th Hussars. 15th Hussars: The Crest of England within the Garter. Motto—"Merebimur." Granted the title "The King's" in 1766 in recognition of service, hence the badge. 19th Hussars. The Elephant superscribed "Assaye." Granted to the former 19th Light Dragoons for service at the battle of Assaye, India, on 23rd September, 1803.
16th/5th Lancers	Formed in 1922 by the amalgamation of the 16th and 5th Lancers. 16th Lancers.—The Cypher of Queen Charlotte within the Garter. Motto—"Aut cursu, aut cominus armis." Granted "The Queen's" in 1766 in honour of Queen Charlotte of Mecklenburg Strelitz, Consort of George III. 5th Royal Irish Lancers—The Harp and Crown with the motto "Quis Separabit." The regiment was raised in Ireland in 1689.
17th/21st Lancers ...	Formed in 1922 by the amalgamation of the 17th and 21st Lancers. Death's Head with "Or Glory." This was the cap-badge of the 17th Lancers for a great many years.
Grenadier Guards ... Coldstream Guards ... Scots Guards ... ... Irish Guards ... ... Welsh Guards	See Chapter X for the list of Badges of the Regiments of Foot Guards.
The Royal Scots	**The Royal Cypher within the Collar of the Order of the Thistle with the Badge appendant.** In each of the four corners the Thistle within the Circle and the motto of the Order ("Nemo me impune lacessit"), ensigned with the Imperial Crown. The Sphinx superscribed "Egypt": granted for service in Egypt in 1801 under Sir Ralph Abercromby, against the French.
The Queen's Royal Regiment	**The Cypher of Queen Catherine within the Garter.** The regiment was raised in 1661 to garrison Tangier on the north-west coast of Africa, which was part of the dowry of the Princess Catherine of Braganza, Portugal, on her marriage to Charles II. The Paschal Lamb with the motto "Pristinæ virtutis memor" in each of the four corners. A Naval Crown superscribed "1st June, 1794." The Sphinx superscribed "Egypt." Motto—"Vel exuviæ triumphant." The Paschal Lamb is also the cap-badge of the regiment. Its

REGIMENT OR CORPS	BADGES, WITH NOTES CONCERNING THEM
The Queen's Royal Regiment (*continued*)	origin as a badge of the regiment is obscure, but it was confirmed to the regiment by the 1747 Regulations. The Naval Crown superscribed "1st June, 1794" was granted for service in Lord Howe's fleet when he defeated the French off Brest on "The Glorious First of June." The Sphinx superscribed "Egypt" commemorates service in Egypt in 1801 against the French.
The Buffs	**The Dragon.** A supporter of the Arms of Queen Elizabeth I, who permitted the forerunners of the regiment to go to the help of the Netherlands against Spain in 1572. The united Red and White Rose ensigned with the Imperial Crown in each of the four corners. Motto—"Veteri Frondescit Honore."
The King's Own Royal Regiment	**The Royal Cypher within the Garter and the Crown over it.** The Lion of England in each of the four corners, believed to have been granted by William III.
The Royal Northumberland Fusiliers	**St. George killing the Dragon.** Origin uncertain, but confirmed to the regiment by the 1747 Regulations. The united Red and White Rose slipped and ensigned with the Royal Crest in each of the four corners. Motto—"Quo fata vocant."
The Royal Warwickshire Regiment	**The Antelope within the Garter.** According to regimental tradition, the Antelope was a badge on one of the flags captured by the regiment in Spain in 1707, and Queen Anne gave the regiment permission to bear it on its Colours. It was confirmed to the regiment by the 1747 Regulations. The united Red and White Rose slipped, ensigned with the Imperial Crown in each of the four corners.
The Royal Fusiliers ...	**The united Red and White Rose within the Garter, and Crown over it.** The White Horse of Hanover in each of the four corners.
The King's Regiment ...	**The White Horse of Hanover within the Garter.** Motto—"Nec aspera terrent." The Royal Cypher ensigned with the Imperial Crown in each of the four corners. The Sphinx superscribed "Egypt": granted for service against the French in Egypt in 1801.
The Royal Norfolk Regiment	**The figure of Britannia.** Origin obscure but regimental tradition has it that it was granted by Queen Anne for service in Spain in 1707. It was confirmed to the regiment in 1799.
The Royal Lincolnshire Regiment	**Within two Clarions the Roman numeral X: above the Clarions a Sphinx resting on a plinth inscribed "Egypt."** This regiment, the old 10th Foot, hence the numeral X, was raised by John, Earl of Bath, in 1685, one of whose badges was a clarion. The Sphinx was granted for service in Egypt against the French in 1801.

REGIMENT OR CORPS	BADGES, WITH NOTES CONCERNING THEM

The Devonshire Regiment

The Castle of Exeter with the motto "Semper Fidelis." From the arms of Exeter, county town of Devonshire.

The Suffolk Regiment ...

The Roman numeral XII within a branch of Roses and a branch of Oak. This regiment was the old 12th Foot, hence the numeral XII. It fought at Minden on 1st August, 1759, and went into battle bedecked with wild roses plucked from briars on Minden Heath as it passed through them, now represented by the branch of roses in the badge. It was raised in 1685 by the Duke of Norfolk, a supporter to whose arms is a horse with a twig of oak in its mouth, hence the branch of oak in the badge.

The Castle and Key, superscribed "Gibraltar, 1779-83" with the motto "Montis Insignia Calpe" underneath. The arms of Gibraltar, granted as a badge in recognition of service at the siege by the French and Spaniards in 1779-83.

The Somerset Light Infantry

A Bugle Horn stringed ensigned with a Mural Crown superscribed "Jellalabad": within the Bugle the Roman numeral XIII. This regiment was the old 13th Foot, hence the numeral XIII. For its distinguished conduct in defending Jellalabad during the First Afghan War (1839-42) it was granted the badge of a mural Crown superscribed "Jellalabad": All Light Infantry regiments have a bugle as their badge.

The Sphinx superscribed "Egypt": granted for service against the French in Egypt in 1801.

The West Yorkshire Regiment (The Prince of Wales's Own)

The Prince of Wales's Plume. The regiment was granted the title "The Prince of Wales's Own" in May, 1876, hence the Prince of Wales's Plume as a badge.

The White Horse of Hanover with motto "Nec aspera terrent." The Royal Tiger, superscribed "India": awarded in recognition of service in India from 1807 to 1831.

The East Yorkshire Regiment

The Roman numeral XV ensigned with the White Rose. This was the old 15th Foot, hence the numeral "XV": the White Rose of York is also appropriate.

The Bedfordshire and Hertfordshire Regiment

A Hart crossing a Ford. This was a badge of the old Herts Militia.

The Royal Leicestershire Regiment

The Royal Tiger superscribed "Hindoostan." This is a green tiger with yellow stripes, granted for service in Hindoostan (India) from 1804 to 1823.

The Green Howards (Alexandra, Princess of Wales's Own Yorkshire Regiment)

The Cypher of H.R.H. Alexandra, Princess of Wales, in gold (thereon "Alexandra"), interlaced with the Dannebrog enscribed with the date 1875, and the whole surmounted by the Coronet of the Princess. The regiment became the "Princess of Wales's Own" in 1881. H.R.H. was a Danish Princess, hence the Dannebrog in the badge. The date 1875 refers to the year in which she presented Colours to the regiment.

REGIMENT OR CORPS	BADGES, WITH NOTES CONCERNING THEM
The Lancashire Fusiliers	**The Roman numeral XX ensigned with the Red Rose.** This was the old 20th Foot, hence the numeral XX. Being a Lancashire regiment, it is appropriately ensigned with the Red Rose of the House of Lancaster. The Sphinx superscribed "Egypt": granted for service against the French in Egypt in 1801. Motto—"Omnia Audax."
The Royal Scots Fusiliers	**The Thistle within the Circle and Motto of the Order of the Thistle.** The Royal Cypher ensigned with the Imperial Crown in each of the four corners.
The Cheshire Regiment ...	**An Acorn leaved and slipped.**
The Royal Welch Fusiliers	**The Plume of the Prince of Wales.** In the first and fourth corners the Rising Sun and in the second corner the Red Dragon (badges of the Prince of Wales and therefore appropriate to the senior regiment of the Principality). In the third corner the White Horse of Hanover with the motto "Nec aspera terrent." The Sphinx superscribed "Egypt": granted for service against the French in Egypt in 1801.
The South Wales Borderers	**The Roman numeral XXIV within a wreath of Immortelles.** This is the old 24th Foot, hence the numeral XXIV. The wreath of Immortelles commemorates the saving of the Queen's Colour at Isandhlwana and the noble defence of Rorke's Drift, Natal, during the Zulu War of 1879. The Sphinx superscribed "Egypt": awarded for service in Egypt against the French in 1801.
The King's Own Scottish Borderers	**The Castle of Edinburgh.** Motto—"Nisi Dominus frustra." The regiment was raised "all in one day" at Edinburgh in March, 1689. The motto is one of those of Edinburgh. In the first and fourth corners the Royal Crest with the motto "In Veritate Religionis confido" (also of Edinburgh). In the second and third corners the White Horse of Hanover with the motto "Nec aspera terrent." The Sphinx superscribed "Egypt": awarded for service in Egypt against the French in 1801.
The Cameronians (Scottish Rifles)	The Sphinx superscribed "Egypt": awarded for service in Egypt against the French in 1801. The Dragon superscribed "China": awarded for service in the China War of 1840-42.
The Royal Inniskilling Fusiliers	**The Castle of Inniskilling with three Turrets and St. George's Colours flying.** Formed in 1689 from the defenders of Enniskillen against the forces of the deposed King James II. The White Horse of Hanover with the motto "Nec aspera terrent" in each of the four corners. The Sphinx superscribed "Egypt": granted for service in Egypt in 1801 against the French.

REGIMENT OR CORPS	BADGES, WITH NOTES CONCERNING THEM
The Gloucestershire Regiment	**A Sphinx upon a pedestal inscribed "Egypt," the whole within a laurel wreath.** Granted for service in Egypt in 1801 against the French. Owing to the regiment fighting back to back it wears a metal badge, identical in design with the above, at the back of its headdress as well as in the front or at the side.
The Worcestershire Regiment	**The Lion of the Royal Crest standing upon a pedestal inscribed "Firm."** A Naval Crown superscribed "1st June, 1794." The Naval Crown was granted for service in Lord Howe's fleet on "The Glorious First of June," when he defeated a French fleet off Brest.
The East Lancashire Regiment	**The Red Rose charged in the centre with a Sphinx resting on a plinth inscribed "Egypt."** Being a Lancashire Regiment, the Red Rose of Lancaster is appropriate. The Sphinx was granted for service against the French in Egypt in 1801. Motto—"Spectamur agendo."
The East Surrey Regiment	**On an eight-pointed star a Lion couchant guardant in front of a Castle, the centre tower charged with an escutcheon of the Arms of Kingston-upon-Thames.** The star, lion and castle are the arms of Guildford, the county town of Surrey. The Regimental Depot is at Kingston-upon-Thames and is represented by the escutcheon.
The Duke of Cornwall's Light Infantry	**The Castle and Lion as shown in the Great Seal of the Duchy of Cornwall, pendent therefrom a Bugle Horn stringed, the whole ensigned with the Coronet of H.R.H. The Duke of Cornwall.** The badge is appropriate to a Cornwall regiment. All Light Infantry regiments have a bugle in their badge.
The Duke of Wellington's Regiment	**The Duke of Wellington's Crest and motto "Virtutis Fortuna Comes."** The great Duke of Wellington served in the regiment as a Subaltern (1787) and as a Major (1793) and was Colonel of the Regiment from 1806 to 1816. He died in 1852, and the following year the title "The Duke of Wellington's" was granted to the 1st Battalion (33rd Foot) and his crest and motto granted as a badge also. An Elephant, with howdah and mahout, circumscribed "Hindoostan," ensigned with the Imperial Crown: granted for twenty years' service in Hindoostan.
The Border Regiment ...	**A Laurel Wreath.** Said to have been awarded in recognition of distinguished service at the battle of Fontenoy on 11th May, 1745. The Dragon, superscribed "China": granted for service in the China War of 1840-42.

REGIMENT OR CORPS	BADGES, WITH NOTES CONCERNING THEM
The Royal Sussex Regiment	**The White (Roussillon) Plume surmounted by the Star of the Order of the Garter.** At the battle of Quebec on 13th September, 1759, the regiment defeated the French Royal Regiment of Roussillon, and took from their hats the tall white feathers they wore and placed them in their own. Later they were granted this feather badge as a distinction and combined it with the Star of the Order of the Garter, previously worn by the Sussex Militia.
The Royal Hampshire Regiment	**A double Red Rose fimbriated gold.** This is popularly called the Hampshire Rose, being granted to the county by Henry V. The Royal Tiger, superscribed "India": granted for service in India from 1805 to 1826.
The South Staffordshire Regiment	**The Stafford Knot** (a badge of the De Stafford family, adopted by the County of Staffordshire and the town of Stafford). The Sphinx superscribed "Egypt": granted for service in Egypt against the French in 1801.
The Dorset Regiment ...	**The Castle and Royal Arms as shown in the seal of the Borough of Dorchester.** Dorchester is the County town of Dorset. The Castle and Key, superscribed "Gibraltar, 1779-83," with the motto "Montis Insignia Calpe" underneath: granted for service during the siege of Gibraltar by the combined French and Spanish forces. The Sphinx, superscribed "Egypt": granted for service in Egypt in 1801 against the French. Motto—"Primus in Indis." Believed to have been granted in recognition of the fact that it was the first King's Infantry regiment to fight in India. It served under Clive at the battle of Plassey on 23rd June, 1757.
The South Lancashire Regiment (The Prince of Wales's Volunteers)	**The Prince of Wales's Plume.** The 2nd Battalion (old 82nd Foot) was designated "Prince of Wales's Volunteers" on raising in 1793, hence the badge. The Sphinx, superscribed "Egypt": granted for service in Egypt in 1801 against the French.
The Welch Regiment ...	**The Rose and Thistle on the same stalk, within the Garter and the Crown over.** This badge was granted before Ireland joined the Union in 1800, hence the absence of the Shamrock. In the first and fourth corners the Royal Cypher ensigned with the Imperial Crown, in the second and third corners the Plume of the Prince of Wales. A Naval Crown superscribed "12th April, 1782": granted for service in Rodney's fleet when he defeated the French on 12th April, 1782. The date "St. Vincent, 1797," is also associated with the Naval Crown. On

REGIMENT OR CORPS	BADGES, WITH NOTES CONCERNING THEM
The Welch Regiment (*continued*)	14th February, 1797, a detachment served in Admiral Jervis's fleet when it defeated a Spanish fleet off Cape St. Vincent, at the south-west corner of Portugal. Motto—"Gwell angau na Chywilydd."
The Black Watch	**The Royal Cypher within the Garter.** The badge and motto of the Order of the Thistle. In each of the four corners the Royal Cypher ensigned with the Imperial Crown. The Sphinx, superscribed "Egypt": granted for service in Egypt against the French in 1801.
The Oxfordshire and Buckinghamshire Light Infantry	**A Bugle Horn stringed.** Identical in design with the metal regimental cap-badge.
The Essex Regiment ...	**An eagle.** At the battle of Salamanca on 22nd July, 1812, during the Peninsular War, the regiment captured a French Eagle Standard and was later granted the badge of an Eagle to commemorate the episode. The Castle and Key, superscribed "Gibraltar, 1779-82," with the motto "Montis Insignia Calpe" underneath: granted for service during the defence of Gibraltar against the combined French and Spanish forces. The Sphinx, superscribed "Egypt": granted for service in Egypt against the French in 1801.
The Sherwood Foresters (Nottinghamshire and Derbyshire Regiment)	**A Maltese Cross charged in the centre with a Stag lodged on water within a wreath of oak.** The stag and oak are emblematic of the forests of Nottinghamshire and Derbyshire.
The Loyal Regiment (North Lancashire)	**The Red Rose charged with the Royal Crest.** Being a Lancashire regiment, the Red Rose is appropriate. Motto—"Loyaute' m'oblige," the motto of the Earl of Lindsey who raised the Second Battalion in 1793.
The Northamptonshire Regiment	**A sprig of three Maple Leaves each charged with a Fleur-de-Lis.** From the arms of Quebec ; symbolic of the regiment's service in Canada in 1758 and 1759 under Major-General James Wolfe. The Castle and Key, superscribed "Gibraltar, 1779-83" and with the motto "Montis Insignia Calpe" underneath: granted for service during the siege of Gibraltar by the combined French and Spanish forces. The Sphinx superscribed "Egypt": granted for service against the French in Egypt in 1801.
The Royal Berkshire Regiment	**A Stag under an oak tree.** A badge of the old Berkshire Militia. The Dragon superscribed "China": granted for service in the China War of 1840-42. Naval Crown superscribed "2nd April, 1801": granted for service in Admiral Hyde-Parker's fleet when he destroyed the Danish fleet on 2nd April, 1801.

P

REGIMENT OR CORPS	BADGES, WITH NOTES CONCERNING THEM
The Queen's Own Royal West Kent Regiment	**The White Horse of Kent with the motto "Invicta."** The Sphinx superscribed "Egypt": granted for service against the French in Egypt in 1801. Motto—"Quo Fas et Gloria ducunt."
The King's Own Yorkshire Light Infantry	**Within a French Hunting Horn a Pomme, thereon the White Rose.** The French Horn is a variant of the Light Infantry bugle. Being a Yorkshire regiment, the White Rose of York is appropriate. Motto—"Cede Nullis."
The King's Shropshire Light Infantry	**Within a Bugle Horn stringed a Leopard's face.** The Leopard's face is from the Arms of Shrewsbury, county town of Shropshire. Motto—"Aucto Splendore resurgo."
The Middlesex Regiment (Duke of Cambridge's Own)	**The Plume of the Prince of Wales.** An old badge of the 2nd Battalion, formerly the 77th Foot. In each of the four corners the late Duke of Cambridge's Cypher and Coronet. The 2nd Battalion became "The Duke of Cambridge's Own" in 1876.
The King's Royal Rifle Corps	A Maltese Cross ensigned with the Imperial Crown. Motto—"Celer et Audax." The motto was granted for service in North America under Major-General James Wolfe in 1759.
The Wiltshire Regiment (Duke of Edinburgh's)	**A Cross Pattée charged in the centre with a Roundle, thereon the Cypher and Coronet of the late Duke of Edinburgh.** The 2nd Battalion, formerly the 99th (Lanarkshire) Regiment, became "The Duke of Edinburgh's" in 1874.
The Manchester Regiment	**A Fleur-de-Lis.** An old badge of the regiment. The Sphinx superscribed "Egypt": granted for service in Egypt against the French in 1801.
The North Staffordshire Regiment (The Prince of Wales's)	**The Prince of Wales's Plume.** The 2nd Battalion, the old 98th Foot, was granted the title of "The Prince of Wales's" in October, 1876. The Dragon superscribed "China": granted for service in the China War of 1840-42.
The York and Lancaster Regiment	**The Union Rose** (the White Rose of York combined with the Red Rose of Lancaster). The Royal Tiger, superscribed "India": granted for service in India during the early part of the nineteenth century.

REGIMENT OR CORPS	BADGES, WITH NOTES CONCERNING THEM

The Durham Light Infantry — **Within a Bugle Horn stringed the letters D.L.I.** A bugle is the badge of all Light Infantry Regiments.

The Highland Light Infantry — **Within a French Hunting Horn the monogram H.L.I.** The French Hunting Horn is a variant of the bugle. The Castle and Key, superscribed "Gibraltar, 1780-83" and with the motto "Montis Insignia Calpe" underneath: granted for service during the defence of Gibraltar against the combined French and Spanish forces. The Elephant superscribed "Assaye": granted for service at the Battle of Assaye, India, on 23rd September, 1803.

The Seaforth Highlanders (Rosshire Buffs, The Duke of Albany's) — **A Stag's Head caboshed, between the attires the Cypher and Coronet of the late Duke of Albany, with the motto "Cuidich'n Righ."** The Stag's Head and motto are from the Arms of the Earl of Seaforth who raised the regiment in 1793. The 1st Battalion, the old 72nd, was granted the title "The Duke of Albany's Own" in 1823 (*London Gazette*, 27th December, 1823), and it refers to H.R.H. Frederick, Duke of York and Albany, Commander-in-Chief from 1795 to 1809. In each of the four corners the late Duke of York's Cypher and Coronet. The Elephant, superscribed "Assaye": granted for service at the battle of Assaye, India, on 23rd September, 1803.

The Gordon Highlanders — **The Crest of the Marquess of Huntly within a wreath of Ivy, with the motto "Bydand."** The Marquess of Huntly became the Duke of Gordon: he raised the 2nd Battalion of the Regiment (the old 92nd Foot) in 1794. The Royal Tiger, superscribed "India": granted for service in India from 1787 to 1806.

The Sphinx, superscribed "Egypt": granted for service against the French in Egypt in 1801.

The Queen's Own Cameron Highlanders — **The Thistle ensigned with the Imperial Crown.** The Sphinx, superscribed "Egypt": granted for service in Egypt against the French in 1801. The Cypher of Queen Victoria within the Garter: granted "Queen's Own" by Queen Victoria in 1873.

The Royal Ulster Rifles ... — The Harp and Crown with the motto "Quis Separabit." The Sphinx superscribed "Egypt": granted for service in Egypt in 1801 against the French.

REGIMENT OR CORPS	BADGES, WITH NOTES CONCERNING THEM
The Royal Irish Fusiliers (Princess Victoria's)	**The Plume of the Prince of Wales.** The regiment was designated "The Prince of Wales's" in 1794, but this was displaced by "Royal" in 1827. In the first and fourth corners Princess Victoria's Coronet. The 2nd Battalion, the old 89th, was designated "Princess Victoria's" in 1866, the title referring to Queen Victoria before her accession to the throne. In the second corner an Eagle with a wreath of laurel: granted Eagle badge in commemoration of capturing a French Eagle Standard at Barrosa during the Peninsular War. In the third corner the Harp and Crown. The Sphinx, superscribed "Egypt": granted for service against the French in Egypt in 1801. Motto—"Faugh-a-Ballagh."
The Argyll and Sutherland Highlanders (Princess Louise's)	**The Princess Louise's Cypher and Coronet.** The 1st Battalion, the old 91st, became "Princess Louise's" in 1872 and Her Royal Highness was Colonel-in-Chief of the regiment from 1914 until her death in 1939. A Boar's Head with the motto "Ne obliviscaris," within a wreath of Myrtle, and a Cat with the motto "Sans Peur" within a wreath of Broom, over all the label as represented in the Arms of the Princess Louise and surmounted with Her Royal Highness's Coronet. The boar's head and motto are from the arms of the Argyll family and the cat and motto are from the arms of the Sutherland family.
The Parachute Regiment	*Regular Battalions.*—**A Parachute between a pair of wings outspread ensigned with the Royal Crest.** On a scroll over the tie of the Union Wreath the Regimental motto: "Utrinque Paratus." *Territorial Army Battalions.*—On the circle is inscribed "Parachute Regiment" and in the dexter canton the Battalion number in Roman numerals. On a scroll over the tie of the Union Wreath the Regimental motto. In addition, in some T.A. battalions, the subsidiary title of the battalion—*e.g.,* "County of London Battalion," "Scottish Battalion," or "Welsh Battalion"—is inscribed on a scroll over the tie of Wreath. In such cases the Regimental Motto is placed below the base of the Wreath.
The Brigade of Gurkhas	**2nd King Edward VII's Own Gurkha Rifles (The Sirmoor Rifles).** The Plume of the Prince of Wales, the Royal and Imperial Cypher of King Edward VII. **6th Gurkha Rifles.** Two Kukries, points upwards, the blades crossed in saltire, their cutting edges outwards; between the handles the numeral 6.

REGIMENT OR CORPS	BADGES, WITH NOTES CONCERNING THEM
The Brigade of Gurkhas (*continued*)	**7th Gurkha Rifles.** Two Kukries, points upwards, the handles crossed in saltire, the cutting edges of the blades inwards; between the blades the numeral 7. **10th Princess Mary's Own Gurkha Rifles.** A Bugle Horn stringed interlaced with a kukri fesswise, the blade to the sinister; within the strings of the bugle horn the numeral 10.
The Rifle Brigade ...	Within a laurel wreath ensigned with a crown, a Maltese Cross, the points terminating in balls, having on each of the four angles a Lion passant guardant, and in the centre a Bugle Horn stringed, ensigned with a crown, within a circle bearing the title of the regiment. A Naval Crown, superscribed "2nd April, 1801": granted for service in Admiral Hyde-Parker's fleet when it destroyed the Danish fleet on 2nd April, 1801.

Appendix "D"

ROYAL WARRANT, 19TH DECEMBER, 1768.

GEORGE R.

OUR WILL and PLEASURE is, that the following Regulations for the Standards, Guidons, Clothing, &c., of OUR Regiments of DRAGOON GUARDS, HORSE, DRAGOONS and LIGHT DRAGOONS, be duly observed and put in Execution, at such Times as the Particulars are or shall be furnished.

No Colonel is to put his Arms, Crest, Device, or Livery, on any part of the Appointments of the Regiment under his Command.

Standards and Guidons

The Standards and Guidons of the Dragoon Guards, and the Standards of the Regiments of Horse, to be of Silk Damask embroidered and fringed with Gold or Silver. The Guidons of the Regiments of Dragoons, and of the Light Dragoons, to be of Silk. The Tassels and Cords of the whole to be of Crimson Silk and Gold mixed. The Lance of the Standards and Guidons (except those of the Light Dragoons) to be nine feet long (Spear and Ferril included). The Flag of the Standard to be two feet five inches wide without the Fringe, and two feet three inches on the Lance. That of the Guidons to be three feet five inches, to the end of the slit of the Swallow-tail, and two feet three inches on the Lance. Those of the Light Dragoons to be of a smaller size.

The King's, or First Standard, or Guidon, of each Regiment, to be Crimson, with the Rose and Thistle conjoined, and Crown over them in the Centre. His Majesty's Motto, Dieu et mon Droit, underneath. The White Horse, in a Compartment, in the First and Fourth Corner; and the Rank of the Regiment, in Gold or Silver Characters, on a Ground of the same Colour as the Facing of the Regiment, in a Compartment, in the Second and Third Corners.

The Second and Third Standard, or Guidon, of each Corps, to be of the Colour of the Facing of the Regiment, with the Badge of the Regiment in the Centre, or the Rank of the Regiment, in Gold or Silver Roman Characters, on a Crimson Ground, within a Wreath of Roses and Thistles on the same stalk. The Motto of the Regiment underneath. The White Horse, on a Red Ground, to be in the First and Fourth Compartment, and the Rose and Thistle conjoined upon a Red Ground, in the Second and Third Compartments. The Distinction of the Third Standard, or Guidon, to be a Figure 3 on a Circular Ground of Red, underneath the Motto.

Those Corps which have any particular badge, are to carry it in the Centre of their Second and Third Standard, or Guidon, with the Rank of the Regiment on a Red Ground, within a small Wreath of Roses and Thistles, in the Second and Third Corners; except those of the Prince of Wales's Dragoon Guards, and Light Dragoons. The Rank of those two Regiments to be under the Plume of Feathers.

General view of the Differences and Distinctions in the several Corps of Cavalry, in the Clothing, Drummers' Clothing, Horse Furniture, and Standards.

REGIMENTS	STANDARDS AND GUIDONS			
Ranks and Titles of the several Corps of Dragoon Guards, Horse, Dragoons and Light Dragoons	Colour of the Second and Third Standard or Guidon	Embroidery on the three standards	Fringe on the three Standards or Guidons	Badge, or Device on the Second and Third Standard or Guidon
Facings: Blue				
1st or King's Regt. of Dragoon Guards	Blue	Gold	Gold	King's Cypher within the Garter.
1st Horse	Blue	Gold and Silver	Gold and Silver	Rank of the Regt. I.H.
1st or Royal Dragoons	Blue	Gold	Gold	Crest of England within the Garter.
2nd or Royal North British Dragoons	Blue	Gold and Silver	Gold and Silver	Thistle within the circle of St. Andrew.*
3rd or the King's Own Regt. of Dragoons	Blue	Gold	Gold	White Horse within the Garter.†
5th or Royal Irish Dragoons	Blue	Gold and Silver	Gold and Silver	Harp and Crown.
15th or King's Light Dragoons	Blue	Gold painted	Gold	King's Crest within the Garter.‡
16th or Queen's Light Dragoons	Blue	Gold and Silver painted	Gold	Queen's Cypher within the Garter.§
Facings: Yellow				
6th or the Inniskilling Dragoons	Full Yellow	Silver	Silver and Blue	Castle of Inniskilling.
8th Regt. of Dragoons	Yellow	Silver	Silver and Yellow	Rank of the Regt. VIII. D.
10th Regt. of Dragoons	Deep Yellow	Silver	Silver and Green	Rank of the Regt. X. D.
14th Regt. of Dragoons	Lemon Colour	Silver	Silver and Red	Rank of the Regt. XIV. D.
Facings: Buff				
2nd or Queen's Regt. of Dragoon Guards	Buff Colour	Gold	Gold	Queen's Cypher within the Garter.
9th Regt. of Dragoons	Buff Colour	Silver	Silver and Blue	Rank of the Regt. IX. D.
11th Regt. of Dragoons	Buff Colour	Silver	Silver and Green	Rank of the Regt. XI. D.

* Motto on the Second and Third Standard or Guidon: "Nemo me impune lacessit."

† Motto on the Second and Third Standard or Guidon: "Nec aspera terrent."

‡ Motto on the Second and Third Standard or Guidon: "Emsdorff."

§ Motto on the Second and Third Standard or Guidon: "Aut Cursu, Aut cominus Armis."

REGIMENTS	STANDARDS AND GUIDONS			
Ranks and Titles of the several Corps of Dragoon Guards, Horse, Dragoons and Light Dragoons	Colour of the Second and Third Standard or Guidon	Embroidery on the three standards	Fringe on the three Standards or Guidons	Badge, or Device on the Second and Third Standard or Guidon
Facings: White 3rd or Prince of Wales's Regt. of Dragoon Guards	White	Gold and Silver	Gold and Silver	The Feathers issuing out of the Coronet; also the Rising Sun and Red Dragon.*
3rd Regt. of Horse or the Carabineers	White	Gold	Gold	Rank of the Regt. III. H.
7th or the Queen's Regt. of Dragoons	White	Gold	Gold	Queen's Cypher within the Garter.
17th Regt. of Light Dragoons	White	Gold and Silver painted	Silver and Red	Death's Head.†
18th Regt. of Light Dragoons	White	Gold and Silver painted	Silver	Rank of the Regt. XVIII. L.D.
Facings: Green 2nd Regt. of Horse	Full Green	Gold	Gold	Rank of the Regt. II. H.‡
4th Regt. of Dragoons	Full Green	Silver	Silver and Blue	Rank of the Regt. IV. D.
13th Regt. of Dragoons	Deep Green	Silver	Silver and Yellow	Rank of the Regt. XIII. D.
Facings: Black 4th Regt. of Horse	Black	Gold	Gold and Silver	Rank of the Regt. IV. H.
12th Regt. or Prince of Wales's Light Dragoons	Black	Silver painted	Silver	The Feathers issuing out of the Coronet; also the Rising Sun and Red Dragon.§

* Motto on the Second and Third Standard or Guidon: "Ich Dien."

† Motto on the Second and Third Standard or Guidon: "Or Glory."

‡ Motto on the Second and Third Standard or Guidon: "Vestigia nulla retrorsum."

§ Motto on the Second and Third Standard or Guidon: "Ich Dien."

Given at Our Court at St. James's, this 19th day of December, 1768, in the Ninth Year of Our Reign.

By His Majesty's Command.

BARRINGTON.

GEORGE R.

OUR WILL and PLEASURE is, that the following Regulations for the Colours, Clothing, &c. of OUR MARCHING REGI-MENTS OF FOOT, be duly observed and put in Execution, at such times as the particulars are or shall be furnished.

No Colonel is to put his Arms, Crest, Device, or Livery, on any part of the Appointments of the Regiment under his Command.

Colours.

The King's, or First Colour, of every Regiment, is to be the Great Union throughout.

The Second Colour to be the Colour of the Facing of the Regiment, with the Union in the upper Canton; except those Regiments which are faced with Red, White, or Black. The Second Colour of those Regiments which are faced with Red or White, is to be the Red Cross of St. George in a White Field, and the Union in the upper Canton. The Second Colour of those which are faced with Black is to be St. George's Cross throughout; Union in the upper Canton; the three other Cantons, Black.

In the Centre of each Colour is to be painted, or embroidered, in Gold Roman Characters, the *Number of the Rank of the Regiment* within the Wreath of Roses and Thistles on the same stalk; except those Regiments which are allowed to wear any Royal Devices, or ancient Badges; on whose Colours the Rank of the Regiment is to be painted or embroidered, towards the upper corner. The size of the Colours to be six feet six inches flying, and six feet deep on the pike. The length of the pike (Spear and Ferril included) to be nine feet ten inches. The Cords and Tassels of the whole to be crimson and gold mixed.

DEVICES AND BADGES

OF THE

ROYAL REGIMENTS, AND OF THE SIX OLD CORPS.

NOTE: The Devices and Badges are the same as in the 1751 Warrant with the following addition.

LXTH OR ROYAL AMERICANS.—In the centre of their colours the King's Cypher within the Garter and Crown over it. In the three corners of the Second Colour, the King's Cypher and Crown. The Colours of the Second Battalion to be distinguished by a Flaming Ray of Gold descending from the upper corner of each Colour, towards the centre.

GENERAL VIEW of the FACINGS, &c. of the several
MARCHING REGIMENTS of FOOT.

Rank and Title of the Regiments	Distinctions in the same Colour
Facings: Blue	
1st, or the Royal Regt.	
2nd, or the Queen's Royal Regiment	
4th, or the King's Own Regiment	
7th, or Royal Fuziliers	
8th, or King's Regiment	
18th, or Royal Irish	
21st, or Royal North Brit. Fuziliers	
23rd, or Royal Welch Fuziliers	
41st, or Invalids	
42nd, or Royal Highlanders	
60th, or Royal Americans	
Facings: Yellow	
6th Regiment	Deep Yellow
9th Regiment	
10th Regiment	Bright Yellow
12th Regiment	
13th Regiment	Philemot Yellow
15th Regiment	
16th Regiment	
20th Regiment	Pale Yellow
25th Regiment	Deep Yellow
26th Regiment	Pale Yellow
28th Regiment	Bright Yellow
29th Regiment	
30th Regiment	Pale Yellow
34th Regiment	Bright Yellow
37th Regiment	
38th Regiment	
44th Regiment	
46th Regiment	
57th Regiment	
67th Regiment	Pale Yellow
Facings: Green	
5th Regiment	Goslin Green
11th Regiment	Full Green
19th Regiment	Deep Green
24th Regiment	Willow Green
36th Regiment	
39th Regiment	
45th Regiment	Deep Green
49th Regiment	Full Green
51st Regiment	Deep Green
54th Regiment	Popinjay Green
55th Regiment	Dark Green
63rd Regiment	Very Deep Green
66th Regiment	Yellowish Green
68th Regiment	Deep Green
69th Regiment	Willow Green

Rank and Title of the Regiments	Distinctions in the same Colour
Facings: Buff	
3rd Regiment, or The Buffs	
14th Regiment	
22nd Regiment	Pale Buff
27th, or The Inniskilling Regiment	
31st Regiment	
40th Regiment	
48th Regiment	
52nd Regiment	
61st Regiment	
62nd Regiment	Yellowish Buff
Facings: White	
17th Regiment	Greyish White
32nd Regiment	
43rd Regiment	
47th Regiment	
65th Regiment	
Facings: Red	
33rd Regiment	
53rd Regiment	
56th Regiment	Purple
59th Regiment	Purple
Facings: Black	
50th Regiment	
58th Regiment	
64th Regiment	
70th Regiment	
Facings: Orange	
35th Regiment	

Given at Our Court at ST. JAMES'S, this 19th Day of December, 1768, in the Ninth Year of Our Reign.

By His Majesty's Command.

BARRINGTON.

Appendix "F."

EXTRACTS FROM REGULATIONS AND ORDERS FOR THE ARMY, 1844.

STANDARDS AND GUIDONS OF REGIMENTS OF DRAGOON GUARDS AND DRAGOONS.

1. The Standards of the Regiments of Cavalry are to be of silk Damask embroidered and fringed with Gold.

2. The Guidons of Regiments of Dragoons are to be of Silk.

3. The Tassels and Cords of the whole to be of Crimson Silk and Gold mixed.

4. The Lance of the Standards and Guidons to be nine feet long (spear and ferrel included).

5. The Flag of the Standard to be two feet five inches wide, without the Fringe, and two feet three inches on the Lance: *the corners to be square.*

6. The Flag of the Guidon of Dragoons to be three feet five inches to the end of the slit of the swallow-tail, and two feet three inches on the Lance. The upper and lower corners to be rounded off at twelve inches distance from the end of the flag.

7. The *Royal,* or First, Standard, or Guidon, of each Regiment is to be Crimson, with the Rose, Thistle, and Shamrock conjoined, ensigned with the Imperial Crown; Her Majesty's motto, Dieu et mon Droit, underneath :—the White Horse, on a green mount on a crimson ground, in a compartment within a scroll, in the first and fourth corners; and the Rank of the Regiment, in Gold Roman Characters, on a ground of the same colour as the Facing of the Regiment, in a compartment within a scroll, in the second and third corners.

8. The *Regimental,* or Second, Standard, or Guidon is to be of the Colour of the Facing of the Regiment, with the Rank of the Regiment in Gold Roman Characters on a crimson ground, in the centre, within a wreath of Roses, Thistles, and Shamrocks on the same stalk, ensigned with the Imperial Crown :—the White Horse, on a green mount on a crimson ground, to be in the first and fourth compartments, with a scroll; and the Rose, Thistle, and Shamrock conjoined, upon a crimson ground, within a scroll, in the second and third corners.

9. Those Regiments which have any particular Badge are to carry it in the Centre of their Second Standards or Guidons, within a wreath of Roses, Thistles, and Shamrocks, on the same stalk; ensigned with the Imperial Crown:—The White Horse, on a green mount on a crimson ground, within a scroll, in the first and fourth corners; and the Rank of the Regiment, on a crimson ground, within a wreath of Roses, Thistles, and Shamrocks, in the second and third corners.

10. The Regimental, or Second, Standard, or Guidon, is also to bear the Devices, Distinctions, and Mottos which have been conferred by Royal Authority: the Motto to be under the Wreath in the centre.

11. The Third and Fourth Standards, or Guidons, are to be of the same description as the Second, and to be distinguished by the figures 3 and 4, on a circular ground of crimson, under the motto.

12. No addition or alteration is to be made in the Standards, or Guidons, of any Regiment of Cavalry, without the Sovereign's special permission and authority.

13. The Standards and Guidons of Cavalry are to be carried by Troop Serjeant-Majors.

14. N.B.—In the making up of New Standards or Colours, application is to be made, through the Adjutant-General, to the Inspector of Regimental Colours for a Drawing of the Pattern as approved by Royal Authority.

COLOURS OF REGIMENTS OF INFANTRY.

1. The *Royal*, or First Colour of every Regiment is to be the Great Union throughout,—being the Imperial Colour of the United Kingdom of Great Britain and Ireland in which the Cross of St. George is conjoined with the Crosses of St. Andrew and St. Patrick, on a blue field— and is to bear in the centre the Imperial Crown, and the Number of the Regiment underneath in Gold Roman Characters.

2. The *Regimental*, or Second, Colour is to be of the colour of the Facing of the Regiment, with the Union in the Upper Canton, except those Regiments which are faced with Red, White, or Black; in those Regiments which are faced with Red or White, the Second Colour is to be the Red Cross of St. George in a White Field, and the Union in the upper Canton. In those Regiments, which are faced with Black, the Second Colour is to be St. George's Cross ; the Union in the Upper Canton; the Three other Cantons Black. The Number of the Regiment is to be embroidered in Gold Roman Characters in the Centre.

3. Those Regiments which bear a Royal, County, or other Title, are to have such designation on a Red Ground round a Circle within the Union-wreath of Roses, Thistles, and Shamrocks. The Number of the Regiment in Gold Roman Characters in the Centre.

4. In those Regiments which bear any ancient badge, the badge is to be on a Red Ground in the Centre, and the number of the Regiment in Gold Roman Characters underneath. The Royal, or other Title, to be inscribed on a Circle within the Union-wreath of Roses, Thistles, and Shamrocks.

5. The Regimental, or Second, Colour is also to bear the Devices, Distinctions, and Mottos, which have been conferred by Royal Authority ; the whole to be ensigned with the Imperial Crown.

6. The Colours are to be of silk; the dimensions to be six feet six inches flying, and six feet deep on the Pike; the length of the Pike (spear and ferrel included) to be nine feet ten inches ; the Cords and Tassels of the whole to be Crimson and Gold mixed.

7. No addition, or alteration, is to be made in the Colours of any Regiment of Infantry, without Her Majesty's special permission and authority, signified through the Commander-in-Chief of the Army.

Appendix "F."

DECKING COLOURS IN THE FOOT GUARDS

Whenever the Queen's or Regimental Colours are carried on duty on the days noted in the following regimental lists, they are decked on the Colour pike by a wreath of laurel.

Day and Month	Battle or Operation Commemorated	Notes
	GRENADIER GUARDS	
16th January	Corunna, 1809	Peninsular War
5th March	Barrosa, 1811	Peninsular War
24th March	Somme, 1916	Great War, 1914-18
	Somme, 1918	Great War, 1914-18
	Bapaume, 1918	Great War, 1914-18
28th March	Arras, 1918	Great War, 1914-18
12th April	Hazebrouck, 1918	Great War, 1914-18
23rd May	Ramillies, 1706	War of Spanish Succession
16th June	Dettingen, 1743	War of Austrian Succession
18th June	Waterloo, 1815	Napoleonic Wars
11th July	Oudenarde, 1708	War of Spanish Succession
31st July	Ypres, 1914	Great War, 1914-18
	Ypres, 1917 (Pilckem)	Great War, 1914-18
4th August	France and Flanders, 1914-18	Great War, 1914-18
13th August	Blenheim, 1704	War of Spanish Succession
18th August	Lincelles, 1793	French Revolution
21st August	Somme, 1916	Great War, 1914-18
	Somme, 1918 (Albert)	Great War, 1914-18
27th August	Arras, 1918	Great War, 1914-18
	Scarpe, 1918	Great War, 1914-18
2nd September	Khartoum, 1898	Sudan Expedition
7th September	Marne, 1914	Great War, 1914-18
9th September	Sevastopol, 1855	Crimean War
11th September	Malplaquet, 1709	War of Spanish Succession
12th September	Hindenburg Line (Havrincourt)	Great War, 1914-18
13th September	Tel-el-Kebir, 1882	War against Arabi Pasha
14th September	Aisne, 1914	Great War, 1914-18
15th September	Somme, 1916	Great War, 1914-18
	Somme, 1918 (Flers Courcelette)	Great War, 1914-18
20th September	Alma, 1854	Crimean War
25th September	Somme, 1916	Great War, 1914-18
	Somme, 1918 (Morval, 1916)	Great War, 1914-18
27th September	Loos, 1915. Hindenburg Line (Canal du Nord)	Great War, 1914-18
2nd October	Egmont-op-Zee, 1799	French Revolution
8th October	Cambrai, 1917-18	Great War, 1914-18
9th October	Ypres, 1914	Great War, 1914-18
	Ypres, 1917 (Poelcappelle)	Great War, 1914-18
29th October	Ypres, 1914 (Gheluvelt)	Great War, 1914-18
	Ypres, 1917	Great War, 1914-18
5th November	Inkerman, 1854	Crimean War
11th November	Ypres, 1914	Great War, 1914-18
	Ypres, 1917 (Nonne Bosschen)	Great War, 1914-18
	France and Flanders, 1914-18	Great War, 1914-18
	Armistice Day	Great War, 1914-18
27th November	Cambrai, 1917	Great War, 1914-18

Day and Month	Battle or Operation Commemorated	Notes
27th November	Cambrai, 1918 (Fontaine-Notre Dame)	Great War, 1914-18
28th November	Modder River, 1899	South Africa, 1899-1902
30th November	Cambrai, 1917	Great War, 1914-18
	Cambrai, 1918 (Gouzeaucourt)	Great War, 1914-18
13th December	Nive, 1813	Peninsular War

COLDSTREAM GUARDS

Day and Month	Battle or Operation Commemorated	Notes
5th March	Barrosa, 1811	Peninsular War
26th March	Douchy-les-Ayette, 1918	Great War, 1914-18
12th April	L'Epinette, 1918	Great War, 1914-18
5th May	Fuentes d'Onor, 1811	Peninsular War
16th June	Dettingen, 1743	War of Austrian Succession
18th June	Waterloo, 1815	Napoleonic Wars
11th July	Oudenarde, 1708	War of Spanish Succession
28th July	Talavera, 1809	Peninsular War
31st July	Pilckem, 1917	Great War, 1914-18
18th August	Lincelles, 1793	French Revolution
21st August	Moyenville, 1918	Great War, 1914-18
25th August	Landrecies, 1914	Great War, 1914-18
27th August	St. Leger, 1918	Great War, 1914-18
1st September	Villers Cotterets, 1914	Great War, 1914-18
6th September	Marne, 1914	Great War, 1914-18
11th September	Malplaquet, 1709	War of Spanish Succession
13th September	Tel-el-Kebir, 1882	War against Arabi Pasha
14th September	Aisne, 1914	Great War, 1914-18
15th September	Ginchy, 1916	Great War, 1914-18
20th September	Alma, 1854	Crimean War
25th September	Les Boeufs, 1916	Great War, 1914-18
27th September	Loos, 1915	Great War, 1914-18
	Canal du Nord, 1918	Great War, 1914-18
9th October	Houthulst Forest, 1917	Great War, 1914-18
	Wambaix, 1918	Great War, 1914-18
21st October	Langemarck, 1914	Great War, 1914-18
29th October	Gheluvelt, 1914	Great War, 1914-18
	Zonnebeke, 1914	Great War, 1914-18
5th November	Inkerman, 1854	Crimean War
11th November	Armistice Day	Great War, 1914-18
27th November	Fontaine-Notre Dame, 1917	Great War, 1914-18
28th November	Modder River, 1899	South Africa, 1899-1902
30th November	Gouzeaucourt, 1917	Great War, 1914-18
13th December	Nive	Peninsular War

SCOTS GUARDS

Day and Month	Battle or Operation Commemorated	Notes
5th March	Barrosa, 1811	Peninsular War
13th March	Egypt, 1801	Campaign against French
5th May	Fuentes d'Onor, 1811	Peninsular War
16th May	Festubert, 1915	Great War, 1914-18
16th June	Dettingen, 1743	War of Austrian Succession
18th June	Waterloo, 1815	Napoleonic War
28th July	Talavera, 1809	Peninsular War
31st July	Ypres, 1914	Great War, 1914-18
	Ypres, 1917	Great War, 1914-18
4th August	Namur, 1695	Campaign in Low Countries
18th August	Lincelles, 1793	French Revolution
23rd August	Somme, 1916	Great War, 1914-18
	Somme, 1918	Great War, 1914-18

Day and Month	Battle or Operation Commemorated	Notes
24th August	Retreat from Mons, 1914	Great War, 1914-18
6th September	Marne, 1914	Great War, 1914-18
9th September	Sevastopol, 1855	Crimean War
13th September	Tel-el-Kebir, 1882	War against Arabi Pasha
14th September	Aisne, 1914	Great War, 1914-18
15th September	Somme, 1916	Great War, 1914-18
	Somme, 1918	Great War, 1914-18
20th September	Alma, 1854	Crimean War
27th September	Hindenburg Line, 1918	Great War, 1914-18
28th September	Loos, 1915	Great War, 1914-18
9th October	Ypres, 1914	Great War, 1914-18
	Ypres, 1917	Great War, 1914-18
10th October	Cambrai, 1917	Great War, 1914-18
	Cambrai, 1918	Great War, 1914-18
26th October	Ypres, 1914, 1917	Great War, 1914-18
29th October	Ypres, 1914, 1917	Great War, 1914-18
5th November	Inkerman, 1854	Crimean War
11th November	Armistice Day	Great War, 1914-18
26th November	Cambrai, 1917	Great War, 1914-18
	Cambrai, 1918	Great War, 1914-18
28th November	Modder River, 1899	South Africa, 1899-1902
13th December	Nive, 1813	Peninsular War

IRISH GUARDS

13th April	Hazebrouck, 1918	Great War, 1914-18
18th May	Festubert, 1915	Great War, 1914-18
23rd August	Retreat from Mons, 1914	Great War, 1914-18
8th September	Marne, 1914	Great War, 1914-18
14th September	Aisne, 1914	Great War, 1914-18
15th September	Somme, 1916	Great War, 1914-18
	Somme, 1918	Great War, 1914-18
27th September	Loos, 1915	Great War, 1914-18
	Hindenburg Line, 1918	Great War, 1914-18
9th October	Ypres, 1914	Great War, 1914-18
	Ypres, 1917	Great War, 1914-18
27th November	Cambrai, 1917	Great War, 1914-18
	Cambrai, 1918	Great War, 1914-18

WELSH GUARDS

24th March	(1st) Bapaume, 1918	Great War, 1914-18
31st July	Pilckem, 1917	Great War, 1914-18
2nd September	(2nd) Bapaume, 1918	Great War, 1914-18
9th September	Ginchy, 1916	Great War, 1914-18
10th September	Ginchy, 1916	Great War, 1914-18
15th September	Flers Courcelette, 1916	Great War, 1914-18
16th September	Flers Courcelette, 1916	Great War, 1914-18
25th September	Morval	Great War, 1914-18
26th September	Morval	Great War, 1914-18
28th September	Loos, 1915	Great War, 1914-18
29th September	Loos, 1915	Great War, 1914-18
30th September	Canal du Nord	Great War, 1914-18
1st October	Canal du Nord	Great War, 1914-18
8th October	Cambrai, 1918	Great War, 1914-18
9th October	Cambrai, 1918	Great War, 1914-18
10th October	Poelcappelle, 1917	Great War, 1914-18
4th November	Sambre, 1918	Great War, 1914-18
28th November	Cambrai, 1917	Great War, 1914-18
1st December	Cambrai, 1917	Great War, 1914-18

Appendix "G."

Extracted from William Maskell's "Monumenta Ritualia Ecclesiae Anglicanae."

"BENEDICTIONES DIVERSAE."

1. "VEXILLORUM PROCESSIONALIUM, VEL MILITARIUM, BENEDICTIO."*

ORATIO.

Inclina, Domine Jesu, salvator omnium et redemptor, aures tuae pietatis ad preces nostrae humilitatis, et per interventum beati Michaelis archangeli tui, omniumque caelestium virtutum, praesta nobis auxilium dexterae tuae, ut sicut benedixisti Abraham adversus quinque reges triumphantem, atque David regem in tui nominis laude triumphales congressus exercentem, ita bene ✠ dicere et Santi ✠ ficare digneris hoc vexillum, quod ob defensionem sanctae ecclesiae, contra hostilem rabiem defertur, quatenus in nomine tuo fideles et defensores populi tui illud sequentes, per virtutem sanctae crucis triumphum, et victoriam, se ex hostibus ecquisiisse laetentur. Per te Jesus Christe, qui cum Patre et Spiritu sancto vivis et regnas Deus, per omnia saecula saeculorum.

ALIA ORATIO.

Domine, Deus omnipotens, cui omnia possibilia sunt et nihil difficile est, bene ✠ dic vexillum istud, sicut benedixisti serpentem aeneum in eremo hasta elevatum, quem quicunque vulneribus sauciati aspexerunt salvabantur, quia unigenitum tuum post lenga saecula cruce elevandum hoc portendebat mysterium; et praesta ut omnes qui illud super se elevari viderint, a quacunque informitate et periocule et occursu male liberentur. Bene ✠ dic etiam, Domine Deus, vexillum istu sicut benedixisti dilectum puerum tuum David, cum adversus Philisten in funda et lapide congressus est, et unigeniti tui virtutem, mundo quandoque venturam, sue praemonstravit praelio; adhuc te petimus, omnium demonator Domine, et bene ✠ dicas illud, sicut benedixisti fluvium Jordanis, in quo unigenitus tuus descendens, totius mundi maculas abolevit, et per baptismum omnes salvandos esse praeostendebat, et quae petere non presumimus aut quae petendo impetrare non meremur, tu nobis concede propitius. Per eundem.

Translation of the above Prayers.

VARIOUS BLESSINGS.

BLESSING OF BANNERS, WHETHER PROCESSIONAL OR MILITARY.

PRAYER:

Incline, Lord Jesus, Saviour and Redeemer of all, the ear of Thy piety to the prayers of our humility, and through the intervention of Thy Blessed Archangel Michael, and of all the heavenly powers, extend to us the help of Thy hand, that as Thou didst bless Abraham when he triumphed against the five kings, and King David when he waged triumphal battle in the

---

* These benedictions are taken from the (so-called) Evesham pontifical in the British Museum. Lansdown MS. 451.

Q

praise of Thy name, so Thou mayest deign to bless and sanctify this banner which is carried for the defence of the Holy Church against the fury of its enemies. So that those who follow it, being faithful in Thy name and defenders of Thy people, may rejoice to have gained triumph and victory over their enemies through the virtue of the Holy Cross. Through Thee, Jesus Christ, Who with the Father and the Holy Spirit liveth and reigneth God through all the ages of the ages.

ANOTHER PRAYER.

O Lord, Omnipotent God, to Whom all things are possible and nothing is difficult, bless this banner as Thou blessedst the golden serpent lifted up on a spear in the desert, which whoever looked upon, being hurt with wounds, was healed; because this mystery foreshowed that Thy only son was to be lifted up upon the cross after many ages. And grant that all who see it lifted up over them may be set free from every infirmity and danger and evil encounter. Bless also, Lord God, this banner as Thou blessedst Thy beloved Son David when he fought the Philistine with a sling and stone and foreshadowed the virtue of Thy only Son, whenever it was to come into the world, by his battle. And we ask Thee, Lord and Ruler of all, that Thou bless it as Thou blessedst the River Jordan in which Thy only Son descended and took away the sins of the whole world, and by His baptism foreshadowed that all must be saved. And these things we do not presume to ask, nor do we deserve to attain them by asking, but do Thou grant them graciously to us. Through the same.

Appendix "H."

LAYING UP THE KING'S COLOURS AT THE INDIAN NATIONAL DEFENCE ACADEMY

BY "EYEWITNESS"

On 26th January, 1950, India became a Sovereign Democratic Republic and as a result Royal prefixes were dropped and it was no longer appropriate to carry the King's Colours on parade.

The decision was taken to lay up King's Colours at the Indian National Defence Academy, Dehra Dun. For this purpose a ceremonial parade was held at the Military Wing of the Indian National Defence Academy on 23rd November, 1950, on the square outside the Chetwode Hall.

THE PARADE

His Excellency Lieut.-General Sir Archibald Nye, G.C.S.I., G.C.I.E., K.C.B., K.B.E., M.C., High Commissioner for the United Kingdom in India, represented His Majesty the King. On his arrival the massed bands played "God Save the King," and he was met and conducted to his seat by General K. M. Cariappa, O.B.E., Commander-in-Chief.

The salute was taken by the Defence Minister, Sardar Baldev Singh, who was flanked on the saluting base by General Cariappa and Major-General K. S. Thimayya, D.S.O., Commandant of the Indian National Defence Academy.

A large number of guests were invited to attend the parade, and the gathering included representatives of Commonwealth countries.

On parade were the Colours of The Punjab Regiment, The Madras Regiment, The Grenadiers, The Mahratta Light Infantry, The Rajput Regiment, The Jat Regiment, The Sikh Regiment, The Dogra Regiment, The Kumaon Regiment, and the Indian Navy.

COLOUR PARTIES

The two senior Colours were trooped. These were those of the 1st (Para.) Battalion The Punjab Regiment and the Indian Navy.

Colour parties consisted of an officer, a J.C.O. (formerly V.C.O.) and an N.C.O. Many of these had earned decorations, British and Indian, and it was obvious that great trouble had been taken in the selection of individuals forming the parties. After the two senior Colours had been trooped there followed a march past in slow time. This was followed by an address by the Defence Minister, who said: "We have gathered here today to witness the solemn ceremony of laying up the King's Colours belonging to some of the oldest and most famous regiments of our Army.

"These Colours, as you know, were awarded by His Majesty the King in the long course of our association with Great Britain. They were held in very great esteem by the units—some of whom have had them for well over a century. In days gone by, these Colours were carried along with the Regimental Colours in action during a war, and many a soldier sacrificed his life to prevent them falling into enemy hands. We recall to our mind the happy association of our soldiers with the British officers who lived with and loved the 'Jawan' and trained him in the arts of war and made the Indian Army the envy of all nations. The King's Colour was a mark of signal honour to a regiment that had excelled in action as a unit. The laying up of these Colours is the end of a glorious chapter in

The Colours of the 1st (Para.) Bn. The Punjab Regiment and the Indian Navy which were trooped at the Laying-Up Parade.

Trooping the Colours of the 1st (Para.) Bn. The Punjab Regiment and the Indian Navy.

the history of these regiments. It is also the beginning of a new one, in which these, and indeed all the other regiments, will build greater and more praiseworthy traditions of bravery and discipline around the new Colours the regiments will in due course receive."

After the Defence Minister's speech the parade formed a hollow square and the Colours were then marched off into the Chetwode Hall to the tune of "Auld Lang Syne."

LAYING UP THE COLOURS

Visitors were seated facing each other in the Chetwode Hall with a central lane between the lines of chairs. At one end of the hall was a dais. The Commandant of the Academy stood on the dais, flanked by two officers, and received each Colour in turn. The Colour-bearer of the senior unit gave his Colour to the Commandant with the following words:

"Since the King's Colour will no longer be carried on military parades as from 26th January, 1950, the date on which India became a Republic, I and the other representatives of units now deliver these Colours to your hands for safe custody in the Chetwode Hall and National Defence Academy, Dehra Dun. I therefore deliver to you the Colour of the 1st Battalion The Punjab Regiment."

The other thirty-five Colour-bearers in turn handed their Colours to the Commandant with a similar statement for their own regiments. When the last Colour had been handed over to the Commandant, visitors were asked to stay in their seats. The Defence Minister then stood up and asked the High Commissioner to convey to His Majesty the King the grateful thanks of the Government of India and of all the regiments which participated in the parade and to assure His Majesty of the high esteem in which the Colours would be held by all concerned. Sir Archibald Nye replied:

Colours marched off parade into the Chetwode Hall.

The Colour Parties.

The Commandant receiving the Colours.

"Mr. Minister, I thank you very much for the message which you have given, which it will be both my duty and my pleasure to convey to His Majesty the King.

"It is but natural that as a soldier I should have viewed the parade today with a critical eye, but I found that the arms drill, the bearing of the troops, the marching and steadiness on parade were all in the highest traditions of the Indian Army and I would like, if I may, to congratulate all concerned on the manner in which the ceremony was performed.

"Nobody who was present today could have failed to appreciate the solemnity of the occasion. Today's ceremony, magnificent though it was, was symbolic and indicative of something very much deeper than appeared on the surface. It is true that this ceremony took place because India has now become a Sovereign Independent Republic, but it is also true that it was held because India has of its own free will and without any pressure from any source voluntarily decided to remain within the Commonwealth and to recognize the King as the symbol of the free association of the independent member nations.

"In these uncertain times this decision was of the greatest importance to both countries.

"May this spirit of friendship and cordiality continue to guide both our two great countries in the years to come."

The whole ceremony was carried out with a very high standard of military efficiency in every respect. It was, moreover, apparent that great trouble had been taken to ensure that the ceremony was carried out with the solemnity that this historical occasion warranted.

It was a very moving occasion, and there was no doubt that all those present were deeply touched.

The King's Colours that were laid up were those of the following battalions of Indian Army regiments and the Indian Navy:

> The Punjab Regiment: 1st (Para.) Battalion; 2nd (1st Guards) Battalion; 3rd Battalion; The Punjab Regimental Centre.
>
> The Madras Regiment: 1st Battalion.
>
> The Grenadiers: 1st Battalion; 2nd Battalion; 3rd Battalion; 4th Battalion.
>
> The Mahratta Light Infantry: 1st Battalion; 2nd Battalion; 3rd (Para.) Battalion; 4th Battalion; 5th Battalion; The Mahratta Light Infantry Regimental Centre.
>
> The Rajput Regiment: 1st (4th Guards) Battalion; 2nd Battalion; 3rd Battalion; 4th Battalion; The Rajput Regimental Centre.
>
> The Jat Regiment: 1st (Light Infantry) Battalion; 2nd Battalion; 3rd Battalion; The Jat Regimental Centre.
>
> The Sikh Regiment: 1st Battalion; 2nd Battalion; 3rd Battalion; 4th Battalion; The Sikh Regimental Centre.
>
> The Dogra Regiment: 1st Battalion; 3rd Battalion.
>
> The Kumaon Regiment: 1st (Para.) Battalion; 2nd Battalion; 4th Battalion; The Kumaon Regimental Centre.
>
> The Indian Navy.

Reproduced from *The British Army Journal,* by kind permission of the War Office.

INDEX

*All regiments of Household Cavalry, regular
R.A.C. and Infantry are listed in Appendix "C".